MW00850094

Praise for *Warrior to Civilian*

"It is a well-known principle of military operations that we are at our most vulnerable during transitions. Through personal experience and extensive research, Rob and Alex remind us that our transitions out of the military are a time of vulnerability too. Importantly, they provide sound advice and encouragement. This is a timely and important book."

—General Martin E. Dempsey, 18th chairman of the
Joint Chiefs of Staff of the U.S. Military (Ret.)

"If you are preparing to transition from a lifetime of service to your nation back to the civilian sector, this is a must read for you. My own personal transition was riddled with surprises—from medical care to emotional challenges—that I would have given anything to have had my hands on this book. This book is full of practicum, shared experiences, and perspectives. It is a must read for those preparing for this life changing experience."

—Lieutenant General Robert Caslen, U.S. Army (Ret.), former
superintendent of the U.S. Military Academy at West Point
and current senior research fellow of the Simon Center for
Ethical Leadership and Interagency Cooperation

"I loved this book. I know of nothing else that meets this threshold of valuable information support for the veteran leaving the military."

—John Broman, brigadier general, U.S. Air Force
and Minnesota Air National Guard (Ret.)

"Transition is hard as most of us will always search for a new purpose— for the next mission. Rob and Alex have provided an honest, realistic, and holistic view of this difficult journey. Use their advice and insights and best wishes as you move forward."

—Rear Admiral Michael Giorgione, CEC, U.S. Navy (Ret.), author
of *Inside Camp David: The Private World of the Presidential Retreat*

"Transformation is challenging because it requires us to break patterns that have made us successful in the past—and learn about others we don't yet know. Alex and Rob have done an incredible job of transmuting what is often isolated as a transition from the military into the civilian world and made it much more principled and universal—the unending transformations that we must all undergo on the Hero's Journey. This is the journey of infinite courage—the courage to surrender to all."

—Commander (SEAL) Curt Cronin, U.S. Navy (Ret.), cofounder and managing partner at Broadway Strategic Return Fund and founder and CEO of Aiki Partners

"This is a MUST READ for anyone to learn how to plan and execute a successful transition into a new company/culture/environment. With this collection of knowledge, more veterans will succeed in transition and be happier, more fulfilled, and more impactful for their families, communities, and corporations."

—Derek Herrera, captain, U.S. Marine Corps (Ret.), founder and CEO of Bright Uro

"The transition from military to civilian life is difficult for almost everyone who undergoes it. Even as a judge advocate (military lawyer), I experienced an adjustment period and steep learning curve when I started practicing in civilian courts. *Warrior to Civilian* will help all service members tremendously—not only because of the resources, checklists, and other practical information it contains, but because it makes clear that those who are facing this life change are not alone. I especially appreciated the effort to include guidance for female service members and their spouses."

—Colonel Terri R. Zimmermann, U.S. Marine Corps reserve, and managing partner of Zimmerman and Zimmerman, PLLC

"Transitions can be disorienting and complicated, especially when your identity is deeply ingrained in an organization like it most often is in our military service members. Not only is the transition difficult for our warriors but it can also be confusing and frustrating for our military families as well. For a more successful transition to civilian life, the whole family has to be involved by arming themselves with information and resources outlined in *Warrior to Civilian*. There is help and there is hope, no one needs to transition alone. This should be required reading before anyone takes the step from war fighter to civilian."

—Jen Satterly, acclaimed filmmaker, photographer, author of *Arsenal of Hope: Tactics for Taking on PTS*, cofounder and co-CEO of the All Secure Foundation, and Army spouse

"*Warrior to Civilian: The Field Manual for the Hero's Journey* is a must read for any person transitioning out of the military into civilian life. Many of us have complained for years of not having the required information for a smooth transition and here it is. Dive in to this manual and give it a good read for a smoother future. The authors have done a spectacular job of gathering resources and advice, including their own, to help everyone in transition."

—Command Sergeant Major Thomas Satterly, U.S. Army (Ret.), 1st Special Forces Operational Detachment—Delta (1st SFOD—D), author of *All Secure: A Special Operations Soldier's Fight to Survive on the Battlefield and the Homefront*, and cofounder and co-CEO of the All Secure Foundation

"This is a first-rate manual for the military folks thinking about making the transition. I wish I had had it when I was getting out."

—Lieutenant Hyonwoo Shin, 42nd Engineer Company, Combat Support Battalion, Berlin Brigade, U.S. Army, and current managing director of FE International

"This book should be required reading for anyone contemplating getting out of the military or going through the process of entering the civilian world. Not only is it spot on with its advice, examples, and useful strategies, but it's funny and engaging as well. Rob and Alex have done a great service to an under-represented and often overlooked group of Americans going through what is a very difficult transition."

—Commander Joshua Klein, U.S. Navy (Ret.) and retired executive and professor of business at Savannah College of Arts and Design

"As a gay, pacifist pastor and also the father of a female officer in the U.S. Marine Corps, I can't say I was wildly excited to read this book. I did not think it was for me. However, it is astonishingly important and rich. I learned so much about a sector of our nation's community and how we need to care for veterans and how they need to care for themselves. I did not understand how much about a life in the military should be brought into our civilian life, and how difficult it is when we do not. The authors write so beautifully and with such authenticity and generosity and love. This book is a real gift for veterans, their families, and all who benefit from their sacrifice and service."

—Reverend Peter Manning, Monie pastoral resident,
Preston Hollow Presbyterian Church, Dallas, Texas

"I love this book! The results of Rob's and Alex's work resonate with the work we do in the Resilient Warrior's Program of the David Lynch Foundation, helping veterans, active-duty personnel, and their families heal from PTSD through Transcendental Meditation, often when nothing else has worked and when veterans have been able to save themselves from suicide. When we offer our brothers and sisters who have served a way to find peace within, we feel we are serving them in a way that fosters true and lasting healing. This is the unique power of *Warrior to Civilian: The Field Manual for the Hero's Journey*—and why I am convinced this incredibly accessible, compelling, informative book will make a huge difference in the lives of veterans—and for the rest of us."

—Bob Roth, CEO of the David Lynch Foundation

"This book is a must read for anyone before they are discharged."

—Private Ron Zaleski, U.S. Marine Corps,
author of *The Long Walk Home*, and founder of
the Long Walk Home Organization

"Regardless of the branch, every officer, enlisted, and civil servant are members of the Profession of Arms. When our time comes to an end, we will inevitably return, in one capacity or another, to the civilian world. *Warrior to Civilian* is the most comprehensive book on the subject. It is full of practical advice, personal anecdotes, and most importantly, real life veteran observations. It is not enough to make a plan. You must know what obstacles will be in the way and harness the strategies necessary to make you a Civilian Warrior. That all starts with this book."

—Captain James M. Shinn, former Army attack helicopter pilot, and assistant district director of the Office of Federal Contract Compliance Programs, U.S. Department of Labor

"In *Warrior to Civilian*, the juxtaposition between the hero and community speaks to the reality that each of our journeys are both unique and interior while at the same time dependent on honest, loving, and supportive relationships. Through tapping into the power of story as a critical piece in transitions this book has the potential to better help us understanding the very nature of what it means to be human."

—Reverend Tom Evans, senior pastor, Brick Presbyterian Church of New York City

"Life after the military is simply executing a new mission, adapting to new terrain, and having the courage to take risks and be vulnerable... and avoiding the pitfalls experienced by so many veterans who try to attack these new challenges alone. And don't forget your allies: we fought together, we need to heal together."

—Lieutenant Steve Williams, U.S. Army (Ret.), former regional president for continental Europe at Lockheed Martin and current chairman of the Veteran Coalition International

"A must read for all service members regardless of rank or component."

—Albert Altro (Ret.), command sergeant major, U.S. Army, and current senior managing director at Traverse Advisors

"*Warrior to Civilian* serves as a remarkably thorough, helpful, and accessible guidebook to all aspects of the difficult transition out of service. This comprehensive manual covers the early and inevitable issues of physical, psychological, and moral wounding and displacement at home, through the many steps and strategies of healing, and finally to restoring purpose and achieving transformation and reintegration into society and family. This book is an essential resource supporting service people in making a successful transition from military to civilian cultures into a new and restored life of meaning and honor."

—Dr. Edward Tick, renowned psychotherapist, healer, author, and educator

"Having spent almost twenty-five years as a professional counselor/ marriage and family therapist, working off and on with military members and their families, my main question is, 'Where has this book been?' This book uniquely balances research-based information with practical wisdom from real world experience. What an incredible resource—Alex's wisdom and experiences as a military parent and Rob's lessons he has learned from his incredible service career and adjustments afterwards are truly outstanding. This is a must read for military leaders, and families of and service members. This should be required reading for service members before they get their DD214."

—Dr. Ryan Rana, LMFT, LPC, ICEEFT certified trainer

"As a service-connected combat Veteran I am certain having had this book when I departed service would have provided some clarity to the fog of transition out of the service. As a therapist I will recommend this for veterans in my care and fellow therapists. This is an invaluable resource that will undoubtedly help ease the transition for active-duty personnel preparing to depart from service, as well as veterans who are struggling to find their way."

—Kenneth MacIntosh, Fleet Marine Force Navy corpsman, former Department of Veterans Affairs suicide prevention case manager and Vet Center readjustment counselor, and current private-practice therapist specializing in veterans' mental health

"The hardest part of my own transition was the nagging suspicion that I was screwing it up in ways no other veteran had before. I was convinced my struggles were unique and a product of my own ineptitude. Only years later did I learn that other veterans; indeed, most veterans; are challenged in some way to adapt. This book does an excellent job of bringing together a diverse cast of former service members to speak of their own experiences that, in many ways, resembled my own. While I hate that any veteran would have to struggle the way I did, we should all take some comfort in knowing that none of us is alone."

—Commander Dan Bozung, U.S. Navy (Ret.) and U.S. Navy Reserves and senior vice president of corporate development and sustainability at WireCo World Group

"This is the most comprehensive and well-written book I've ever read with respect to military-to-civilian career transition…it's a must-have if you're interested in betting on yourself, setting you and your family up for greater success, and thriving within the new chapters of your life. I only hope that every military member reads this before their transition."

—Eric Potterat, PhD; performance and clinical psychologist; and retired commander, U.S. Navy; former head psychologist for the U.S. Navy SEALs and the Los Angeles Dodgers

WARRIOR
TO
CIVILIAN

**THE FIELD MANUAL
FOR THE HERO'S JOURNEY**

WARRIOR
TO
CIVILIAN

**LIEUTENANT (SEAL) ROB SARVER
AND ALEX GENDZIER**

balance

New York

This book is not intended as a substitute for medical advice of physicians. The reader should regularly consult a physician in all matters relating to his or her health, and particularly in respect of any symptoms that may require diagnosis or medical attention.

Copyright © 2025 by Rob Sarver and Alex Gendzier

Cover design by GCP/BALANCE

Cover copyright © 2025 by Hachette Book Group, Inc.

The poem "Unless You've Been a Soldier," on page 94, is by Clive Sanders. Used by permission.

The poem "Sentry" by Kate Dahlstedt, on page 118, originally appeared in *Lessons from the Garden: Selected Poems and Essays* by Kate Dahlstedt. Used by permission.

Hachette Book Group supports the right to free expression and the value of copyright. The purpose of copyright is to encourage writers and artists to produce the creative works that enrich our culture.

The scanning, uploading, and distribution of this book without permission is a theft of the author's intellectual property. If you would like permission to use material from the book (other than for review purposes), please contact permissions@hbgusa.com. Thank you for your support of the author's rights.

Balance
Hachette Book Group
1290 Avenue of the Americas
New York, NY 10104
GCP-Balance.com
@GCPBalance

First Edition: January 2025

Balance is an imprint of Grand Central Publishing. The Balance name and logo are registered trademarks of Hachette Book Group, Inc.

The publisher is not responsible for websites (or their content) that are not owned by the publisher.

Scriptures taken from the Holy Bible, New International Version®, NIV®. Copyright © 1973, 1978, 1984, 2011 by Biblica, Inc.™ Used by permission of Zondervan. All rights reserved worldwide. www.zondervan.com The "NIV" and "New International Version" are trademarks registered in the United States Patent and Trademark Office by Biblica, Inc.™

The Hachette Speakers Bureau provides a wide range of authors for speaking events. To find out more, go to hachettespeakersbureau.com or email HachetteSpeakers@hbgusa.com.

Balance books may be purchased in bulk for business, educational, or promotional use. For information, please contact your local bookseller or the Hachette Book Group Special Markets Department at special.markets@hbgusa.com.

Print book interior design by Bart Dawson.

Library of Congress Cataloging-in-Publication Data
Names: Sarver, Robert, author. | Gendzier, Alex, author.
Title: Warrior to civilian : the field manual for the hero's journey / Lieutenant (SEAL) Robert Sarver, and Alex Gendzier.
Description: First edition. | New York : Balance, 2025. | Includes index. |
Identifiers: LCCN 2024032476 | ISBN 9781538769966 (hardcover) | ISBN 9781538769980 (ebook)
Subjects: LCSH: Veteran reintegration—United States. | Veterans—Services For—United States. | Veterans—Life skills guides. | Retired military personnel—Life skills guides. | Families of military personnel—Services for—United States.
Classification: LCC UB357 .S27 2025 | DDC 362.860973—dc23/eng/20240905
LC record available at https://lccn.loc.gov/2024032476

ISBNs: 9781538769966 (hardcover); 9781538769980 (ebook)

Printed in the United States of America

LSC-C

Printing 1, 2024

To those still serving and standing the watch,
we are grateful to you beyond words.

To the veteran, whose service in defense of our country is
something we honor, we seek to support your transition
to civilian life with everything we've got.

To those who made the ultimate sacrifice,
we serve humbly in your honor, and may we see
each other again where the stars and seas meet.

CONTENTS

"Our debt to the heroic
men and valiant women
in the service of our country
can never be repaid.
They have earned our
undying gratitude."

—HARRY S. TRUMAN

PREFACE

I am a combat veteran who has lived many parts of the pages of our book. What I would tell you out of the box is that this is not a book that glorifies war. In fact, this is the antithesis. In the pages that follow, you'll find real stories of transitioning service members, both officers and enlisted, as well as their spouses and families; stories that highlight hardships, regrets, trauma, and success as they left their war-fighting days and returned to civilian life. These revelations are an integral part of the book.

As you read, you'll receive input from a wide range of service members, from airmen and privates to admirals and generals who have served in the U.S. Army, Navy, Air Force, Marines, and Coast Guard (the U.S. Space Force is so new that we weren't able to contact any transitioning service members).

Through our outreach to veterans and their spouses, it became clear that regardless of background, experience, age, gender, race, or sexual orientation, enlisted or officer, service members have much more in common than not. There's one distinction to mention: The struggles of injured veterans go beyond what many others encounter; from them, we draw great inspiration, and parts of this book will focus on their experiences specifically.

What emerges from the stories we collected is that fellow veterans and military spouses not only speak with great commonality in their voices, but they also have gone out of their way in helping us to express a strong wish to help you, future veterans and military spouses, make one of the most important steps in your lives—the transition from military to civilian.

Alex and I have put together (in our opinion) a good cross section of input and practical knowledge to help the widest demographic group of veterans and their families. That said, I feel it is out of benevolence and inclusion as a "cake eater" (this is how enlisted service members often refer to officers, if you're not familiar) that I say something to my enlisted brethren (and even some officers) who may not want advice:

We are not attempting to tell you what to do. You have likely taken orders your whole career, and the last thing you want to do is read a book written by a naval officer and a lawyer full of "do-this-not-that." One of my best friends from high school, Joe Dickman, who served in the Ranger Regiment as an enlisted shooter, told me he'd never had the desire to pick up a book and read about transitioning from the military, though in hindsight he wishes he had. That's okay. You may just want to figure it out on your own. I commend you for going your own way and taking the road less traveled, as Robert Frost would advise you to do. But if you're here and have made it this far, I assume you're searching for advice and mentorship as you take these first steps out of your existence as a service member. The better prepared you are for this journey and the more willing you are to see the world through a different lens, the less chance you'll have of failing and looking back on lost time and cursing decisions you made or failed to make. I encourage you to exercise your self-preservation instinct and listen to those who have struggled before you. Spoken like a true cake eater, I know, but there is real meaning in the ancient Chinese proverb "The more you sweat in peace, the less you bleed in war." You are about to step into a new kind of proverbial fog of war as you leave the service and return to civilian life.

The successes Alex and I have achieved were earned after learning from our mistakes. As the saying goes, "To be old and wise, you must first be young and stupid." Not the mantra I was aspiring to live by, but what the hell, it happened. And, along this path I found some of my closest friends—both enlisted and officers—while serving in the military and living on the edge, an edge that sometimes landed me standing tall in front of "the Man," answering for my actions. At the Virginia Military

Institute and the Naval Academy, I had mediocre grades and poor conduct and I was rebellious. I was a breath away from being awarded the so-called "badge of envy" (meaning dishonor) during my plebe (freshman) year at the Naval Academy. My time in the fleet as a surface warfare officer wasn't exactly a step up in my performance. But, along the way, I learned about myself and was able to finally prioritize my life to serve my country in the greatest way I knew how.

Once, one of my instructors at Basic Underwater Demolition/SEAL (BUD/S) training—he is now a chief warrant officer—admonished me and each in our group to "be a savage, leading savages to do savage shit for our country." I am mindful that this sentiment may make some senior officers frown, but those words gave meaning to me as I searched for a path forward for myself in service of something worthy. I had been training for war, not making grades in courses that didn't make sense to me. I was training to lead SEALs into combat in service of our country and one another. Later, when reflecting on my life, I was struck by the words of the late Senator John McCain during a Forrestal lecture at the Naval Academy about the days he had spent on restriction. He said, "Virtue is not determined in moments of public attention to our behavior. Courage, devotion, humility, compassion—all the noble qualities of life—are not practiced in pursuit of public approval."

I would never compare myself to Senator McCain, nor have I walked in your shoes, but Alex and I have earned our stripes, and we now serve as the messengers for what your own peers wish to tell you. I developed an uncommon desire to help my friends and those who stand ready to defeat evil. But, that said, I gladly sat behind my computer and helped the men and women who served with me to get out the door and deliver the full force of combat to our enemies...that was my job. Now, I sit behind the computer to give the most practical advice to help those who have served have a better experience transitioning than those before us.

When I consider my own transition, I think back to the time I realized my war was over and the role of rituals in how I marked that. I had experienced seven deployments over nine years as a surface warfare officer and Navy SEAL. A ritual that was meaningful to me came through one of my mentors, Rich Gray, who aided me through my transition from the SEAL teams into the world of finance. I met Rich in 2010 when I was still serving at SEAL Team 3. In 2012, I visited New York City to interview for a position, through the Veterans Integration Program, with Goldman Sachs. Rich took me to the Fraunces Tavern in Lower Manhattan in the Financial District. Rich wanted to share in the same symbolic gesture that General George Washington, in the Long Room at that very tavern in which we sat, partook of, on December 4, 1783, by giving his officers a final farewell speech as their commander in chief, marked by sharing a toast with them. General Washington said, "With a heart full of love and gratitude, I now take leave of you. I most devoutly wish that your latter days may be as prosperous and happy as your former ones have been glorious and honorable." After his farewell, he took each one of his officers by the hand for a personal word.[1] We can understand that this was a unique moment, wrapped in rituals of honor, shared sacrifice and service, and one with tremendous meaning and emotion for all involved. Having a drink at this hallowed place marked the end of a chapter in my life. Rich knew this, but he was also implying that a greater, new beginning was awaiting me, one, he hoped, that would be as prosperous and happy as my former ones had been glorious and honorable. Interwoven with this ritual were symbolic commonalities between Rich and me. I was sitting in the epicenter of the financial capital of the world. This was where Rich had started his finance career in 1985 and where I was aspiring to do the same.

I have helped many officers and enlisted go on and apply to college and master's programs, get jobs or find better jobs, and seek to become more whole. I have also tried to help them become better fathers and spouses and become more at ease in the civilian world. I have seen them excel as investment bankers, entrepreneurs, company owners, and many other successful career paths. And, I also have had friends, both enlisted and officers (me included), that have bounced from career to career and struggled in other parts of their lives and could have been better prepared for that figurative punch in the face. In the end, remember why you signed up to serve your country—what motivated you and what got you through your training and service to this great nation. We were all driven to serve a higher cause than self. It is time to apply that same passion, desire, and grit to your transition. Jim Rohn, an author and motivational speaker, said, "The problem with waiting until tomorrow is that when it finally arrives, it is called today. Today is yesterday's tomorrow."[2] Seize today.

—Rob Sarver

There is nothing more humbling and thought-provoking than having your children remind you about what matters in life. My sons have blessed me with that and much more. They have reminded me about service to one another and to country. My younger son has challenged me about helping those we have encountered who needed help; I have heard stories of him kneeling beside impoverished veterans and others, feeding them on the street; I have heard stories of him standing up to bullies twice his size to defend a young lady. My older son now serves our country in the military, seeking to be the warrior, as Heraclitus put it, that brings the rest home. The outlook and actions of these young men have challenged me to do more, to be better, to live according to a higher standard.

For one reason or another, Rob and I struck up a friendship. This led to discussions about life, transitions in life, what it means to be a father, moments of success, moments of failure, and moments of brokenness and regret. We've talked of ultimately finding growth and healing and how to live a life of meaning, success, and service. Along the way, we've had moments of sidesplitting humor and a few stories not appropriate for this book. In other words, we've had the kind of conversations one is lucky to have with true friends. In our lives, we each have been underestimated and had to overcome, which led to looking back over our very different yet parallel experiences. We got the idea that maybe we could use what we have had to learn (did we actually learn it?) and our ability to rope in others and then go solve problems—to unfuck any problem—and to make a difference to veterans and their families. Unwittingly, we somehow conceived of this as a project being built from our different experiences and skills, and yet coming from a common mindset, values, and goal—a rare military-civilian partnership. Thus arose the idea of writing this book together. But an idea is one thing—getting it done is another. Rob and I did not quite realize what lay ahead. Working on this book has been a four-year journey—fitted in around our day jobs and our families. The path took on the profile of a large project—from an idea after too much coffee in the morning and then too much beer at night in conversation, to moments of discouragement and picking ourselves up and moving forward. Our discussions with more than two hundred veterans and their spouses, from E-2s to celebrated flag officers, have been the animating center of the project. These conversations were enlightening, revealed great heartbreak at times, and were often inspirational. The stories of wounded veterans and heroes made us even more committed to the project and to our involvement in it.

For Rob, this is terrain that he has walked—serving, finding, and refinding great purpose; sorting through all that comes with that while building a new life afterward; having lost brothers; having seen extreme sacrifice for one another, for the Constitution, and for our country; and having a relationship with teammates that few can understand or experience. For me, to do this competently and to honor the sacrifice and service I saw in front of me required me to understand the experience of the veteran at a deeper level, what their words meant, the emotions inside them, their search for new purpose after getting home, and their differing senses of their experiences. We saw clues left behind of success and failure in the transition to civilian life.

Through our work, we also saw some common patterns in veterans' stories. What came into focus was nothing less than the epic tale of the hero's journey, an archetype or pattern of how to understand the epic tales of all time, such as Homer's *Odyssey*. When thought about in this way, what these veterans' stories revealed was the same pattern, a common story in all of our lives that involves an ordinary person who goes on an adventure, encounters challenges of great proportion, and is victorious at decisive moments before returning home transformed, able to change the world around him or her. Veterans' stories are epic tales. They leave the comfort of civilian life (whether for a cause or a calling or something else); they encounter adventure, combat, loss, and suffering, all while overcoming odds stacked against them and accomplishing great feats of courage. They experience inner growth inside and love and respect for comrades. The journey home at times involves struggle, a sense of loss, and dealing with difficult emotional, physical, and spiritual challenges. Broken hearts and marriages and job and career stumbles follow for some. But life's promise of redemption beckons in the finding of new purpose, the search for healing, and the finding of new joy and new or renewed love. There are new challenges to conquer and opportunities for continued service to others. The journey gives us a chance to become better and bigger and to find a sense of inner peace, a transcendent purpose, and a higher-level perspective. We then are able to more clearly envision why we are here and what we are meant to do in this life. The transition to civilian life—like any major life transition—offers the chance for personal transformation, resulting in a greater sense of dignity and even nobility of purpose and service.

Our work together began by collecting stories from veterans. In them, we also witnessed the power of storytelling to transform. When listening to stories, we have a chance to process life's moments and our emotions that are, at times, too concentrated to unpack in one sitting or simply by reading some instructional manual or workbook. We get to hear about heroes that call upon and inspire us to become our better selves. We witness how some harnessed their energy to heal or to find a new path in life as civilians by envisioning a changed, more positive story or self-narrative coupled with taking action to actualize those visions— getting results in not only their lives but the lives of others. From all of this, we also were reminded of the power of speaking and listening to one another. Frankly, nothing is more healing or more productive in this transition than veterans' gathering to exchange thoughts and ideas. In those moments, the act of speaking difficult things to comrades who inherently understand you is a first and perhaps more poignant step in this journey. The act of listening and serving as a witness is a generous act of support and even love. The generosity of veterans in giving of themselves to this project and to us was an inspiring and heartwarming encouragement—and, ultimately, a sobering challenge.

One late night, when my work was done at my day job, it occurred to me that the challenges in transition that the veteran faces are no different than what a man goes through when he loses his wife (whom he loved so dearly beyond words, and who was the mother to their young children); when he decides he must find a new career in his mid-fifties; or when he has to adjust and find new purpose when his kids, who have been the center of his mission, leave the house. I thought of that statement in the abstract. Then I realized that I was not somehow special—remarking to myself, "Well, shit, all three of those things are me." No one gets through life unscathed. As my father told me, everyone gets hit, so you'd better realize it's how you get up off the canvas that defines you and makes a difference to you and those around you. So, I said to myself that if I didn't use what I somehow had learned along the way and the ability to harness the wisdom of others, then rising above these challenges would not really be available for the betterment of those around me. Worse—if I didn't pursue this and put all of myself into it, then I would be passing up a chance to lift others up. A line from a speech given by Admiral William McRaven rang in my head—to never pass up an opportunity to lift others up around you. As my friend and former commander (SEAL) Curt Cronin, U.S. Navy (Ret.), said to me, while staring at me with his disarming ease and innate intensity and jabbing his finger into my chest, "What would you be giving up by not pursuing this with everything you had and by not putting yourself into this?" at an early breakfast one morning, granted, with slightly different lingo than he had come to master in the Navy. The questions came to me: What kind of a model or legacy would I be leaving my sons if I let that happen? Would I be truly honoring the memory and meaning of the incredible life and heart of my late wife if I did not put into use for others the lessons from her life? How could I let down my coauthor? What of the many veterans who spent time with us, thinking that the book would actually get published and go somewhere and so their time with us was worthwhile? I cannot say I have lived up to these standards, but these questions stayed with me and pushed me. What a journey and what a privilege and honor to have had the chance to speak with veterans, their spouses, and those that care for them, to partner with Rob and to work on this book.

Thank you.

—Alex Gendzier

"You don't develop courage by being happy in your relationships every day. You develop it by surviving difficult times and challenging adversity."

—HERACLITUS

INTRODUCTION

"Warriors who were so proud, so audacious, so terrible abroad could not be very moderate at home. To ask for men in a free state who are bold in war and timid in peace is to wish the impossible."

—MONTESQUIEU

We love our country, but we as a country and as a people have not honored the promise we *should* make to our veterans, that we as a country will help them when they transition out after they have served and sacrificed. The transition to civilian life has proved difficult for many of our veterans, particularly for those who have suffered and are injured, whether the wounds are visible or not. The statistics speak for themselves: an epidemic of roughly twenty-two veteran suicides per day;[1] substantially higher rates of post-traumatic stress disorder (also referred to as PTSD) and traumatic brain injury (also referred to as TBI), particularly among combat veterans, substance abuse, sexual assault, physical injury, homelessness, and a range of other sufferings compared to the civilian population. Beyond the statistics are deeper challenges of divorce, alienation, loss and grief, and, for many, a feeling of emptiness at losing a life purpose. Putting aside these kinds of issues, reintegrating to civilian life, finding a new job or career, and, for those with spouses and families, the adjustment required when beginning to live full-time with your family, are things to be taken seriously.

We do not intend to paint a picture of our veterans as troubled. We believe that image is a misconception among some portion of the civilian population—a negative myth that is just that—a myth. In fact, a large portion of the problem in veteran transition lies within the society—our society—to which the veteran returns after serving our country. And, in fact, in this transition, there is great opportunity, hope, and the possibility of a great life in the civilian world. In our work over the last five years on this book, which has included conducting hundreds of interviews and many hours of research, we have found that there are many stories of success and failure, each of which leaves clues. In other words, there are many lessons to learn from those who have transitioned and those still undergoing the process. We want to do something to help.

WHO IS THIS FIELD MANUAL FOR?

We have been inspired to serve by writing this book to be a complete, practical guide—a field manual—for the active-duty military personnel considering transitioning out and to veterans going through it, whether recently or ongoing for decades.

We have also written this book with the spirit of being inclusive. If you are wearing the uniform now or have taken it off, we hope this manual will help you. That's what we intend—it's for everyone, regardless of where you come from, how you look, differences within, what you may have suffered, and even how you think of yourself.

Finally, this field manual is also for military spouses of warriors, whether of active-duty personnel considering leaving the service or of those who have become civilians. By "spouses," we mean those who are married or those who form a significant partnership with their other halves. Spouses figure equally as veterans from the beginning to the end of this field manual. In chapter 1 ("The Preparation Phase: Plan Your Dive; Dive Your Plan"), we strongly advise the warriors to involve their spouses in every phase of the preparation process; we devote the sixteenth and final chapter ("The Transition for Spouses and Families") to spouses and families; and, in between, every chapter is critical for spouses, especially to help in understanding what their warriors are going through. So, the veteran's hero's journey is equally the journey of the military spouse.

WHY THE TRANSITION IS DIFFICULT, WHY IT IS WORTHWHILE, AND ETERNAL HOPE

So, your last assignment ended, you signed your papers to leave the military, and you are back home. This is the first time you have been out of the military in a while. For some, this was a voluntary decision, and you may even have yearned to be back home; for others, you may have suffered a physical or psychological trauma that took you out of your unit. For some, you had already made plans for life after the military; for others, planning may have been hard to do and you didn't know where to start, so you put it off. Or maybe you thought it would be easy or a friend told you it would be a walk in the park after what you'd experienced in the military, so you thought planning wouldn't really be necessary. But now that you're in this moment, you're realizing that going from military life to civilian life is complicated.

It is worth pausing to recognize why the transition can be difficult:

- The loss of having a mission larger than oneself—often referred to as a transcendent cause—and the loss of even your identity, having been symbolized by the uniform you wore for many years, can make life after the military feel without meaning.
- At a deeper, primordial level, the loss of community can be understood for many as the loss of your tribe. The move from living in a small community, with an intense sense of purpose and identity, to a society and a culture that is alienated, fractured, and materialistic, as Sebastian Junger has described it, can be jarring. The coming home of veterans during the wars in Vietnam, Afghanistan, and Iraq has been substantially more difficult when compared to how our country embraced the warriors returning from World War II.
- There is simplicity and structure to living by a code of honor and all of what that means in terms of integrity, service, and

country, as well as courage and selflessness. These are seemingly hard to replace in civilian life, at least at face value.

- Returning to being a civilian after having become a warrior
  isn't a simple two-step. This is understandable in light of the
  fact that transforming civilians into warriors requires *intense
  training*, a gargantuan effort, accomplishment, and even a
  re-creation of one's "ego structure," in psychological terms.
  Are you supposed to just press a button and be transformed
  into being Johnny or Joanna Civilian? Very simply, you may
  feel lost and disoriented; if not now, those emotions may come
  later. Some have been exposed to horrific things when overseas and in combat. You may be suffering from post-traumatic
  stress disorder or traumatic brain injury. Often, divulging
  or explaining this to your family or close friends may prove
  daunting and may lead to emotional distance and even alienation and separation.

- Whatever difficulties you brought into the military with
  you—drug or alcohol abuse, family dysfunction, job stress
  or instability, or emotional difficulties, among others—are
  likely to persist and go back with you when you transition out.
  Civilian life offers a greater degree of freedom and choice,
  but navigating these things can be a shock to the system.
  When you were in the military, many things were taken care
  of, including housing, medical care, childcare and schooling;
  there was even easier access to shopping. Now, on the outside,
  you have to figure out these aspects of life for yourself. There's
  no doubt this can be initially disorienting.

Regardless of the reason, the reality is that the transition to civilian life is rarely easy. In fact, it is a disservice to the veteran to suggest as much or not to warn veterans about this and provide assistance
in the transition. Few are immune from one or more of the above,
from entry-level enlisted to flag-ranking officers. Yet, make no mistake: While the terrain is different from what you encountered in the

military and there are no enemy combatants, it is no less challenging to navigate.

Are there worthwhile things to look forward to in civilian life? Hell, yes. The picture should not be gloomy. It's the opposite. In this next chapter of your life, the possibility of great things lies ahead. There is great opportunity and hope for healing, refinding purpose and mission, ambition in one's work, a full life, adventure, discovery, fulfillment, and joy. Why do veterans need a new guide now? There are a few reasons: Today, there are more living veterans (about 22 million); more family members of veterans (about 15 million); and more veterans transitioning out every year (about 200,000) than ever before in our history. In addition, the last two decades of war have had an effect on any veteran's transition to civilian life and it's time for a new guide, with fresh insights and some lessons learned from the past.

For many, the path requires tough love, discipline, and the help of brothers, sisters, and strangers, as well as a commitment to finding a new life full of meaning, purpose, and promise. More than that, from the patterns we have observed in the stories shared with us by veterans, we believe that there is a recipe for success. It does require making a decision—and setting an intention—to transition effectively, realizing that this new world will require a new campaign. This mission of transitioning will involve developing new skills and reconfiguring the many skills you already have, creating a vision for your new life, finding fellow veterans along the way, receiving coaching and finding a mentor, and paying attention to the lessons in each of this book's chapters. As Command Sgt. Maj. Tom Satterly, U.S. Army (Ret.), observed, "You trained intensely to prepare for combat; what makes you think you can get away without training for the transition to civilian life?"[2]

Having said the above, there is not one formula for a successful transition to civilian life that works for everyone. We can tell you, though, that those who have done so effectively have executed on the preparation in advance, initiating a job search and other practical components we discuss. These folks have found some measure of healing and peace within and have come to a vision of themselves that includes a new purpose. In addition, having balance in one's life and having a "fulfilling community, family and spiritual life," as Dr. Eric Potterat, U.S. Navy commander (Ret.); and Alan Eagle observe in *Learned Excellence*, are often key ingredients to a successful transition.[3]

From our interviews with veterans, our research, and Rob's own experience, a central paradox of the transition to civilian life for many veterans is that everything that made you a warrior, all of what you were trained to do, all of what you experienced, often feels like the exact opposite of what you need to be successful in civilian life, whether at work or at home. And while there is some truth and also lessons to be learned from that understanding, the very essence of the warrior mentality, including the inner strength, resilience, discipline, courage, and devotion to things larger than oneself, are the great traits inside veterans that can lead to success, happiness, and fulfillment in the civilian world.

You have served our country and our country may have sent you into harm's way. For that reason, we intend this book to represent the spirit of leaving no one behind. That includes those of you who have left the military and are seeking a future that includes everything you deserve and have worked for.

RANKS AND TITLES

We have been careful to reflect military ranks and designations accurately when we refer to veterans in this book. We hope that these conventions don't offend you.

THE HERO'S JOURNEY

What is the hero's journey and what does that have to do with you? The idea of the hero's journey came from a way to interpret the epic tales of our history, such as Homer's *Odyssey*, which we'll take up again in chapters 11 and 12 on refinding purpose. This is the journey all veterans take. It involves the leaving of home for the military (regardless of the reasons for that); the untold challenges you meet and risks you take when in uniform (including the sacrifice and loss involved in service) and how those things affect you; and, after all of that, how you return, a changed person, and are able to transform the world around you. For many, the sense of loss and grief is inevitable, if only due to leaving one's unit and the military, let alone from the grief that arises with losing friends in battle.

There are many ways returning warriors are changed and can transform the world around them on their return. In practical terms, many warriors have faced and overcome enormous challenges. In doing so, they have developed greater moral and physical courage, discipline, leadership, resourcefulness, problem-solving, and a host of other skills that were not evident before they joined the military. These attributes and skills can be put to good use for themselves and for their families, community, and country.

At a deeper level, the returning warrior often faces the need to heal themselves. In doing so, they are also given a chance to see the need for healing in others around them and to assist in that process.

All you have to do is pick your head up and look around and you will see that opportunity—meaning other veterans in need. In sitting with the pain inside us and in seeking to heal it in others—an act performed out of love for our brothers and sisters in arms around us—something profound happens. We get the chance to be more human, to live more fully and humanly. Making use of one's own loss in this way is a great privilege. And in performing this service, perhaps we will inspire others to action.

Taking these steps gives us a chance to serve others from the place inside of us that was changed by our journey in and back home from the military, the place we had to become bigger and better versions of ourselves from these experiences. In Homer's *Odyssey*, the hero, Odysseus, has to grapple with how to live in the mundane world to which he has returned from his military service and also how to control that part of him that had been called on to wrestle with demigods, serpents, and nature's destructive forces. In doing so and in putting to good use how he became transformed in the process, Odysseus lifted up his family, community, and country. When we use what we have learned, when we put to good use the skills that have enabled us to become bigger and better people in the name of something higher than ourselves, we earn a chance at redemption.

The hero's journey is a story and a way to conceive of your life after leaving the military. Every veteran is on a hero's journey. If you think of your life story in these terms and understand the power inside you, power you gained from your military experience, you have the potential to bring back great lessons and transform yourself, your friends and family, and the civilian world around you. The story of your return has the potential to be as full of inspiration, courage, selflessness, and devotion to team and teammate as was your time in the military. It reflects the nobility in you and what you can inspire in others.

A NOTE FROM ROB ON RITUAL

In the preface, I mention why rituals are important. They serve as building blocks for individuals, families, and communities. For example, Friday-night high school football games are often accompanied by a series of acts that serve to create a cohesive, memorable expression of the community: the pep rally, parents gathering in their section, students avoiding their parents in their own section, the band, and, of course, the athletes. These acts, whether fun or solemn, serve a higher purpose. They can be used to create and mark important moments in time, define a journey and a transition, and bring light to darkness in difficult times. In these ways, rituals transcend our past, present, and future. At a profound level, rituals evidence our values, symbolize the things that matter to us and what we stand for, and even serve to represent an important piece of our identity. In these ways, rituals can also define a transition. Many have observed that transitions tend to have three parts to them:

- The beginning: The leaving behind of what we have known, where we have been, and what has heretofore been comfortable, even if imperfect.

- The journey: The voyage through new terrain where we seek something new, which is exciting and uncomfortable, can be a huge test, and can give us opportunities to grow and become bigger and better people in a new place.

- The destination: Finding our new place, which may seem uncomfortable at first but is also one that we find ourselves in for a reason, even if that reason is not understandable to us at the time. It is a place of new opportunities for a different kind of contribution to our life and society, and a chance to find new meaning and purpose, as well as success in whatever way we define it.[4]

Leaving the military is a prime representation of such a journey and nowhere is it more true that rituals can serve a helpful, powerful, and healing moment than in that journey.

A NOTE TO THE ENLISTED SERVICE MEMBER

In speaking with dozens of veterans during our research for this book, we were reminded that the enlisted man or woman is probably tired of being told what to do, especially when they no longer have to listen to officers after they leave the military. We're not doing that—and we hope this book doesn't come across that way. And while there are differences in the experience of the former enlisted service member compared to that of the former officer, the lessons learned and available to you are very much the same. We found that so much of this period of transition out of the military is universal, and we want to help every veteran, regardless of service branch or rank. We are all one team.

In researching and writing this book, we have been struck by—and moved and honored by—the willingness of veterans to give of themselves to help us put this resource together. Veterans' stories and observations fill every chapter. We believe at the core of this generosity lies a continued devotion to service and country and to one another. Dr. Jonathan Shay, a psychiatrist who worked at the Boston VA, noted that the "most fervent wish of the veterans I serve" is to help future generations of veterans, to save them from the sufferings they faced and mistakes they made.[5] Beyond that, the presence of veterans to your left and your right appears as a great resource in every chapter of this book, whether in the value of preparing in advance, networking for jobs, and comparing notes on civilian life, or the more profound and difficult challenges in healing and finding new purpose. In one way, this presence of veterans is at the heart of a successful transition because there is immeasurable value in being able to speak with others who have been through what you have been through and to bear witness to others' stories and experiences. There is a unique quality of community that is nourishing and that can be supportive in intangible and tangible ways. These themes run through every chapter. And that has been the case since the beginning of recorded history, when every generation that returned from war found resources of a practical nature, comfort, healing, and meaning in the transition to civilian life.

KNOWING YOUR WHY

When we interviewed her, Rear Adm. Katherine McCabe, U.S. Navy (Ret.), said, "Own the *why* of your retirement or separation and determine how *you* define success." As you approach milestones, you need to keep focus on the mission, the "why." This will give meaning and serve as a guide to your preparation for the transition; it will sustain you on tough days when you encounter headwinds in your every move to becoming a civilian; and it will enhance your fulfillment on the good days because you are acting in alignment with *what matters to you*. Admiral McCabe continued, "Success is different for each of us. For many, it is tied to salary, prestige, or recognition. It can also be independence of schedule or location, or time for family... and is often a combination or a particular sequence. If you can't articulate this to yourself and others, you may pour a lot of precious time and effort into a post-transition solution that does not help you achieve your actual goals."

In the following chapters, we will discuss the different aspects of how to transition successfully. Each chapter provides a brief explanation of its purpose, along with stories from veterans, and what we believe are the key takeaways. We have collected insights and wisdom from many quarters, from veterans who have made the transition successfully and from those who have not. You'll also hear from coaches and therapists who have studied these matters and have had a meaningful, positive impact on people's lives, and you'll hear from those who have hired veterans into their businesses—perspectives that often differ from those of other veterans.

"The happiness of your life
depends upon the
quality of your thoughts."

—MARCUS AURELIUS

LET'S CUT TO THE CHASE— WHAT DO YOU NEED TO KNOW?

If you want to cut to the chase, here is what you need to know about this field manual.

THE IMPORTANCE OF PREPARING IN ADVANCE

If you are still in the military, take advantage of the time you have to prepare for the transition to civilian life. This can take up to two years—though the time required is different for everyone. However you choose to go about it, realize that the process won't happen on its own after the last time you put on your uniform. Read chapter 1, "The Preparation Phase: Plan Your Dive; Dive Your Plan."

THE RETURN TO CIVILIAN LIFE

Every generation that has come back from war and left the military has had to find a way to return. While that path is different for everyone, most share some common patterns and paths. We provide an overview of the process in chapter 2, "I Am the Master of My Fate: The Return to Civilian Life"; and an outlined approach in chapter 3, "The Four Stages of Reintegration."

The return to civilian life also involves some tough and difficult challenges, including grief and loss, substance abuse, recovering from moral injury, dealing with physical injury, and addressing PTSD and TBI. If you don't address difficult emotions, they will weigh you down, like continuing to wear a fifty-pound rucksack around your house, family, and job. Read chapter 4, "Loss and Grieving"; chapter 5, "Substance Abuse"; chapter 6, "Moral Injury and Physical Injury"; chapter 7, "The Silent Assassin: PTSD"; and chapter 8, "Traumatic Brain Injury."

Psychedelics and other plant-based remedies represent a new frontier for treating depression, PTSD, TBI, and other ailments, which gives a new reason to hope for many. Read chapter 9, "The New Treatment Frontier: Psychedelics and Plant-Based Remedies."

Achieving any important goal requires advance preparation and training. The same goes for the transition to civilian life. If you want to do well at it, then use the best training and performance strategies and tips around. In addition to the best practices for healing we cover in chapters 4 through 8, additional tips include the use of meditation, harnessing fear, and learning to regulate your system. Read chapter 10, "Final Performance Tips."

REFINDING PURPOSE

Most warriors struggle to refind their purpose when they return to civilian life. There is great insight available from the learned knowledge of other veterans' journeys and even epic stories of warriors from ancient times. Because of what's involved in refinding purpose, we have broken it down into two parts: (1) an explanation of the challenge and some useful guidelines; and (2) veterans' stories about how they have approached it. Read chapter 11, "The Hero's Journey: A Guide to Refinding Purpose"; and chapter 12, "Veterans' Perspectives on Refinding Purpose."

SUCCESS IN SMALL STEPS AND WHAT IT MEANS TO BE A CIVILIAN WARRIOR

There are many practical steps involved in landing on your feet as a civilian. In fact, this will be difficult for many—something that is not really spoken about candidly. We're not just talking about the job here—we are also referring to the overall transition. But there are ways to do this and there are great insights from veterans about what worked for them and what was a waste of time. Success doesn't always come right away—it comes one step at a time. Read chapter 13, "Practical Steps in Looking for a Job."

You're no longer wearing a uniform, but the challenges are not over. It will take time, and there is value in recognizing and celebrating the small steps of success along the way. You will also need to fight just as hard in civilian life to become whole and heal yourself and your family (if you need to), and to find success and accomplishment for you and your family, as you did in the military. Becoming a civilian warrior has great meaning and power, and there are effective ways to achieve that. Hear from veterans who have made successful transitions. Read chapters 14, "Small Steps to Success," and 15, "Be a Warrior Inside the Wire as Much as Outside."

THE HOME FRONT—WHAT ABOUT SPOUSES AND CHILDREN OF VETERANS?

Spouses and families have always been our unsung heroes and form the backbone of the military. When a veteran transitions to civilian life, so does their family. Their experiences, lessons learned, new relationships forged or existing ones strengthened or weakened, and new purposes and beginnings are an important part of the veteran's journey and are vital to consider. Read chapter 16, "The Transition for Spouses and Familes."

RESOURCES

The Annexes on our website, www.heroes-journey.net, contain references to many practical resources for veterans and their families, including guides on how to apply to college and how to prepare a financial plan, as well as sample résumés, cover letters, and thank-you notes for prospective employers.

"A hero is someone who can keep going even when they have every reason to quit."

—RICK RIORDAN, *THE BLOOD OF OLYMPUS*

CHAPTER 1

THE PREPARATION PHASE: PLAN YOUR DIVE; DIVE YOUR PLAN

"Those in the service need to start early in planning the transition—at least one year out, if possible. It will be difficult and take some time. For those that served in combat, this is likely to be even more so. Some, including senior officers, resist acknowledging what is coming and the need to get serious about it. In this regard, veterans need to understand what they are about to go through and to get serious about it well before the last time you wear the uniform."

—GEN. DAVID H. PETRAEUS, U.S. ARMY (RET.),
former commander of the Surge in Iraq and the International
Security Assistance Force in Afghanistan; former director
of the Central Intelligence Agency; current partner,
KKR & Co.; and chairman, KKR Global Institute

You have arrived at that critical decision to leave the military, pursue another career, or maybe leave one position for another or even for a chance to be your own boss. With your plan in mind and the mental math working in your favor, eliminating enough variables, you have convinced yourself the time is right. You have earned your stripes—they might be a different color than everyone else's, but the civilian world is not that different, or so you think.

What could go wrong?

In the military—or, honestly, just about everywhere—this statement is usually delivered in a sarcastic tone. It is most often uttered in situations where it is glaringly obvious something will highly likely go wrong. You can't see the variables hiding in your blind spots, or the unknowns that will postpone your goals, sideline your ambition, and create volatility in your life plan that rips all security away from you and leaves you exposed, vulnerable, and off-balance. To help try to mitigate all of that, this chapter has one purpose: planning. A good rule of thumb is to start thinking through your plan to leave the military at least one to two years in advance; in fact, doing so is critical to your future success. We've outlined a transition planning schedule based on the outlines you find in military field manuals that describe the best way to prepare and plan for missions; to double down, you're going to need at least twelve months, if not twenty-four. This process takes time, as you'll often revisit and refine your plan and goals and how to execute them.

That said, if you are being involuntarily separated from the military, time may not be on your side. We recommend reviewing this chapter at a high level so you can consider any military benefits you have earned and then revisit this chapter when you can. Chapter 13 contains more specific practical steps about looking for a job.

KEY TAKEAWAY

Do not wait until your terminal leave to start planning your transition process. Give yourself twelve to twenty-four months to prepare.

For more detail about the endless paperwork needed to separate from the military, we recommend Janet I. Farley's book *Military-to-Civilian Career Transition Guide.*[1]

A word to the wise: If you want to be effective on the home front—let alone loving and caring for your spouse and family (if you have one)—it's best to involve them in your planning process from the beginning. Your family will undergo their own transition as you undergo yours. There are a host of concerns to anticipate and address, from benefits to making sure your children understand what is happening. Such a major life transition usually touches on deeper emotional issues for you and your family. What we have learned from our discussions with military spouses is that a veteran dedicated to being effective and loving regarding this transition will bring their family into it, anticipate their needs and desires, and collaborate about the transition as a team.

A NOTE FROM ROB: WHAT COULD GO WRONG?

Calvin: Look, stop being such a baby and help me push the car into the driveway. We'll move it ten feet. What could possibly go wrong?
Hobbes: Whenever you ask that, my tail gets all bushy. [2]

—*CALVIN AND HOBBES*

We do not know what lurks beneath the sea. What seems calm at the surface can surrender to a wild, cold, dark, and unforgiving environment beneath, one we would be foolish to think we can control. This is why, before you dive into uncertainty, you plan your dive and you do not deviate from your plan, which induces risk and obscurity in one of the cruelest environments on earth.

No plan is perfect. In SEAL teams, we demand and train for perfection in hopes of a flawless execution and outcome. This is the optimal goal. We spend hours planning operations, trying to account for every variable, and look at the problem through multiple lenses. It does not matter what armed service, command, or rank you held in the military, at some point you were involved in a planning process for a real-world mission or training evolution. I'm willing to bet you were intimately involved in a planning process that, well, just didn't go as planned at all.

Before I was selected to go through Basic Underwater Demolition/SEAL training (BUD/S), the initial screening to become a Navy SEAL, I was a surface warfare officer (SWO) onboard the USS *Crommelin* (FFG-37) stationed out of Pearl Harbor, Hawaii. I had just earned my SWO pin, the last step I needed to submit my package to be selected for BUD/S. All I had to do now was not screw up and blow my chances to fulfill my dreams of becoming a SEAL.

As an officer in charge of deck division, I was expected to plan, write, and brief the crew prior to evolutions that involved my department. This meant all small boat operations, man-overboard drills, and helicopter operations, to name a few. This particular training evolution was simulating a catastrophic fire onboard our ship and hailing a friendly vessel, role-played by a U.S. Navy destroyer, for help. The destroyer would respond by lowering their rigid-hulled inflatable boat (RHIB) into the water to send additional firefighting crew members over to combat the fire. At the conclusion of the exercise, the ships would switch roles and the simulation would start over, with our ship sending members of our casualty control team to combat the simulated fire on the destroyer. The plan also included a subset of the training while the fire drill was in process. The RHIB, to train new boatswain's mates to be coxswains, would make approaches alongside the vessels to practice off-loading and embarking personnel. For this exercise, the RHIB had an officer, rescue diver, and two boatswain's mates, acting as coxswains, onboard. All three vessels would be operating on the same radio frequency.

On the morning of the evolution, I briefed the crew members participating in the drills. Most of my brief involved standard operating procedures that the ship and crew had adapted from previous evolutions and that the crew had internalized over months of training. However, during this exercise not every department would be involved, including the engineering department, which was conducting its own internal training in addition to the simulated fire. I was the standing officer of the deck, the officer in charge of driving the ship, coordinating the emergency response on the radio and aiding the safe embarking of the firefighters from the destroyer. Also, it was predetermined that our ship would deploy our ladders on the port (left) side of the ship, and we would request that the RHIB make a port side approach when hailing the other vessel.

What could go wrong?

Everything was going just as planned. Our ship simulated a catastrophic fire, causing us to go dead in the water. We hailed the Navy destroyer and within minutes their RHIB was being lowered. While this was happening, the commanding officer from the destroyer hailed our ship on the radio and requested that the ladder be moved to the starboard side to accommodate the same side their RHIB was entering the water. It seemed like a harmless request, so I yelled from the bridge down to the boatswain's mates to shift to the starboard side and prep the ladder. Minor change to the plan, but everything was back on track. The RHIB made its approach on the starboard side and the firefighters onboarded with no issues. And, just as planned, the RHIB cast away from the starboard side, made a large loop off to our starboard side, and began to make its approach to come back alongside our ship. As this sequence of events was underway, my commanding officer was seated in his captain's chair on the starboard bridge. I stayed inside the bridge during the drill to answer radio traffic. As the RHIB made its second approach and came alongside, I suddenly heard yelling and the RHIB broke away, speeding off to the front of the ship's bow and coming to a stop. *Well, this can't be good.* The officer in charge of the RHIB abruptly came over the radio to inform his CO, "Sir, the *Crommelin* just emptied the CHT onto us and the RHIB is covered in shit!" On a U.S. Navy frigate, the opening for the collection and holding tank (CHT), or sewage discharge, is on the starboard side. When the commanding officer of the destroyer requested that I move the ladder from port to starboard, I forgot to notify the engineering department, and, as they were still carrying on normal business, they discharged hundreds of gallons of sewage, about twenty gallons of which ended up covering the RHIB.

What could go wrong, indeed.

Needless to say, my commanding officer quickly hailed the other captain, apologized, and offered to clean the RHIB. What awaited me was a verbal lashing I will not forget, and luckily my transfer package for SEAL training was not mentioned. I guess you could say I got lucky as shit!

Just when you think you have a good plan, some external force makes it all go to hell, and in the words of Forrest Gump, "Shit happens."

HOW TO MITIGATE THE RISKS AHEAD:
PREPARATION STEPS AND TIMELINE

While our research and discussions with veterans led to our recommended planning timeline of twelve to twenty-four months, we suggest an even longer timeline for those transitioning out of active duty. In this case, it may be advisable to begin planning even three years out so you can adapt to a process that will likely be alien to you. Janet Farley advises: "I can't stress enough how important it is that you visit the Military Transition Assistance Office as soon as possible. If you are concerned that your presence there might send the wrong message to your colleagues or your boss, call or email the office instead of visiting it. Most counselors will be happy to answer your questions or point you in the right direction over the phone or by email."[3]

A word about the list of things to consider and the checklists and samples we provide below: Review them and rereview them in whatever order and at whatever time best suits you. We have organized them in this way for the sake of global practicality, but some may not be as useful to you. Take what you need and leave the rest. Some may be applicable now; some will be helpful later.

If you are married or in a long-term relationship, we urge you to include your spouse or significant other in this—for a host of reasons we'll discuss further in chapter 16.

Beginning Phase: Twelve to Twenty-Four Months Ahead of Separation

Use this time wisely, aggressively, and creatively to plan your next critical twelve months until you take off your uniform for the last time. In hindsight, you will look upon this time as a great luxury. Take advantage of it.

Treat this like a warning order. A warning order is a preliminary notice of an order or action that is to follow. It is issued by the commander at the outset of receipt of an order from higher in the chain of command. The warning order is issued prior to beginning the planning process in order to allow subordinate leaders and units to maximize their preparation time. If you are receiving this message, you are currently in your preparation time for transitioning out of the military. This warning order will provide you with information to help focus your efforts and time.

Below is a sample warning order diagram that was part of our manual in the SEAL teams.

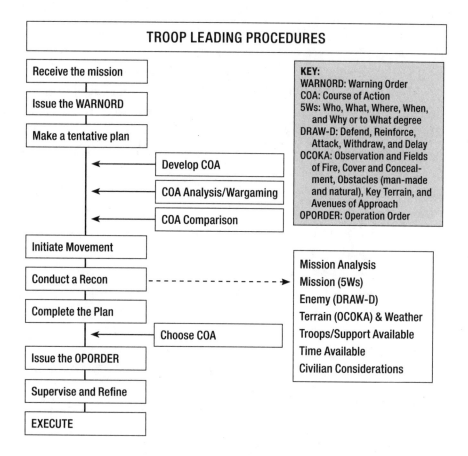

TROOP LEADING PROCEDURES

Receive the mission

Issue the WARNORD

Make a tentative plan

→ Develop COA

→ COA Analysis/Wargaming

→ COA Comparison

Initiate Movement

Conduct a Recon - - - - - - - - - - - - - →

Complete the Plan

→ Choose COA

Issue the OPORDER

Supervise and Refine

EXECUTE

KEY:
WARNORD: Warning Order
COA: Course of Action
5Ws: Who, What, Where, When, and Why or to What degree
DRAW-D: Defend, Reinforce, Attack, Withdraw, and Delay
OCOKA: Observation and Fields of Fire, Cover and Concealment, Obstacles (man-made and natural), Key Terrain, and Avenues of Approach
OPORDER: Operation Order

Mission Analysis
Mission (5Ws)
Enemy (DRAW-D)
Terrain (OCOKA) & Weather
Troops/Support Available
Time Available
Civilian Considerations

Brainstorm. Think about where you want to land, speak with friends and veterans, and make phone calls and investigate, all with the goal in mind of forming a specific plan. Chris Grillo, former U.S. Navy lieutenant commander, noted the following about this process: "Do not hesitate to ask a friend, contact, or a contact of a contact to go get a cup of coffee so you can ask them some questions about your next steps. If they can't help you, ask if they know someone who can. And, by the way, beer works just as well as coffee or maybe even better." As Cdr. Curt Cronin, U.S. Navy (Ret.), said, beer can often be a truth serum. It may take a hundred such meetings before you have all the information you need. It is a process of networking and gaining information, and none of it will be time wasted. It's also important to prepare yourself on how you'll ask questions during these meetings. The more specific your sense of direction, and the more specific your questions, the more informative the response will be. Don't stop. This brainstorming process will continue until you complete your transition—and then likely after that.

Find a mentor. Different from a fellow veteran or someone who occasionally gives you advice, a mentor is someone with whom you develop a trusted relationship and who has experience and wisdom to impart to you—someone who doesn't mind calling bull when required. Ideally, this is someone who has walked this path and has a network of contacts and friends. An adviser is someone you will be able to bounce ideas off. That process will last until you find your first job and afterward. Finding a mentor who understands and sees you is also essential for veterans in diverse groups or communities, such as African American, Asian American, female, LGBTQ+, and others. There are many organizations set up to provide mentorship to veterans, such as heroeslinked .org. Visit Annex 1 on our website, www.heroes-journey.net, for a list of resources.

Visualize. The practice of visualization is a powerful tool to develop a concrete, actionable vision of what your life will be like in the future. We recommend you learn visualization practices and develop the discipline to keep them going. Some of the most successful athletes, business leaders, and mastery coaches use this technique, including Tom Brady, Michael Jordan, and Lindsey Vonn. We also recommend the instructional videos of Tony Robbins and Joe Dispenza that you can find on YouTube and other online resources. You only need to follow a few simple steps to practice visualization:

- Begin by breathing for a few minutes, focusing on your breath; this gets your energy up but keeps you calm.
- Think of a few things about which you are grateful—because that's the cure for fear and anger.

- Imagine that you have accomplished your goals and picture what that feels, smells, and tastes like in detail. Put yourself in that space.

Plan leave days. Consider that you may need to accumulate leave days. A smart use of leave days can include going to networking events, doing research, and developing a plan of action, which are hard to do while you have your active-duty job. If you're considering an internship for a specific job or company, plan ahead and review the time commitments—this may require additional leave days.

Speak with friends and fellow veterans about jobs. Most veterans who have been in the military for any length of time probably will not be able to understand what jobs in civilian life are like, what they require, and what will lead to success or failure. Go speak with friends and fellow veterans about their civilian jobs.

Weigh Your Educational Options

Investigate trade schools and alternatives. Trade schools offer the chance to transition the skills and experience you built in the military into many civilian jobs. Call them and ask about the application process, timelines, requirements, cost, and jobs available after graduation. You might also consider certificate programs, online courses, internships, or skilled trades training as other options.

Consider applying to college. College may not be for everyone, but getting a college degree will widen your life and career options. One veteran lamented to us that he wished he'd taken the time after getting out to get a college degree—it would have expanded his job, career, and compensation options. If you need to start earning a salary right away, consider sequencing your transition in that order. But use your time when you are still in to plan these things. Like all aspects of the transition, applying to and getting accepted by a college requires advanced planning and preparation. There are many military-friendly colleges and universities. Check Annex 2 on our website, www.heroes-journey .net, for guidelines on how to apply to college, which will include the need to request a copy of your high school transcript.

All of your military courses and training may transfer into college credits. Be sure to ask any college you're interested in how to go about having those credits recognized.

- If going to college has been a dream of yours, don't give up on it so easily. James Hatch, a former Navy SEAL, started college at age fifty-two, thirty years older than most of his classmates, and transformed his college and those around him.[4]

- Don't give up on college because of the cost. There are several ways to pay for college, including by working and with scholarships. Consult the VA for benefits to help pay for college. Some colleges and universities participate in the VA's Yellow Ribbon Program, which helps make college tuition more affordable for veterans and their dependents. You can find a partial list of scholarships in Annex 2 on our website, www.heroes-journey.net.

- Become familiar with Yellow Ribbon Programs and other veteran-friendly programs at the universities. There are several organizations that maintain lists of military-friendly graduate schools and programs. And, once admitted, many of these have valuable veteran support groups.

Consider applying to graduate school. Graduate school is one way many veterans have leapfrogged from the military into careers. Getting an advanced degree can also make the transition into civilian life more gradual, compared to being thrown into a sink-or-swim job environment. The decision as to what kind of graduate school will involve some searching, research, and discussions with friends, former teammates, and former professors. It will also require a substantial preparation in advance—knowing about deadlines for application, standardized tests (such as the GMAT and the LSAT), and getting transcripts and letters of recommendation as well as records from the military.

- There are many military-friendly universities to which you can apply—and they usually advertise themselves as such on their websites. See www.militaryfriendly.com for one list of military-friendly schools.

- If you are accepted to college or graduate school and are not ready to leave the military, see if you can defer a year. Don't waste time on regrets. Several of Rob's friends have gotten out of the military and went back into the Reserves so they could continue to serve because they did not feel they had fulfilled their original intent of being in the military. Sometimes the transition happens in steps.

Is politics of interest? Many veterans have run for and won political office, made a difference, and found fulfillment by representing their constituents and giving a veteran's perspective on how our country should be run.

How close are you to retiring? If you are a stone's throw from retirement, consult with your loved ones and weigh thoroughly the pros and cons of separating from the military before being eligible for full retirement benefits. Use some of the suggestions mentioned earlier in this section, like planning leave days, to help you anticipate what your next steps may be after leaving the military. It may be worth it to delay your transition out, or it might be better to just go ahead and start your new life. For those retiring due to only statutory requirements: You are leaving to make room for all those you led. It's time for you to put your skills and talents to work for another purpose.

- If you are planning to separate from the military and also stop working completely—what in civilian terms is considered "retirement"—you will need to plan for two major life transitions in one: the end of your military career and the end of your work life, at least in conventional terms. While much of this book focuses on the first transition, it applies equally to the second as well. These days, retirement allows for many creative, life-enhancing possibilities. We have found that most veterans never stop working or being engaged in some productive way.
- If you are retiring, the Transition Assistance Program will require an approved copy of your retirement orders (DD Form 2656).

- A complete list of documents that you will need for retirement can be found at www.va.gov/records/discharge-documents/.

Begin major life transition planning. The military takes care of food, housing, health care, and a paycheck. Beyond these tangible pieces, it also provides a sense of identity, community, and mission. After you separate, you will need to take care of these things on your own—and we urge you to review all of this with your spouse and family. Consider the following:

Anticipate monetary needs and engage in financial planning. It's a good idea to start saving money and budgeting for your expenses. While the military will cover some transition costs, the reality is that it is usually more expensive than you think, so start now. If retiring, become familiar with the specific retirement benefit options offered by TRICARE (the health care program for active-duty, National Guard, and Reserve members and their families, as well as all retirees and their families). Take a look at www.tricare.mil/About. Don't forget to check on your Thrift Savings Plan (TSP) and how to manage it going forward. See Annex 3 on our website, www.heroes-journey.net, for more information on how to prepare a financial plan.

The Cost of Living Adjustment (COLA) Trap. When you are retiring you need to be aware of pay inversions and how your retirement will be calculated. Over a longer period of time, a better COLA can add up to more retirement pay than a few more months in uniform. For a full explanation, we suggest the article "How to Avoid the Military 'COLA Trap' by Getting Smart About Your Retirement Date" on www.Military.com.

Where will you live? There are several factors that you might consider, including proximity to family and friends, best educational and job or career options, best schools for your children, the presence of a veteran community, a place that shares your values, access to veterans hospitals, and proximity to commissaries and exchanges. Review your relocation options and entitlements, especially if you are retiring. Consult www.dmdc.osd.mil/sites—it provides a list of every American military installation in the world. Look into VA home loans if buying a new home. As you think about where to live and what career you would like to pursue, use a cost-of-living calculator to see the geographic differences in living expenses.

Plan for moving practicalities. The military will pay for your final move, but only the costs of getting to your official home of record—including the expenses of driving your car. Anything beyond that will have to come out of your own pocket. For details on all of your moving and permanent change of station (PCS) benefits, visit www.militaryonesource .mil/moving-pcs/plan-to-move/moving-benefits.

When packing for your move:

- Make sure you supervise the movers. Items can be misplaced or taken and/or sent to the wrong place.
- It will take time for your belongings to arrive at your new home. Shipping from overseas takes longer. Consider bringing some essentials with you (like cooking utensils, dishes, sheets, etc.).
- Pad your budget to deal with delays, lost items, and the cost of replacing all of the everyday perishables, condiments, and cleaning supplies that couldn't be moved but will have to be purchased for your new home.

Review a checklist of VA and other available benefits. In planning your transition, we urge you to spend time in advance educating yourself and your spouse (if applicable) about the many benefits available to you from the VA and other sources. There is paperwork to complete, requirements to meet, and deadlines. You should set an objective of learning to navigate VA benefits and the VA system—that is a job in itself at times and requires one to really learn how it works and how to receive the care you need. We list below some of the more important benefits, but there are many others. See Annex 1 on our website, www.heroes-journey.net, for a list of resources that will help you navigate the VA.

Inquire about separation pay. Inquire if you are eligible for separation pay.

Enroll in the Transition Assistance Program (TAP). This consists of a three-day workshop designed to help service members in transition. It includes pre-separation counseling, Department of Labor employment workshops, VA benefit briefings, a Disabled Transition Assistance Program, and an online course.

Joint transition assistance. The Departments of Veterans Affairs, Defense, and Labor created a website for wounded warriors, the National Resource Directory (NRD), at www.nationalresourcedirectory.gov. It is a comprehensive online tool that provides access to thousands of services and resources at the national, state, and local levels to support recovery, rehabilitation, and community reintegration.

Federal Recovery Coordination Program. This is a joint VA and DoD program that helps coordinate and access federal, state, and local programs for benefits and services available to seriously wounded, ill, or injured service members.

Pre-Discharge Program. This is a joint VA and DoD program that gives veterans the opportunity to file claims for disability compensation and other benefits up to 180 days prior to separation or retirement.

Health Care. You can enroll online at the Department of Veterans Affairs website or at your local VA medical center. Be aware that VA health care does not extend to dependents and is available only for the veteran. If you have dependents, plan accordingly. If you have a spouse who has a job, will their employer offer health coverage for your spouse and children—and perhaps yourself? Combat veterans may receive free health care for up to two years after release from active duty for any illness or injury related to service against a hostile force in war. Call 877-222-VETS (8387) to learn more about health benefits, or visit www.usa.gov/veteran-health.

Education and training benefits. There are many benefits programs, including those that help pay for college, graduate study, technical or vocational training, and correspondence and flight training. Some examples include the Montgomery GI Bill, the Veterans' Educational Assistance Program (VEAP), and the Post-9/11 GI Bill. These benefits do have term limits and will expire. If you have a serious service-connected disability, check out the VA's Veteran Readiness and Employment (VR&E) website, formerly Vocational Rehabilitation and Employment. The VA will pay for any training costs and special services you require.

This may be used in place of some college and graduate programs if you qualify.

Disability. You can file claims for a variety of disabilities, though they must be service-related.

Life insurance. Veterans' Group Life Insurance (VGLI) and Service-members' Group Life Insurance (SGLI) are available for most veterans and are less expensive than other civilian options. If you apply within the first 120 days after your separation date, you may save some unnecessary paperwork.

Small Business Administration (SBA) loans. These are helpful if you are starting a new small business.

Job search assistance. Every branch of the armed forces offers seminars and courses, which include information on résumé and cover letter preparation, interview coaching, career counseling, educational counseling, job searches, and other concerns regarding employment. Read chapter 13 for a comprehensive discussion of looking for a job.

Burial. As a veteran, you and your eligible family members have the right to be buried in a VA national cemetery. Burial benefits are not limited to a military cemetery; the VA will provide a standard-issue headstone to any veteran who wishes to be buried in a private cemetery free of charge. Depending on the veteran's service history and where the veteran is buried, the VA may pay an allowance of up to $2,000 to cover burial-related expenses, and the VA will cover transportation expenses to the final resting place.

Family and survivor benefits. If a veteran is disabled or deceased, some family members may be eligible for the following benefits: education, home loan guaranty for surviving spouse, medical care (CHAMPVA), death pension, burial, and Dependency and Indemnity Compensation (DIC), which is a monthly benefit paid to eligible survivors of a service member who died while on active duty or a veteran whose death resulted from a service-related injury or death. To apply, review VA Form 21P-534.[5] If you are retiring, schedule and attend a Survivors Benefit Plan (SBP) briefing and have your spouse attend with you. See "Survivor Benefit Plan Overview" on the Department of Defense website

(https://militarypay.defense.gov/Benefits/Survivor-Benefit-Program
/Overview/).

We've given you a lot of information here. As stated, it may not all
be immediately relevant to you, but nevertheless it's a full meal to digest.
So, a necessary suggestion is to *budget time to decompress.* As part of your
separation from the military and after you are out, we recommend that
you take time to sit with yourself and create the space necessary to clar-
ify your thoughts. Taking a moment to rest only further supports your
efforts to redefine your purpose and motivation for the road ahead. You
will encounter many stressors as you plan and execute your transition to
civilian life; it's essential to take breaks. Doing so creates an opportunity
for clarity of thought, which can lead to new opportunities or a different
way to approach a complicated issue. When you give yourself time—
time to sit with yourself—space can be created around you and opportunities start arising and you allow yourself a moment of clarity of thought.
This will support your refinding your purpose and provide motivation
for the road ahead. It will also give you a break from the stressors that
enter the picture.

Your Illustrative Plan—Ten to Twelve Months Ahead of Separation

Ask yourself simple and basic questions as you plan your transition.
Here are four to get you started:

1. What industry do I want to work in?
2. What function do I want to serve?
3. What region do I want to live in?
4. What kind of people and community do I want around me?

If you cannot answer these questions now, no sweat. But these are
good questions to consider and research.

We recommend approaching this by conducting a full mission
analysis:

- *Enemy analysis.* There could be two enemies lurking in the
  shadows. The first could be you. It might be your ego or a

health issue. There are a lot of ways we become our own worst enemy. The second enemy is your own blind spots—meaning, you don't know what you don't know. You have been living within the regimented structure of the military for so long you may see things your own way and need help seeing differently. Therefore, we recommend taking the time to learn everything you can about transitioning out. What critical skills are needed for your transition? What are your unknowns? Who is your competition for the job you want?

- *Troops and fire support.* This is your veteran network. Do you know any veterans who have already transitioned? Can you reach out to any of them for support? Who will mentor you?
- *Terrain analysis.* This is different from landforms we would study on a map. Consider these to be gaps in your intelligence and gathering atmospherics. If the civilian environment is a type of battlefield, what are your capabilities and the environmental features that must be considered during your preparation? Treat this as a deep dive into the industry or company you would like to work for. Study the culture of the organization. Reach out to former and current employees and get a sense of the people who work in the organization.
- *Recon—seek out the friendlies.* As part of your terrain analysis and mission planning, seek out fellow veterans to get their intelligence on the road ahead.
- *Time analysis.* How realistic is your timeline? What are the deadlines? How far in advance do you need to begin to meet a deadline? Do you need letters of recommendation, to take tests, to obtain your high school or college transcript, et cetera?
- *Civilian considerations.* These are not considerations for collateral damage. This is building your nonveteran network. Consider your neighbors, family, and friends in your established network or the network you need to build. Consider what kind of support, therapy, or larger issues they can help you with.

- *Train for the mission.* Consider practicing what you might be doing. Rear Admiral Michael Giorgione, U.S. Navy (Ret.), told us, "What I knew then was that eventually I would do my own thing and focus on teaching and coaching others. I created my company name that I still use today in 2005—Leading Leaders—bought the domain name, and set up the first website. I also started writing blogs, though not posting them, and material for classes. I just parked it all away, but I enabled myself to become more aware of everything that would cross my path over the ensuing years."

Develop a Specific Course of Action—Nine Months Ahead of Separation

In this last phase, refine your plan and what it will take to execute it.

- *Make a ledger to plan job searching.* On a sheet of paper, write down everything you know about the industry/function/region you are thinking about entering. Underneath that, draw a line down the middle of the page and make lists of pros and cons.
- *Prepare a skills inventory.* Ask yourself what skills and values you have gained in the military that will help you enter your industry of choice and begin to add value quickly. How do they align with what an employer wants? One hiring manager said, "I'm willing to take a chance on veterans because I know the work ethic of the military. But they still have to bring value to the company, and I want that as quickly as possible." For more ideas, see the "Skills Transition" section in chapter 13.
- *Every decision involves trade-offs.* You will face some basic trade-offs, so consider how much risk you should take. For example, think about the risks and rewards associated with transitioning into a start-up or smaller company versus a big corporation. It can be easier to go to a big-name firm first

and get the training and then move to a smaller boutique company or start-up later, but often smaller companies may offer more attractive incentives, like stock options, to get you to join.

- *Remember that it takes time.* Remember that it takes five seconds to buy the gear, five days to learn the lingo, and five years to learn the job. Rob observes: "I find a lot of this is true in business—it takes time to develop expertise."

- *Trade school application prep.* Continue to investigate trade schools and alternatives. Call them and ask about the application process, timelines, cost, requirements, and jobs available after graduation.

- *College and graduate school application prep.* Continue to map out the application process, including obtaining transcripts from your prior schools, lining up letters of recommendation, outlining school and standardized test deadlines, and coming up with an initial list of schools to which you want to apply. Because this process requires knowing these deadlines and other aspects, noted in Annex 2 of our website, www .heroes-journey.net, we do not repeat this piece of your planning below. Consult the VA for benefits to help pay for college. As mentioned, some colleges and universities participate in the VA's Yellow Ribbon Program, which helps make college tuition more affordable for veterans and their dependents.

- *Rereview the lists of questions and ideas in the previous section.* Create and refine your list of objectives, things to do, questions, and where you need input or help. Many veterans were trained to be effective warriors by solving problems on their own. In civilian life, that skill will come in handy, but you must realize that your ability to get help in this sometimes strange new world is a virtue, not a vice. Captain Derek Herrera, U.S. Marine Corps (Ret.), said, contrary to the military, in civilian life, one's ability to solve problems and find solutions is often tied to the extent of your network of friends, colleagues, and resources and your ability to access your network effectively.

Initiate Movement and Take Action—Six to Nine Months Ahead of Transition

In this phase, focus on continued exploration and implementation:

- *Write a résumé.* It may sound simple, but it's not. Résumés take time to think about and write. They can be the only basis upon which someone will decide whether or not to speak with you. Take time and get advice from nonmilitary contacts to make sure that what you write is understandable to people who have not served and do not have visibility into the way the military works. Note that for some industries and companies, résumés need to be tailored specifically to the company or job you're applying for—in fact, this is a good rule for all résumés.

- *Train for résumé preparation.* You might consider taking a seminar or course to help learn résumé and cover letter writing skills; these are often provided by your branch of the armed services. Rear Admiral Katherine McCabe, U.S. Navy (Ret.), reminded us that "your college's alumni or career offices are good resources. They will often do résumé reviews, hold online and in-person job fairs, and host alumni networks. You have to do the legwork, but it's one relationship you already have, even if it needs dusting off."

    There are many online resources, including some specifically for veterans, to help you create a résumé. We list tips for writing a résumé in chapter 13 under "Building Your Résumé," and sample cover letters are provided in Annex 4 on our website, www.heroes-journey.net.

- *Take Courses.* Consider a seminar or courses available about résumé and cover letter writing provided by your branch of the armed services.

- *Find out when you can start a new job.* Most employers are not going to commit to hiring you full-time more than three to six months out. Build this into your planning.
- *Check out job fairs.* Go to job fairs with a folder containing your résumé. There are many places to find them online, including www.success.recruiting.com, www.victory.com, and www.military.com (search for upcoming job fairs).
- *Continue to network.* Talk to civilian friends and ask fellow service members if they know anyone in the job industry you're considering. Continue to have those coffee and beer sessions and build out your network.
- *Consider getting an internship.* See if you can do an internship with the company (another reason for saving up your leave days), go visit the city where you want to live, and check out the schools if you have children. Some of this can be done online, but nothing replaces boots on the ground gathering atmospherics. Be aware that many internships are not paid. Look into the Department of Defense Skillbridge Program. Since inception in 2011, this program allows members of the military to spend a final portion of their active-duty service in an internship with a company. Check with your branch of service for the latest instructions regarding how much time you will be allotted based on rank and current billet.
- *Make sure to check VA deadlines.* For example, you'll need to schedule your VA physical to take place at least six months before your separation.
- *Check out deadlines to apply for reserve duty.* If you are interested in the Reserves, speak with a reserve recruiter before you separate to ensure that you don't get tripped up over deadlines. Combining reserve duty with a civilian job or career has worked well for many who have left active duty.
- *Are you going to stay overseas?* If you are stationed OCONUS (outside the continental United States) and wish to remain in that location, you must seek approval through your personnel office.

- *Reach out to a Transition Assistance Program office.* If you have not already done so, this is the time to reach out to your Transition Assistance Program (TAP) office. All service members who leave the military must complete a DD Form 2648, Preseparation Counseling Checklist, which covers by-law information to include benefits, entitlements, and resources for eligible transitioning service members. Additional resources for transition assistance by military branch:
  - Army: Army Career and Alumni Program (ACAP)
  - Air Force: Military and Family Readiness System
  - Navy: Fleet and Family Support Center
  - Marine Corps: Transition Readiness Program
  - Coast Guard: Work-Life Programs

Things to Anticipate

Here are some things to anticipate and do:
- Plan your retirement ceremony, if applicable.
- Once you have your separation orders, schedule an appointment to finalize your shipment and storage of household goods and potential benefits at your transportation office.
- Visit the area where you plan to live. Revisit the cost-of-living calculator. Has there been inflation since you first started planning? Try to set aside reserve funds for unexpected expenditures or if things start to cost more than you had planned.
- Prepare and update your will and estate plan, including any tax planning, such as setting up trusts for your children, if necessary. A will does not necessarily have anything to do with the transition to civilian life. Rather, it is an important part of life planning for your loved ones that everyone should consider, especially veterans and their spouses, given the nature of the life transition occurring. Before you separate, speak with a JAG (Judge Advocate General's Corps) officer who may be able to help you with this.

A NOTE FROM ROB

I was fortunate to have several networks to rely on. I had friends in finance who helped me guide my civilian career decision. I had military veterans at Goldman Sachs who were giving me input along the way. Jack Daly, a partner at that firm, served as a tremendous resource as I was leaving the military and beginning my work at Goldman Sachs. This is the most critical step. It's okay if you have not completed every step of the framework and you still have unknowns. Just start moving. You cannot stay stagnant in life or business, just like on the battlefield.

Complete the Plan—Six Months Ahead of Separation

In this next phase, start to make conclusions about your future direction:

- *Conclude your situation assessment.* This is your critical analysis of all the groundwork you have done, intelligence you have collected, and blind spots you have identified. Now it is time to weigh the risks and your go–no go criteria (shorthand for the factors for and against your next decision or move).
- *Finalize your course of action.* This may be a plan you developed in your head or formulated during a family gathering at the dining table. Keep a record of the detailed plan and the decisions you have made regarding which course of action you're going to take.

The following practical steps all work toward implementing your course of action. Some need advanced planning, and some may take time to accomplish.

- *Get and review your personnel or military service records.* Six to nine months out, request a copy of and review your personnel or military service records (DD Form 214: Certificate of Release or Discharge from Active Duty). There are several sources from which you can get these records, including MilConnect at the VA website, the National Archives, and DD214Direct .com. It can take six to eight weeks to update your records if corrections are necessary.

- *Complete your VA disability application (VA Form 21-526).* We recommend that you start completing this form six to nine months before your planned transition because you may need to get additional documentation to justify a claim. For example, if you hid injuries to stay in the game while serving, this is the time to document and get statements from corpsmen, or your command, about your injuries.

  If you do not think you will receive any disability, we still recommend that you apply for a status. Even if you receive a 0 percent rating, this will allow you to be reevaluated in the future and you could have a service-connected disability in the future. Additionally, there are some educational benefits for which you may qualify even with a 0 percent disability rating. Visit the benefits section on www.va.gov, or call 800-827-1000. Always check with the VA for the most current and accurate information.

- *Schedule a separation physical if you have not had one yet.* You can schedule this while in the military, and you can also visit the VA website (search for Separation Health Assessment for service members).

- *Schedule a final dental exam.* That sounds like fun.

- *Attend a transition assistance workshop.* We recommend you bring your spouse.

- *If you are obligated to join the Reserves,* verify that you are meeting all requirements and have completed the necessary paperwork.

- *Request your Verification of Military Experience and Training form (DD Form 2586).* To order online, go to https://milconnect .dmdc.osd.mil/milconnect/public/faq/Training-VMET.

- *If you are considering federal employment, begin to put your package together now.* Begin to apply for jobs with the final version of your résumé. We outline considerations for résumé preparation in chapter 13 and include sample résumés, cover letters, and thank-you notes for employers in Annex 4 on our website, www.heroes-journey.net.
- *Choose replacement benefits and schools.* Once you figure out some foundational decisions (where you'll live and what your job will be), you will need to pay attention to the list of things the military once provided for you and, if relevant, for your family. This includes health and medical plan benefits, choices of doctors, schools for children (if relevant), and other concerns. If you have a spouse, make sure you plan out these things in advance; get intelligence from friends and budget time for appointments, to check things out, and so on.
- *Review your course of action.* Rereview your options and your plan. Stress-check and sanity-check it. Consult with fellow veterans and friends and solicit their analysis of your course of action.

CRITICAL ADVICE

If you feel you were exposed to one or more traumatic events, consult a doctor or counselor about PTSD. If you think that you were exposed to blast waves, that you have suffered a concussion, or that you have symptoms of traumatic brain injury (or TBI), sometimes referred to as breacher syndrome, see a doctor and be sure to get records of your baseline exams or take a baseline assessment test. See chapter 8 for a more in-depth discussion of traumatic brain injury. If your medical file has no record of these conditions by the time you separate, you may face a difficult time having your care covered, whether provided by the VA or a private doctor.

Refine Your Plan, Get Supervision, and Execute—Three Months Ahead of Separation

Since you are now close to leaving, give your plan one last look and get a mentor's advice. Don't work in isolation. A mentor can help refine your plan and supervise. This may be a veteran who has already transitioned, or even your significant other, parent, or a close friend.

VETERANS' VOICES

"When I was contemplating leaving the Navy I felt that I was moving into a world that was potentially very different from the one I had been living in for the past seven years, but not really knowing what those differences were going to be. I was quite fortunate that my final tour on active duty (not counting all the subsequent recalls) was teaching NROTC while also getting my MBA, so I was living and working in a small military bubble in a civilian and academic environment. Broadly, this was helpful because it gave me a chance to readjust to the civilian world before completely leaving the military."

—Cdr. Joshua Klein, U.S. Navy (Ret.); currently professor of business, Savannah College of Art and Design

"Leaving active duty was kind of scary at first, even when submitting the paperwork request for a temporary separation. That's a program that the Coast Guard has that allows members to serve in the Standby Reserve or the Individual Ready Reserve for six months to three years while exploring options on the outside, taking a pause from service, or taking care of family issues."

—Lt. Cdr. Jono Parkhurst, U.S. Coast Guard Reserves

"When I was leaving the Marine Corps, I knew that I wanted to get a college degree, I had mapped that out. In hindsight, though, the most important preparation I did was my decision to put my military career and tactical mindset behind me. That wasn't easy. I thought I would relish taking time off and being back at home, but instead, I felt a huge part of me was missing, including the lack of structure. But, I toughed it out and decided I needed to focus myself on my new direction, my new career. I think this allowed me to move forward without looking backward, like I saw a lot of guys do. This gave me a blank slate. And, I pursued college and my career with everything I had."

—Anonymous veteran, former sergeant, U.S. Marine Corps

"One of the biggest lessons I learned: Prepare to change your plans and adapt. My plan essentially was to get a degree and figure out a career decision based on my interests in college. Even though I went to business school, I got hooked up with a federal law enforcement recruiter and decided that was the path I wanted to take, so I started that process prior to graduating. Simultaneously, I started the officer process for the Air Force and thought I would be able to do both. However, both processes took so long, I had to find that interim job to stay afloat, which was never a part of my plan. In hindsight, it was a great learning experience and really diversified my knowledge and I was able to serve the veteran community in my new position with Veterans Lending Group, but at the time, I was highly frustrated and discouraged. So my biggest takeaway from the transition process I tell people is to have a plan, have a backup plan, and probably a third backup plan, but ultimately be prepared to just shoot from the hip and make the best decision with the information at the present and don't lock yourself into one way of thinking."

—Josh Pelto, former staff sergeant, U.S. Air Force

"During my last year on active duty, I spent a great deal of time preparing for my next move in education planning. I was a high school dropout and had enlisted in the Navy with a GED via waiver because my ASVAB score exceeded whatever the minimum was for kids with my background. I had a traumatic childhood, like many in the military, particularly within the enlisted ranks. I used the Navy as a one-way ticket out of town and now I was ready to enter the civilian world with a chip on my shoulder. I knew where I wanted to go to college and what I wanted to major in. I even knew what I needed to do in a summer course load to graduate with my BA in two and a half years. I knew all the details of the Post-9/11 GI Bill. It was important for me at the time to graduate as soon as possible, as I wanted to go to law school because I wanted to become a sports agent, and thought being close to thirty years old was too old to have my first real civilian job. I was ready to kick down the door and pursue my dream of working in the sports industry. In my mind, there was nobody going to stop me."

—Dustin Bennight, former seaman apprentice, U.S. Navy

"A hero is someone who has given their life to something bigger than oneself."

—JOSEPH CAMPBELL

CHAPTER 2

I AM THE MASTER OF MY FATE: THE RETURN TO CIVILIAN LIFE

"One of the biggest impediments to veterans healing themselves and their relationships is themselves. We all need to own this part of ourselves, take responsibility for it, and act on it."
—COMMAND SGT. MAJ. THOMAS SATTERLY,
U.S. Army (Ret.), First Special Forces Operations
Detachment–Delta; author; and current CEO
of the All Secure Foundation

One of the most memorable and life-changing parts of our military experience is the transformation we endured through our indoctrination into the service of our country. We were all molded into one common, uniform body to protect the person standing next to us and serve the Constitution. Rob notes that, countless times, he's heard how, after this experience, veterans cannot relate to their civilian friends anymore. It makes sense, as only about 6 percent of the U.S. population are veterans and would have remotely any idea of the transformation you have experienced.[1]

A deeper look into the psychology and physiology of our training reveals that all indoctrination has the same overarching goal: to train recruits or cadets physically and mentally, instilling in them an understanding of, and willingness to live by, the values held by each branch of the U.S. Army (TRADOC Regulation 350-6). We were taught physical and psychological reflexes, survival skills to become warriors. Said differently, indoctrination incorporates civilian individuals into a collective group that shares a unique identity and purpose. It has three specific goals: (1) to remove characteristics that are detrimental to military life (that is, to subordinate self-interest to follow orders); (2) to train individuals to kill when necessary; and (3) to enable recruits to view themselves in collective terms.[2]

Along with these changes, we were pushed to our limits both mentally and physically and taught to never quit. Asking for help and revealing pain were signs of weakness and a lack of commitment to the cause. There are times when you need to muscle through everything— whether it be an emotional difficulty or trauma, continued exposure to combat and its physiological toll, head injury, or other challenges. Recalling the wisdom of then gunnery sergeant Cobb, U.S. Marine Corps, from Rob's Plebe Summer at the Naval Academy in 2000: "If you want sympathy, you can find it in the dictionary between shit and syphilis!" Like a broken record, this would play in his mind through the hard times he endured in the service, flipping the pages of a dictionary looking for definitions of body excrement and an STD, and there it was—"sympathy"! *Mind blown*. We all have our internal mantra to keep muscling through adversity in our lives, never stopping to get help. And now as you look to transition, you will automatically default to what you know. Put the dictionary down—this way of thinking is behind us. We no longer need it, and it is in fact detrimental to the terrain in which we are now operating. Before we move on, a disclaimer: We are neither psychotherapists nor mental health experts. This chapter is not meant to replace the advice of trained professionals. Our objective is to present the best advice we have found, both as consumers and as fellow travelers.

To the veteran who observes, "They say, 'Thank you for your service—and good luck restoring your soul.' The baggage doesn't just go away"—please pay particular attention to this chapter. Command Sgt. Maj. Tom Satterly, U.S. Army (Ret.), remarked, "We are each responsible for our own healing." Or as William Henley wrote in his poem "Invictus," "I am the master of my fate; I am the captain of my soul."

THE WOUNDS OF WAR

We know from our own lives that any serious life transition involves profound emotional, physical, and even spiritual issues, and their ramifications on an even deeper level affect our ability to function optimally and feel fully alive. Many returning warriors suffer from one or more of four major categories of ailments:

- *Challenging emotions.* By this we mean the kind of grief, depression, anger, and confusion experienced on a deeper level, whether from a sense of loss, moral injury, or an overwhelming experience. These can affect the deepest parts of ourselves. They can change our physiology, as well as alter our equilibrium and ability to adapt and respond to our situation and life circumstances. While these ailments are not really just "emotional" in nature, we use that label here for the sake of convenience.
- *Substance abuse.* Whether on its own or in combination with other ailments, substance abuse has a distorting impact on one's life, particularly during a major life transition such as becoming a civilian.
- *Physical injury.* Dealing with physical injuries, whether serious or disabling, can be a life-changing event.
- *PTSD and TBI.* These are complex and challenging conditions for many veterans, with a wide variety of symptoms and degrees of injury.

The wounds of war can be physical, but also hidden from sight. There is no neat dividing line between physical and mental injury. If you feel that you were exposed to one or more traumatic events, make it a point to speak with a doctor or counselor about PTSD. If you think you were exposed to blast waves, have suffered a concussion, or may have symptoms of TBI (sometimes referred to as breacher syndrome), see a doctor and be sure to get records of your baseline exams or take a baseline assessment test. See chapter 1 for an overview of the medical assessments you'll need before you leave the military. If your medical file has no record of these conditions and you ultimately require care for them by the VA or a private physician, it will be much more difficult for your expenses to be covered.

Comorbidity Incidence

Any of the four categories of ailments we introduced above often exist simultaneously within an individual, and they often have a complex reinforcing effect on each other, like a Ping-Pong ball caught between paddles. This is sometimes referred to as an incidence of "comorbidity." For example, moral injury, physical injury, PTSD, and TBI often coexist and are often accompanied by depression and substance abuse. As a result, they tend to build on each other and become more difficult to diagnose, treat, and heal. From our research and via interviews with doctors, we have collected pieces of wisdom that can be applied on a case-by-case basis:

- If possible, pick them off one at a time, like a sniper.
- The whole person needs to be understood and treated. Distinctions between psychiatric disorders and physiological injury are often unhelpful. Rather, a holistic approach to treatment can be effective, including varying types of therapy, exercise, good diet and sleep, meditation, and other powerful healing strategies
- Harnessing the power underneath fear, tapping into hope, and developing a new self-narrative, or story, are essential elements in managing any of these conditions—as well as the other aspects of the transition to civilian life.

Why Don't Veterans Get Help?

In 2022 the *New England Journal of Medicine* revealed that less than half of the soldiers and marines who were experiencing serious PTSD and depression received medical help.[3] The reasons warriors resist help are varied and include the following:

- The remaining stigma of what are believed to be mental health problems
- Lacking sufficient insurance coverage
- Issues with the VA (not having access to VA services, not knowing how to access services or navigate the VA system, or a poor opinion of the VA, particularly given its general reputation among veterans, lack of trust, or bad prior experience with VA services)
- Challenges associated with family life (arranging care for children while seeking treatment, concerns about losing custody of children, particularly for treatment of mental health disorders or taking unpaid leave from work)
- Practical difficulties in accessing treatment (long wait times, having a hard time reaching providers, and not having reliable transportation, particularly in rural areas)
- Concerns that seeking treatment will have a negative impact on employment

For understandable reasons, most combat veterans feel the need for the person caring for them—whether in a professional or personal capacity—to understand their story, something that they do not want or expect from mere civilian doctors.[4] While there are resources available to veterans,[5] including from the Department of Veterans Affairs (which we also refer to as the Veterans Administration or VA) and other sources, many do not take advantage of these.[6] As Tom Satterly has said, getting help is not a sign of weakness but a desire to become stronger and better. And today, there are many more new, innovative, and helpful resources available to veterans than ever before. There is an arsenal of hope, as Jen Satterly has reminded us.[7]

THESE ISSUES ARE REAL

Much has been written about depression, suicide, other mental health issues, substance abuse, PTSD, TBI, and other ailments plaguing many veterans. These conditions make more challenging the already difficult feat of transitioning to civilian life. The statistics are startling.

More than 30 percent of active-duty and reserve military personnel deployed in Iraq and Afghanistan reported a mental health condition requiring treatment (or approximately seventy-three thousand men and women), and those are the ones who were willing to report the PTSD and major depression; the real numbers of those suffering are most certainly larger.[8]

There is an epidemic of veteran suicide. Current estimates vary, but the general consensus is that veteran suicides total roughly twenty-two per day (with some minor reduction in 2021, as stated in the *2023 National Veteran Suicide Prevention Annual Report*, with some estimates as high as forty-four per day.[9] Whatever the number, it is far higher than that of the civilian population. Suicide has become more deadly than enemy forces. Per Dr. Michael Glick, more Vietnam veterans have died by suicide than were killed in the war itself. This has been linked to a variety of factors that can be interrelated: substance abuse, homelessness, mental health issues, medical concerns, and chronic pain. According to Pew Research, 30,177 Global War on Terror veterans have died by suicide, compared to the 7,057 who died while deployed in support of it.[10] Veteran suicide rates have been increasing since 2001,[11] no doubt coinciding with these wars.

"Laying beneath the surface [of suicides] were the homeless, incarcerated, drunks, addicts, dysfunctional families, spousal abuse, divorce, disrepair, victimization, and the insidious impact returning soldiers would have on society as a whole as they affect people close to them," wrote Ron Zaleski, author of *The Long Walk Home: A Veteran's Barefoot Journey Across America*.[12] A study of Iraq and Afghanistan war veterans revealed that many suffer a sense of guilt over the inability to have prevented a comrade's death, whether in battle or by suicide, which makes acceptance of the loss more difficult. The attribution of blame for the deaths creates anger and often a sense of detachment from the civilian world, which may make it more difficult to cope with the loss.

Between 13.5 percent and 30 percent of deployed and nondeployed veterans screened positive for PTSD,[13] with as many as five hundred thousand troopers who served in Afghanistan and Iraq having been diagnosed.[14] The risk of PTSD has been shown to increase among younger soldiers, racial minorities, those with limited education, those who have had prior psychological issues, those with a lack of support from family, friends, and community, and those who have endured longer deployments.[15] The incidence of comorbidity of PTSD with other challenges among veterans is high. Veterans with PTSD may start drinking or using drugs to try to relieve their symptoms. If you already have an issue with substance use, it may worsen if you develop PTSD. Nearly 25 percent of veterans have PTSD, and veterans who have a substance use disorder (SUD) are three to four times more likely to be diagnosed with PTSD. Among veterans with SUD who served in Afghanistan and Iraq, 63 percent also had PTSD.[16]

The trauma and high incidence of physical and sexual assault and harassment is very real. About 30 percent of female veterans have experienced some form of sexual trauma (meaning sexual assault or sexual harassment, among other things) during their time in the military.[17] Male soldiers are not immune from sexual harassment or assault, although it is reported less frequently.

Adding to the veteran's emotional burden is the fact that there is even less attention paid and support given to spouses, children, and the extended families of active-duty military personnel and veterans, even though it has been established that the lengths of deployments are associated with a higher incidence of emotional difficulties among military children and more mental health problems among spouses.[18] Spouses' and children's issues are addressed separately in chapter 16.

Veterans are also disproportionately affected by homelessness. This is due to a variety of factors including mental and physical health disorders, difficulty adjusting to civilian life, trauma, substance use, and difficulty accessing resources and treatment that may be available.[19]

Estimates show about 8 percent of homeless adults in 2020 were veterans, accounting for more than thirty-seven thousand people.[20] Recent media reports have identified a spike in veteran homelessness.

Combat veterans in particular, or anyone who has experienced a traumatic event, tend to suffer from one or more of the ailments illustrated by the concentric circles below. Keep this in mind as you read the rest of this chapter and chapters 3–10.[21]

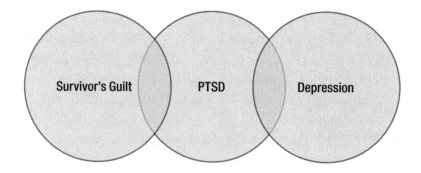

Post-Service Challenges Unique to Some Marginalized Populations

We want to pause here and highlight the experiences of female veterans, members of the LGBTQ+ community, and those of color because, based on our research and interviews, their experiences are often little regarded.

When you have served and then take off the uniform, the change in identity and the feeling that you have lost your identity (which we discuss in chapters 11 and 12 on refinding purpose in life) can lead to a sense of isolation. The list of practical tasks you need to accomplish while working to reorient yourself to your new terrain can be taxing, requiring a new kind of mission planning and adjustment along the way. On top of these transition challenges, if you believe that your own situation or life experience is different from that of your fellow veterans and civilians, then the emotional reactions and sense of isolation and challenge can be made more difficult. That hill may look steeper and harder to climb. These particular groups of veterans are deserving of our support in a respectful way that acknowledges their needs while understanding their equal commitment to duty.

Female veterans face challenges that are unique:

- They report feeling largely invisible, with about 91 percent in one survey feeling that civilians do not understand their experience.[22]
- They experience significantly higher rates of military sexual trauma (MST) than their male counterparts. Most studies vary in their reporting of this statistic (from within the 67 percent reporting MST,[23] one-third reported sexual assault and 71 to 90 percent reported experiences of sexual harassment[24]); some have found the rate to be 2.5 times greater than for women in the general population.[25] It is difficult to know with precision, however, because MST is underreported for a variety of reasons, including shame, stigma, and the risk of career damage.
- They face higher rates of domestic violence compared to their male or civilian counterparts.[26]
- They have double the risk of developing PTSD, are prone to developing SUD if they have PTSD or specific medical issues, and are at greater risk for suicide.[27] Several studies attribute these factors to the incidence of MST, poor health conditions while having served, biases against mothers (and particularly single mothers), and the other factors listed here.[28]
- Shame, stigma, and difficulty accessing childcare may make it difficult for veterans who are mothers to seek treatment in male-dominated VA facilities.[29] In our research, we found a common complaint regarding the lack of sensitivity to women's issues at the VA.[30] One study reported that female veterans were awarded benefits for PTSD at lower rates than men.[31] In 2019, 43 percent of female veterans who used the VA were diagnosed with mental illness, with depression being the most common type.[32]
- The Veterans Health Administration (VHA) identified mental health as a research priority in its Women Veterans Research Agenda after reviewing frequency data indicating that women

veterans have higher rates of mental health conditions, such as post-traumatic stress disorder and depression, compared to male veterans and nonveterans.[33] These result from a combination of stress, stigmatization, and discrimination from other people, as well as overall policies within the military and VA health-care system.

- Female veterans are at higher risk of homelessness compared to their civilian counterparts.[34]

LGBTQ+ veterans face similarly difficult challenges and are more likely to have worse physical and mental health outcomes.

- According to one study, the estimated 1 million LGBT veterans face higher levels of economic insecurity, housing instability, and mental health concerns compared to their non-LGBT counterparts.[35]
- Many LGBTQ+ veterans have complained of mistreatment, discrimination, MST, and the negative consequences of being dishonorably discharged as a result of the "Don't Ask, Don't Tell" policy, including with respect to having their careers ended early and a loss of benefits, among other concerns.[36]
- More than half of LGBTQ+ veterans say they have experienced some sort of discrimination at a VA facility and in receiving health care.[37]
- Discrimination and stigma from health-care providers can cause LGBTQ+ veterans to withhold personal information or avoid seeking care. Half of lesbian veterans are concerned about discrimination if a VA provider becomes aware of their sexual orientation; 10 percent have been harassed, and 10 percent have been denied treatment.[38] Additionally, since the VA does not accurately track sexual orientation and gender identity, providers may fail to recommend suggested screenings for physical and mental health conditions for LGBTQ+ veterans.

VETERANS' VOICES

"When I arrived in Afghanistan, it was a twenty-hour-a-day operations tempo, with constant difficult decisions, attending memorial services for fallen soldiers, and great difficulties. During stressful moments, I threw myself into my work and worked out twice a day. By the end of the day, I was exhausted and was able to recuperate with sleep for the next day ahead. After I left the military, these experiences, including how I dealt with them, helped me in my civilian life."

—Gen. David H. Petraeus, U.S. Army (Ret.); currently partner, KKR & Co., and chairman, KKR Global Institute

"When you leave the military and return to civilian life, it feels like you are starting over—and you are. You need to be prepared for that because it will be difficult and frustrating. At the same time, once you find the right place for yourself at a job or a career, the essential qualities and values you learned in the military will come back to you and serve you well. That will help other parts of your life. These qualities are being unselfish and committed to the team and something bigger than yourself, being a good employee and follower, respecting the chain of command of the organization, knowing how to lead and take responsibility, and having the bearing of discipline and integrity. In this regard, the military trains you to be better, to achieve more. These qualities will be translatable into the new work environment, will be valued, and will attract followers who will want these things around them. These things inside you are things you can control. Others have done it before. They will be there to help you. There is a way also to find a new family in your work that is meaningful and real. These things translated for me into my overall reintegration as a civilian."

—Pat Patalino, former captain, U.S. Marine Corps; currently general counsel, Baron Funds

"The disconnect you have from civilian life when you get out can cause some vets to isolate themselves. This is very detrimental to mental health and can often lead to suicide. Luckily for me, I started college as soon as I got out. This helped keep me from being isolated and I was able to focus my energy in a positive direction."

—Jessi Border, former senior airman, U.S. Air Force

"When I left service I packed away my uniforms and gear into a thirty-gallon drum and forgot about them. When I passed the two New York National Guard soldiers posted at the Port Authority bus terminal in New York City every day on my way home from work at U.S. Customs and Border Patrol, I did not speak to them. I remembered the sense of distance we were supposed to maintain between ourselves and civilians instilled in us by our training and told myself that these National Guard soldiers probably wouldn't appreciate me walking up to them for conversation. Another part of me was doing its best to focus on being a civilian so why would I reengage now. After all, I had packed away my military life in a thirty-gallon drum in the closet. But years later, and to this day, remembering certain things makes me nostalgic about my time in service, and the soldiers I served with. I sometimes wear my old PTs while cleaning house or doing chores and I communicate often with my friend and staff sergeant who retired just a couple of years ago and now lives with his family in Virginia."

—Kelli Asamoah, former sergeant, U.S. Army; currently security consultant and agriculture specialist at AkkAco

"As we express our gratitude,
we must never forget that the highest
appreciation is not to utter words,
but to live by them."

—PRESIDENT JOHN F. KENNEDY

CHAPTER 3

THE FOUR STAGES OF REINTEGRATION

"Between who you once were and who you are now becoming, is where the dance of life really takes place."

—NATIVE AMERICAN PROVERB

To provide veterans a useful framework to structure the journey home, we consulted Dr. Michael Glick, a Vietnam-era Marine and therapist who works with veterans, and Dr. Edward Tick, a renowned author, poet, and therapist who has focused on veterans returning from war.[1] Over the decades, Dr. Glick has identified four stages that many veterans pass through on the path to reintegration and reentry to civilian life. Keep in mind that these are general observations from Dr. Glick, as supplemented by Dr. Tick and others, meaning we have tailored these observations to individual situations. The four stages of reintegration are as follows:

Stage #1—Uncovery: the recognition of feelings we have about leaving the military and transition and the beginning of uncovering them

Stage #2—Discovery: talking about and discovering these
   emotions
Stage #3—Recovery: the ways healing can begin
Stage #4—Reintegration and reentry into civilian society

If emotional baggage is not addressed, it will resurface in unexpected and often unhelpful ways. Colonel Charles W. Hoge, MD, U.S. Army (Ret.), one of the preeminent doctors in the field of veteran return and who spent decades downrange treating warriors, said, "Emotions are like water; they will always find a way to seep through the surface, through any crack or imperfection in defenses."[2] To put it another way, the training we received in the military taught us to compartmentalize physical and emotional injury and to ignore and override the symptoms on the battlefield, but this becomes a liability at home if left unaddressed, leaving the veteran with a heavy load as they transition to civilian life without any cognitive flexibility. Life is much easier—the transition is much easier—if we lighten that load. The perhaps harsh reality is that, unless we can regain at least some of our well-being, it is even more difficult to find a new purpose in life outside the military or to stay focused successfully in an effective way on whatever we're doing, at work or at home.

At every stage, dealing with one's fears and being able to regulate one's emotions and nervous system are critical tools. We provide practical suggestions for doing so in chapter 10.

STAGE #1—UNCOVERY

If you have not been trained to recognize signs of dehydration when camping or out in nature, then it's hard to manage the situation when it begins to affect your performance. If dehydration continues, it can ultimately lead to a serious medical emergency. The same goes for recognizing the signs of emotional pain and distress or just the dislocation of the transition. It isn't just that many of us have not been schooled in recognizing difficult emotions. As has been mentioned, warriors are trained to *not* get help for their emotions, as the military environment often discourages that. In fact, many units are extensively trained to compartmentalize difficult emotions and thoughts for the sake of combat effectiveness, mission success, and survival. But these short-term techniques can last a career and a lifetime. And for some, they can become distorting in a number of ways, ultimately affecting relationships and job performance outside the military. Some would argue that this distortion also causes damage while in the military, but that is for another book.

So how do we recognize the signs of pain and emotional distress in ourselves and in those around us who may also need help? Here are some things to look for:

- Experiencing lethargy, or an increasing lack of energy
- Dramatic mood changes, or getting irritated at things that would not have troubled you before
- Hypersensitivity to outside factors and feelings
- Excessive anger or having a short temper
- Resenting and feeling anger at civilians around you for not understanding what you and your fellow veterans went through or not appreciating the cost of actually defending this country and their lifestyles
- Withdrawal from others, self-isolation, and a sense of estrangement from others
- Problems with sleep, including an inability to fall asleep or not being able to fall back to sleep once awakened in the middle of the night, or other disruptions to normal sleep patterns
- Lack of appetite or lack of interest in eating
- Unwanted weight loss or gain
- Increased susceptibility to illness
- Lack of interest in healthy behaviors and possible negative or destructive behaviors
- Increased alcohol or drug use
- Feeling hopeless, that there is no way out or what you can do does not have meaning or impact
- Lack of motivation to accomplish even everyday tasks
- Feeling guilt or shame at being a survivor

- Thinking or talking about dark memories or feelings, including suicide

Being able to recognize these symptoms is an important first step toward self-discovery and healing.

Deciding to take positive action—no matter how small it may seem— is the next step. Many veterans develop feelings of anger and estrangement at some point during their return to civilian life. If that's you, you are in good company. Our research has shown this to be a common experience of returning veterans from every war, for a variety of reasons.[3] It's okay to acknowledge these feelings, but you want to avoid getting stuck in them. Emotions are fleeting. You can identify and process them, then let them go, so you can continue to make positive progress.

Essential elements of Stage #1 include a sense of safety for the veteran (both physically and emotionally), sobriety and avoiding substance abuse, and the beginning of self-care. Self-care includes meeting health and nutritional needs and seeking to end negative behaviors, including sabotaging and danger-seeking behaviors.[4] It goes without saying that, as part of this step, veterans must care for themselves including by seeking medical care if needed. As Eric Burleson, an Army Special Forces veteran, writes in *Separating from Service: The Mental Health Handbook for Transitioning Veterans*, critical aspects of the first stage of reintegration include (1) stopping the bleeding (whether from visible or invisible wounds); (2) reassessing, triaging, and continuing basic care; and (3) beginning the cultivation of your long-term health.[5] If you feel you need an extensive guide, Burleson's book can walk you through the mental challenges leading to healing, growth, change, and continuing to rethink your lifelong mental health needs.

What matters most at this stage is that we take a step and continue to just take one more step. An anonymous poet once said, "The journey into healing is the walk in the darkness, whose first step invites light to shine."

In some way, this is the most deeply self-caring behavior of them all—the outward manifestation of your internal desire to become stronger and find wholeness. In this aspect of the journey, applying essential skills learned in life in general and in the military can make the difference between staying in a dark place and moving toward light. You were trained to never quit, develop a plan, and solve your way out of a difficult situation. When applied to your emotional life, this may take time. Understand that it is all part of the journey to healing and wholeness.

As with every stage, veterans finding other veterans with whom to speak can be a substantial help. Locating that community may prove to be an enduring and valuable resource.

STAGE #2—DISCOVERY

If we are lucky, we discover these symptoms and triggers on our own or someone we trust points them out to us in a way that we can hear it. Being able to recognize our symptoms is the single most important next step. In his work with veterans over four decades, Dr. Glick observed to us that one of the biggest challenges of veterans is that it is often hard for them to hear—or they don't want to understand—what is blocking them from recognizing and beginning to address their own pain. The stigma of seeking help or even opening up about one's emotions remains a profound inhibition in veterans and their spouses seeking help. Command Sgt. Maj. Tom Satterly, U.S. Army (Ret.), wisely counsels that "one of the biggest inhibitions to discovery is the resistance of someone suffering to be willing to listen to themselves and others. Left to their own devices, these folks can flounder, with potentially dire consequences. It is up to each veteran to take responsibility for their lives and find a way to move on." As several veterans have reminded us, seeking help to get better is a sign of strength, not weakness. That takes courage.

So, how do you discover your own emotional state? There is no single formula or approach. But, if you were in the desert, dehydrated and suffering from wounds, your training as a warrior would kick in and you would have some sense of how to proceed. Dealing with emotional wounds is no different, though navigating emotions can seem a world away from the training you received that helped you thrive in the military. Becoming mindful of the triggers to your own hurt, anger, or damaging behavior takes time, but the signs are likely all around you. Take a look at the list of signs and symptoms listed above. Do any of them resonate with you? Are you experiencing reactions to people and events that are not normal for you? Can you ask your family or friends if this is the case? What feedback are you getting—or could you go get—from colleagues at work?

Discovery also means dialogue. It means talking—beginning by just uttering words. This can be the hardest part of the journey. It takes courage and a determination to get to a better place, to speak the unspeakable and the unspoken. What we have observed from our own lives and from our interviews with veterans is that nothing is as important as having a network of support. Beginning to talk is the first step. Speaking regularly with friends, and especially with fellow veterans—creating that ritual and habit—may seem strange at first, but it is one of the best, and well-worn, paths to this journey. This is a process of engaging the heart. You must put your mind aside and allow the heart to speak. Finding a way to get your feelings off your chest is also the best way to do away with stories you may carry inside yourself about who you are that no longer serve you. Everyone does it at some point; we all have this chatter in the back of our minds. It takes courage and skill to find and dispel these false truths. But remember that the courage, discipline, and skills you learned in the military can be applied to this most inner, quiet, and essential part of yourself—the ability to speak about your heart. And beyond that, creating a positive, empowering self-narrative is a powerful tool in one's transition.

If you need to connect with someone immediately, one good place is Vets Town Hall, a space where veterans can gather to talk. For more information, see Vetstownhall.org.[6]

The heart carries its own truth and wisdom. The body stores this and keeps the signals the heart sends, whether positive or negative.[7] Speaking from the heart opens a door to discovery of the truth and wisdom we all have inside us. This is the fundamental insight and premise of all our healing and therapy. It does not mean all our feelings and per-ceptions are accurate, are being expressed in a healthy way, or should be acted upon. Nor does it mean becoming someone we are not—no one is asking us to go on daytime TV and bemoan our lives with high drama. But being able to experience the feelings, witness them, and allow them to be aired is the only way to truly release them. This is a process of engaging one's feelings, putting the mind aside, and allowing the heart to speak. We must find a way to get these feelings off our chests and clear our own air. This may also be the best way to get rid of stories we may carry inside about how we define and even limit ourselves that no longer serves us. It takes courage and skill to find and uncover these pieces. The courage, discipline, and skills we learned in the military can be applied to this most inner, quiet, and essential part of ourselves—the ability to speak about our hearts.

STAGE #3—RECOVERY: THE WAYS HEALING CAN BEGIN

The road to recovery is one of recovering from wounds, whether visible or invisible—in other words, healing. Throughout chapters 4 through 9, we include the best therapies and treatments available and also a list of best practices in chapter 10. Having said that, healing is, by nature, an idiosyncratic journey, one that does not follow a straight line or lin-ear process—and there isn't an easy definition or formula for it. It is a life story that takes its own course, with its own twists and turns and highs and lows. From that, two powerful truths emerge. First, a way to understand this journey is to listen to stories of fellow veterans. Many of the stories illuminate the path forward. In *The Long Walk Home*, Ron Zaleski tells the story of his return home in 1972 from his service in the Marine Corps, whereupon he was plagued by feelings of anger and guilt; and then, in 2006, as an act of penance, he walked barefoot on the Appalachian Trail, where he learned self-forgiveness and empathy and found a purpose greater than himself again. Second, nothing is more powerful as a method of healing than simply gathering with fellow vet-erans and not only listening to but speaking with one other. From the wisdom of those who have tended to veterans and the stories of veterans themselves, our goal in this chapter is to provide a practical guide to the world of emotions, which will serve as the basis for the rest of the practical steps in this book.

At some point, getting help from a therapist and from family and friends, including fellow veterans, may be an essential element in the healing that you have to do to seek wholeness in your life and to truly reintegrate. Acknowledging the need for help is not a sign of weakness; it is an expression of the desire to become stronger. It also reflects a fundamental truth of the path to civilian life: that the challenges in civilian life are no less daunting than those in the military but are, rather, just different challenges on a different terrain. Having said that, we are not suggesting that working with a therapist is somehow required or that it is the only thing one needs to do. But, talking about oneself, one's pains, regrets, traumas and the prospect for new dreams and joy, can be an irreplaceable component in the healing that is needed to reenter civilian life.

Part of the honor, integrity, and code by which warriors live is defined by their sense of purpose—to serve one another, the country, and the Constitution. When transitioning to civilian life, a major challenge and an equally major opportunity is to refind purpose in your life. Refinding this purpose can be part of a successful reintegration. Later in chapters 11 and 12, we will discuss frameworks for refinding purpose and feature veterans' stories of how they went about it. One of the frameworks is connected to this aspect of reintegration: Hierocles espoused the idea that we should contract with each other to bring our communities closer to our innermost focus (the self). This allows us to recognize ourselves in others, and others in ourselves. This often entails an adjustment in our way of thinking because it encourages us to open our lives to others. It should also lead us to treat people fairly and with respect, mindful that we all share the capacity for reason. In turn, this requires us to recognize our obligations toward those we might not especially like or agree with.

Closely related to that is the narrative many veterans develop about themselves, whether they are conscious of it or not. Constructing a positive self-narrative often encompasses a way to think of your military service as having served a greater good and connects to a refound purpose.

Later, in chapter 10, we'll further discuss the idea of the self-narrative and how it supports the reintegration process. In short, in the military, our sense of purpose was connected to our being in service of one another; however, once you transition you don't have to construct your self-narrative alone. This will require help from friends, family, and professionals.

STAGE #4—REINTEGRATION AND REENTRY

This stage involves reintegrating into civilian society and creating a healthy civilian life. Doing so includes a variety of challenges—including dealing with the visible and invisible wounds of war, including trauma, grief, depression, anger, PTSD, and TBI, as well as managing new stressors that you were never trained to handle—but it also presents paths forward. Finding methods to adjust to civilian society will allow you to live a full, happy, productive, and successful life—in a way that works for you. Doing this work may put you on the path to becoming a better spouse or partner, family member, friend, parent, worker, and a more functional and productive member of society in general. It's not easy, and you should be prepared for a longer, more challenging journey home than you expected. Still, it is a necessary journey, and there are practical steps you can take to make it an empowering one.

From our interviews with veterans, psychotherapists, clergy, our research, and reflections on our own lives, we have witnessed several fundamental truths about the successful journey of reintegration. And while there isn't a single way to accomplish Stage #4, we can offer the following observations:

Healing and reintegration can fully happen only with others in community. Given the uniqueness of their experiences, veterans have an essential need to share stories, to speak and to listen to others. This can occur in many ways, from a weekly meeting, getting together for a beer or coffee, or planning organized outings like hikes or visits to natural landmarks.[8] There is really nothing quite as cathartic and healing as voicing one's experiences out loud to other veterans; being heard and hearing others. Beyond that, veterans can share truly practical information with each other—from advice on job searching, to sharing tips on how to manage the Veterans Administration benefits process, to learning from other veterans about how their spouses and families are managing the transition.

Your community and our country should play a role in your reintegration. The recognition of veterans' experiences by the community and the country itself is critical and historically has had a positive impact on how veterans return and reintegrate. This recognition signifies a welcoming, a validation of your service, and an appreciation of your sacrifice. This occurred in our country at the end of World War II when small communities and big cities welcomed warriors home, which greatly aided one aspect of their return—neighbors knew of and were thankful for the service of their returning warriors. The reverse is true, perhaps nowhere more so than in the negative example of the difficulty of the reintegration process for most Vietnam veterans on their return. If we don't participate as a community and country in the reintegration of our warriors, we likely compound the challenges veterans face. As Sebastian Junger put it, perhaps the difficult issues in a veteran's return have more to do with our society than the often exaggerated, negative image of the traumatized warrior. Beyond this, if we fail to participate in this reintegration, we forgo the enormous benefits returning warriors can provide to our communities. Our returning warriors can offer us the wisdom they have attained through experiencing great adversity and transformation. They can teach us the true costs and consequences of war. An elder warrior class could take a prominent seat in political decision-making, including regarding when is it appropriate to send young men and women into harm's way for us as a country, a point Senator John McCain articulated in his speeches and books. We elaborate on Dr. Tick's approach to veteran reintegration in the context of healing trauma in chapter 7.

Refind purpose. One of the challenges of reintegration for warriors is overcoming the emptiness many feel at losing the sense of purpose they had in the military and struggling to find new purpose in civilian life. We discuss this in more detail later on, but to put it briefly here, any successful reintegration in the longer term is heavily influenced and aided by finding a new purpose or purposes in civilian life.

Recognize the paradox of coming back to yourself. At some point during this stage, veterans may feel that they have refound a part of themselves that was lost in war or in the act of transitioning to civilian life. Recovering that part may allow them to see themselves in a new light or identify pieces of themselves that were lost or damaged. It may also renew or restore positive emotions of joy, love, and ambition. The concept of ambition is inherently forward-looking—and therefore positive—because it represents a desire to accomplish things in the future. These are all dimensions of recovery and the basis of reintegration.[9]

At the same time, returning to oneself in this way is often accompanied by a recognition of what one suffered or experienced. It's an exercise in emotional muscle memory—life's experiences are embedded in our bodies, and they come out or back to us at some point. Many veterans bear wounds of war, whether visible or invisible, that mark them as different to themselves and others compared to how they were before. You may be experiencing this now, depending on where you are in your service or transition. Just when you feel normal or yourself again (when you smile, for example), you may also experience difficult memories or the realization that you changed due to war (with the smile then comes sadness or heartache). This is part of the nobility of the warrior: their ability to bear their wounds well and to see their scars as carrying a beauty that comes only with sacrifice for their brothers and sisters, community and country. This has been described by our own Native American warriors, and by modern writers such as Erwin Raphael McManus in *The Way of the Warrior: An Ancient Path to Inner Peace.*[10]

The role of redemption in reintegration. Redemption carries many meanings; for our purposes, we refer to the concept that the cost of service, sacrifice, and loss for the veteran offers them a chance to have a new civilian life of meaning, joy, happiness, and fulfillment, and—if relevant—on a deeper level, for their souls to be saved. At the risk of sounding too spiritual for some, there's not a cleaner way to frame this idea. The wounds of war often involve deep injury to the soul, and so recovery necessitates taking care of and healing those wounds, which can fully happen only on a spiritual level. If you're skeptical, many doctors, therapists, journalists, and veterans themselves talk about it in these terms. In fact, one of the most respected writers and healers about veteran transition, Dr. Edward Tick, offers "a new, holistic, hope-filled and heart and soul-centered understanding of war trauma and healing."[11] Ultimately, the idea of redemption is simply to have made one's life—its efforts, challenges, sense of purpose, joys, and love—worthwhile and meaningful and provide a basis to think about your life in the present and look to the future. For many veterans, these ideas have aided their reintegration.[12]

Everyone's journey is different—and yet we all share a common humanity. The journey to healing and reintegration into civilian life is different for everyone. Notwithstanding that, the story of how veterans integrate is universal. There is something fundamental to the human condition about being together in these moments and in sharing—one's return, efforts at healing, service to others, and perhaps even the redemption available to us when doing these things.

Some practical tips. Through our research, interviews with veterans, and from our own lives, here are some essential and practical tips for the kind of healing that a successful reintegration requires and some observations about that process:

- Take the best, most healthy practices that we summarize in chapters 3–10 and apply them to your life. Use the time of reintegration to ground yourself with healthy eating, sleeping, and physical training and discipline. Reconnect with friends and family; begin a new job, career, or family; and avoid unhelpful coping mechanisms, such as substance abuse. Find time for yourself in nature, get a dog or other pet, or explore doing art of any kind. In chapter 10, we summarize the best critical tools for veterans, including the power of harnessing fear, self-regulation, self-narrative, and sources of inspiration and hope. We urge you to consider how to best integrate these tools into your life.

- The journey to healing—even the beginning of healing— takes time, commitment, discipline, grit, the help of others, and grace.

- Find the medicine for your soul and life that is right for you.

- Holding on to things that matter to you, as well as a sense of purpose in your life and how you can add value or make a contribution to others is often what animates one's own healing.
- Family and close friends can play a very important role in reintegration and giving you a sense of belonging.
- Finding a community of like-minded veterans and others you respect can be critical.
- Time heals. Just the passing of the days of your life, alongside committed action, will help you find wholeness.
- The signs of healing are varied. You may experience renewed energy or refreshed interest in things that used to be meaningful, or find new interests altogether. This can also lead to a renewed self-confidence and sense of resilience and a new feeling of purpose in life.
- There is a back-and-forth nature to dealing with emotions, finding purpose again, and moving forward in civilian life. Positive moments of success in one area feed the positive moments of the others. As Pastor Tom Evans pointed out, for some, there is a restlessness inside until you sort these things out.

OBSERVATIONS OF LANCE CORPORAL
DANIEL P. CORTEZ, FIFTH MARINES

In our conversation with Lance Corporal Daniel P. Cortez, he described his memories of the Vietnam War beginning with the first day he arrived in South Vietnam, which was his nineteenth birthday. He stepped off the transport plane into 102 degrees Fahrenheit, intensely humid heat, to observe stacks of coffins headed back to the United States, with the continuous sounds and stench of war. As a lance corporal, H&S Company, Second Battalion, Fifth Marines, he served several tours. He spoke of the anguish of war, made more difficult by how our government at that time sacrificed the truth about the "unwinnability" of the war for political gain, the racism that existed unchecked, and the reception service members received when returning home, something that is only now being addressed by our leaders. He spoke of trauma and stress from combat and seeing comrades killed and of survivor's guilt, which persists today, more than fifty-three years later. One particular story still haunts him: He was supposed to join his executive officer, Maj. Cornelius (Corky) Ram, to save two wounded Marines who were trapped in the face of oncoming ARVN troops, but Ram warned him off, telling Daniel that he would go, and that Daniel was to stay back—"Greater love has no one than this: to lay down one's life for one's friends," says John 15:13. The pilot of the command helicopter refused to put Ram and Captain Ford down close to the wounded Marines, because that would have been in a minefield, in the path of the oncoming enemy troops. So, Ram and Ford set down at a distance and were killed. Daniel describes Ram as a remarkable Marine, an even more remarkable man, a father figure, a true leader and patriot; one who exhibited constant honor, integrity, courage, service, and sacrifice—"If ever there was an American hero, it was him." He honored us with his confession that "still, to this day, I think of him every day, how he warned me off, how he went, and I didn't."

When we asked Daniel what he would tell other veterans in their reintegration process, his response was very clear:

- *"It's okay to be angry; it's okay to let the rage out,"* Daniel said. "If you don't let it out, it just stays inside and it does damage to yourself, those whom you love, and how you relate to others, such as employers and coworkers. The key is to let it out in healthy and productive ways."
- *"Stop beating yourself up; find a way to have peace."* Whether from what you witnessed, or were a part of, or other challenges, find a way to forgive yourself, to seek healing.
- *"Hold on to the flag."* Daniel confessed that one thing he has held on to, despite trauma, anguish, and the politics of the 1970s, is the promise of this country, the promise that "a more perfect union" remains. "It is one thing that still guides me, that is still worthwhile, despite all the pain and difficulties. I

am still moved by our flag. It gives it all meaning, what we sought to serve."

- *"Ensure that your life has meaning and positive impact."* He explained, "For me and many others, I have sought to live a life of integrity after I left the Marines, to serve others and to help fellow veterans. It has made a difference in my life and I hope in the lives of others." Daniel has helped fellow veterans since the day he got out; he founded and is currently the chairman of the National Vet Court Alliance, which aims to prevent suicides and the incarceration of veterans suffering from PTSD and other ailments. He is also a commissioner of the President's Advisory Commission on Hispanic Prosperity. "This is my therapy," he said.

VETERANS' VOICES

"Be prepared for initial emotional stress as you make the transition. This can come from normal life circumstances—such as moving houses or even locations, children moving in with you, the cat getting sick—things that, in the context of heightened concern about your transition, may cause you to take on added stress."

—Gen. Stanley McChrystal, U.S. Army (Ret.);
currently cofounder and CEO, McChyrstal Group

"I didn't think transitioning would be difficult, but it was one of the most challenging times in my life. That would probably surprise a lot of people who know me. Although I was fortunate and found a good job almost immediately after retiring from the Army, the real transition took a few years for me. I felt deep down that I had lost my purpose since leaving the Army. I didn't recognize (or I denied) that it had impacted me so deeply, and subsequently, my physical and mental health suffered, and my substance use increased. My wife didn't really recognize the downturn and I never let her know where I stood with my physical and mental health diagnosis, let alone why I was often very difficult to get along with or why I rarely wanted to do anything fun together. The one person who cares the most about me did not know what was happening to me or why. She took on a lot, just trying to figure it out and trying to help. I wish I had talked more honestly with her early on about what I was thinking and experiencing. Now we talk about our physical, emotional, and our mental health. But we recognize that we have to do the work needed every single day to stay healthy and happy. We are stronger than ever together now."

—Col. Shawn Prickett, U.S. Army (Ret.); currently director of Rotary Wing Training Programs, FlightSafety International

"Going through the four stages that Dr. Glick describes is normal for everyone, not just the people who have physical or mental health issues. It does not make you broken and weak to feel grief, anger, anxiety, fear, et cetera. Those stages apply even to the veterans who walk out of the military more physically and mentally healthy than when they walked in. Understanding and paying attention to all those stages becomes so, so, so important to veterans with any of the ailments you mention because PTSD and TBI, among others, can magnify the negative impacts of each stage, but those stages and feelings happen to everyone regardless."

—Siobhan Crawford, former U.S. Navy lieutenant; currently civilian contractor, Department of Defense

"If I had to give advice to veterans, I'd tell them to be true to yourself, to who you are, just as you did on the day you raised your hand to defend the country and the Constitution. I'd also tell them to use the time to take care of yourself when you get out. If I had read about the four stages of reintegration, I would have been much better off and I would have cared for myself better than I did."

—John Sheehan, former petty officer third class (radioman), U.S. Navy; currently CEO, Sheehan and Sons Security

"There are a lot of ingredients to making a successful transition. What worked for me included having a clearly defined support network, not isolating myself, renewing a sense of purpose (which took time), celebrating small victories, finding an outlet or distraction (fishing, hunting, working out, fixing an old car), and getting help in therapy. Don't underestimate the power of therapy. The roughest and toughest operators in the theater will be in the group sessions when you walk in the door. Psychological changes from combat are hard to anticipate unless you've been trained to do that. When I got back, there were times when I was not myself. Therapy is one of the things that really helped me uncover these things, find some healing, and allow myself to return."

—Paul Lukas, former staff sergeant, U.S. Army and New Jersey National Guard (Ret.); currently compliance risk management executive, chief compliance officer—Office of Fair Lending, JPMorgan Chase

"Grief is the price
we pay for love."

—QUEEN ELIZABETH II

CHAPTER 4

LOSS AND GRIEVING

"You will survive, and you will find purpose in the chaos. Moving on doesn't mean letting go."

—MARY VANHAUTE

Grief" is a term often mentioned without much understanding or explanation. What is grief? In its most simple form, it is a natural reaction to loss.[1] In more human terms, experiencing grief can be like an ocean wave that unexpectedly hits you and knocks you over, leaving you with deep mental and emotional anguish, sometimes triggered by the memory of the person or thing lost or just for no reason that is easily apparent to us.

Loss can arise from many occasions: the loss of a comrade (whether during one's time in the military or after, particularly if you have left the military and those still in have died), loss of a spouse or other loved one, the end of a marriage, losing or leaving your job, children growing up and leaving the house, the end of relationships, the loss of innocence, or a sense of the loss of yourself after you suffer a moral injury. Survivor's guilt is a variation on grief. A feeling of loss often arises just from leaving the military—in a way that may be surprising. In hindsight, for many veterans, leaving the military means losing something that has provided structure, comfort, community, a sense of common and transcendent purpose, and a sense of identity. There is an insufficient sense of awareness about the loss that even comes from leaving combat and its potentially addictive qualities.

These kinds of losses are profound, life-altering moments of suffering. Grief goes beyond mere sadness or bereavement. For many of us, grief arises at the time of the loss and for many years after—for some, for their entire lives—because processing the loss simply cannot be done quickly, then stored away or buried. Grieving is a way of coping.

Experiencing grief has, for some time, been considered by psychotherapists as an emotional response to loss, for which there is a set pattern of stages of grieving.[2] However, more recent studies of grief have recognized that there can be dimensions to our grief, such as physical (pain); cognitive (failing to recognize and adjust to one's surroundings, failing to fully focus or engage mentally in an appropriate manner); behavioral (crying, pacing); social (engaging in self-isolation or antisocial behavior); and cultural or spiritual (anger at God, losing faith). Psychotherapists may suggest the role of the unconscious in resolving this suffering, but that's just too hard for us to know and there is nothing practical about that observation for us, particularly for this field manual.

A DEEPER DIVE INTO GRIEF

While there are many kinds of grief—and we cannot address all of them *and* the full waterfront of theories of grieving—there are certain patterns within the grieving process that are universal. The notion that grief follows five stages, as outlined by Elisabeth Kübler-Ross (denial, anger, bargaining, depression, and acceptance), may hold some truth, but can be too formulaic and simplistic and doesn't offer much of a practical path forward out of the dark place.[3] In recent years, we have deepened our understanding of grief. The idea that grief is simply feelings or emotions is outdated. In our discussions with Dr. Ryan Rana,[4] he asserted that grief is a physiological function; it is not "just feelings." The state of grief is a natural and healthy, albeit painful, way our brains and hearts process significant change of any kind, particularly changes that involve loss. When that loss is part of a larger world the veteran loses when separating from the military, with its associations of purpose and deeper meaning, the power of grief and the hold it has on us can be profound. For the veteran, one could also say grief represents the body's and the heart's way of having a battle debriefing that lasts longer than it might normally. Grief can also be understood to be the cost of love, particularly when we lose those closest to us. If we allow ourselves to walk through the times when we are grieving, we are on the right path.

Try to pursue positive responses to grief:

- Eat well and sleep enough every night.
- Work out or engage in physical activity (when you can, at twice the rate compared to normal).
- Put the skills and discipline from your time in the military to use to address your feelings of grief.
- Talk with friends, family, and fellow veterans about your loss.
- Seek out veterans' groups in your community at your local VA, VFW troop center, or nearest military facility.[5]
- Enjoy time in nature, in whatever form you can find it. Whether it's the ocean, lakes, mountains, forests, state parks, or something similar, many veterans have found solace, healing, and valuable time in these places. Many state parks and beaches offer free passes to veterans.
- Consider going on an adventure with fellow veterans and friends.
- Invest your time and self into other things of importance, particularly your job. There are times when it's crucial that you throw yourself into your work and other commitments as a way of getting through a rough patch, even if you also have to attend to your emotional health.
- Get curious about it. Read about what grieving means and does, and ask yourself in what areas of your life the sense of loss arises and how this affects you.
- Engage in positive visualization and self-talk of what your life will look like when you're in a positive place. We lay this out in more depth in chapter 10.

- Seek help from a licensed therapist and grief counselor, particularly if you have symptoms of depression, or feel that you are at risk of hurting yourself or others.
- Compartmentalize your moments of emotional pain. Allow them to come out, but don't allow them to dominate and immobilize you; make sure you still attend to the important parts of your life, like your physical health, spiritual health (if you are a believer), your family, and your job.
- Serve others and seek out volunteer opportunities. In serving others, particularly fellow veterans, we have some chance at redemption in our own lives.
- If you don't already have a meditation practice, consider establishing one. Meditation is simple to learn. We've included some resources for getting started in chapter 10.
- If spirituality or religion is or could be a part of your life, now is a good time to ask God, a higher power, or whatever you refer to it as, for guidance. Contact a chaplain, pastor, rabbi, imam, or other religious figure, and attend group meetings at your local church, synagogue, mosque, or other place of worship.[6]
- Remember to give yourself time to heal—it won't happen overnight, but it will happen.

Avoid negative responses to grief:
- Avoid alcohol and drugs while grieving. Substances may dull the pain in the short term but ultimately work to compound grief and make it much more difficult to get through. If you are in the throes of addiction, you can find resources for getting help in Annex 1 on our website, www.heroes-journey.net.
- Avoid denial. Grief will not go away, nor will it get easier to bear on its own. You will need to take an active approach to your mental and emotional health.
- Avoid hurting those closest to you as you work through your grief. A short temper, failure to communicate, and not being

present for your family or friends will only alienate you further.

- Avoid self-sabotaging behaviors—bar fights and other kinds of physical or verbal fighting, illegal activities, or recklessness.

To this last point, rage is a common emotion many veterans contend with upon their return. It can come up as a mischanneled reaction to the sort of experiences one has in war. Rage is also the body's and the heart's way of not letting go, perhaps of a friend or an experience or a way of being. However, there are healthy and safe ways of expressing the emotions underlying rage, such as grief, at the right time and at the right place.[7]

Isolation and the power of community. Our society has a tendency to isolate those who grieve, which is unfortunate since isolation is the worst place to be at that moment. Communities with strong cultures and bonds, whether in small villages or military units, are better able to circle the wagons and support a grieving person and their family. We have much to learn from communities like this. Nothing replaces talking about your feelings of loss with friends, family, and fellow veterans.

You can't avoid it. Grief is not something we choose to experience and, therefore, cannot be avoided. It is the natural reaction to a loss that is too concentrated to be processed all at once. Attempting to avoid experiencing grief is futile. In a sense, the healing power of grief is the experience of it.

Re-grieving. As mentioned, grief doesn't go away or fully heal. The body and spirit have their own wisdom in such matters, beyond the control of our minds. The loss or event that gave rise to the grief is usually so painful that the healing from it takes time, and the strong feelings can always rise to the surface. Re-grieving is a normal part of the healing process. It can occur suddenly as a wave of emotion that hits you like an ocean wave and knocks you down. It can occur when you do not expect it. Even happy moments can trigger a grief spell, as there may be an intersection with the memory of your loss. Remember one thing: Just as it came, it will pass. You can't control when the grief will erupt, but you can prepare yourself for the inevitability that you will meet grief again.

Find resources and get help. There are many doctors, therapists, and organizations that are trained and effective at helping veterans, their spouses, and family members deal with loss and grief. One of them is the Tragedy Assistance Program for Survivors (known as TAPS), a Veterans Service Organization that has conducted and supported research on surviving loss and grieving. TAPS was founded by Bonnie Carroll, former logistics officer and executive officer, Air National Guard; and chief, Casualty Operations, U.S. Air Force, who has survived the loss of her husband, Brig. Gen. Tom Carroll. Go to www.taps.org, or see Annex 1 on our website, www.heroes-journey.net, for their articles on loss, grieving, and suicide prevention.

A PERSONAL STORY FROM ALEX

One of the things that Rob and I connected over was loss and how to deal with it. Rob lost many friends in combat—SEAL brothers, such as Lieutenant Brendan Looney; Special Warfare Operator Chief Petty Officer Charlie Keating IV; Special Warfare Operator First Class Patrick Feeks; and Special Warfare Operator Second Class David Warsen. In 2010, my wife died, leaving me with our two sons, who were six and ten years old. It was the most searingly painful challenge I have faced, leaving me disoriented. At her memorial service, someone came up to me and said, "You feel like dying, I can see that. But you will live for your sons. You will make it through because of these two boys." I knew that, but it strengthened me to hear it. The period of loss, tears, and grief that this chapter describes was long. Re-grieving happens, even today. It changed me; it made me grow to become a better father and a better man. While I don't claim to be the model for healing through grief, I can confess to you that, in those days, I promised myself that I would never engage in self-pity or complaint; that I had our two most precious sons to heal, love, and raise according to the dreams my wife and I had created, according to the highest standards of what a man and a gentleman should be—and that I was solely accountable for that. I had to get my game up for it; I had to decide between choosing light and strength over the opposite—and that decision helped us get here. Whether I knew it or not, I took one small step after another. I tried to do one good thing every day, no matter how small. Along the way, many friends and family members helped me and us.

It's also not as if it just all goes away at some point. After our discussion with Lance Corporal Cortez, I realized I carried survivor's guilt for many years. When my wife was dying and I was rushing between the hospital to be with her and making sure our young sons were off at camp and were okay, I went to a nearby church. On my knees, I prayed, "God, I don't know if it works this way, but I ask that you take me and leave her. My sons need their mother. So please hear my prayers. Please take me and leave her." This didn't happen.

I kept that guilt, for being the one that was still around, for a long time. Later, I realized that this struggle came down to the way my body was having a hard time letting the grief go because my heart wasn't ready for that. Letting go of it took an affirmative decision and action on my part to address it. I saw it as a vestige of that impossible moment but something I needed to address, for myself and my sons, so that I didn't carry it forward beyond what was right, what I needed to do.

Working on this book with Rob has been a powerful healing chapter in my life. We talked about how we had stowed some pain and stored it in a box, compartments that got opened by these last four years of interviews of veterans, their spouses, and their therapists. Hearing Rob's and others' stories about their walking through it was inspiring. Hearing the stories of injured veterans and their huge hearts and determination to heal and make a difference in the world around them on their hero's journeys made me stop and take notice on the inside of what they were saying. Ultimately, I told myself that if I didn't use what I thought I had learned from all of this in aid of others, then I would be wasting a life opportunity to serve, that I would be failing to honor my late wife, and that I would be failing to pay my share of the rent we all owe from being here. No grand claims from me, but this is a necessary part of my own journey—that I help others. In serving others, I pray that I have some small chance at redemption in our own lives and in the lives of those we love.

VETERANS' VOICES

"You will miss the camaraderie you had in the military even if you don't miss the people themselves. You were living and working with people often in adverse situations and circumstances where sacrifice at all levels was expected and endured. We forged a bond that is hard to describe. You will mourn this loss more than you ever expect to and likely struggle for some time in trying to replace it. Like the loss of a loved one, you'll be reminded often of its absence and you will miss it. The transition exposed me to a number of pain points. One example I recall was sitting in one of my MBA classes and watching a fellow student blatantly sleeping in the back of the class while many others were seemingly paying little to no attention to the professor. What I learned from this was that the anger inside me was coming more out of my pain at losing my brothers and sisters and less out of the immature behavior of one student. I eventually learned to let that moment of anger go."

—Cdr. Joshua Klein, U.S. Navy (Ret.); currently professor of business, Savannah College of Art and Design

"I have carried pain inside me for fifty-three years, since Major Ram took my place on a rescue mission and was killed in South Vietnam. I've carried that with me every day. It haunts me every morning when I awake and realize he took my place; he gave his life for mine in trying to save two stranded Marines about to be overrun by Army of the Republic of North Vietnam. I have found ways to try to let it out of me, which were helpful, which gave me some small measure of peace, at least for a moment. I also realize that I have needed to stop beating myself up, that my seeking peace for myself was okay, that I was worthy of that. One thing that also helped me was visiting Major Ram's gravesite and spending time with his family. That took me several decades to do, to find the courage to do. We all cried at his gravesite. We walked away together in that moment. That also helped me."

—Daniel Cortez, former lance corporal U.S. Marine Corps; currently chairman of the National Vet Court Alliance and commissioner of the President's Advisory Commission on Hispanic Prosperity

"True heroism is remarkably sober,
very undramatic. It is not the
urge to surpass all others at
whatever cost, but the urge
to serve others at whatever cost."

—ARTHUR ASHE

CHAPTER 5

SUBSTANCE ABUSE

"If you can quit for a day, you can quit for a lifetime."
—BENJAMIN ALIRE SÁENZ

Substance abuse is a serious problem afflicting many veterans. It is also a problem that makes addressing mental health difficulties, loss and grief, PTSD, and TBI substantially more complicated and challenging. Just like other emotional and related difficulties that many veterans suffer, if these issues are not addressed in a healthy manner, the transition to civilian life will be that much more difficult, as will life in general. Let us also be reminded of a powerful and practical observation: "Getting help is not a sign of weakness. It's a sign of wanting to get stronger," as Command Sgt. Maj. Tom Satterly, U.S. Army (Ret.), said.

THE SCOPE OF THE PROBLEM

According to the National Institute on Drug Abuse, "Veterans may abuse substances in response to mental health disorders, to cope with readjusting to civilian life, or to manage pain. Substance use has been linked to trauma, homelessness, mental health disorders, physical health issues, increased risk of suicide, and problems in relationships and at work."[1] Substance abuse may also have originated as a response to the exposure to combat and suffering combat-related injuries. Approximately 11 percent of veterans who visit a medical facility run by the VA[2] for the first time have a substance use disorder.[3] This is an alarming number if we consider that nearly half of the veterans in the U.S. use VA facilities, based on 2016 statistics and only first visits. This means that there are approximately 9 million veterans not represented in these statistics who may not be seeking help or who are seeking help through a private provider. If only half of the veterans in the U.S. visit a VA facility, then the following statistics are only addressing a small sample size of the greater veteran population, masking the true gravity of the problem. However, even this small subset of data is enough to understand that veterans are suffering, and, sadly, most are doing so quietly.

The statistics tell a staggering story:[4]

Overall substance use disorder (SUD). Statistics on substance abuse among veterans show that of those who have SUD, more than 80 percent (nearly 900,000) abuse alcohol; nearly 27 percent (about 300,000) abuse illegal drugs; and about 7 percent (almost 80,000) abuse both alcohol and illegal drugs. Veterans with SUD or co-occurring disorders are more likely to experience homelessness, and homeless veterans are at increased risk for suicide.[5] In addition, nearly three-quarters of those homeless veterans have an SUD.[6]

Alcoholism. Veterans who abuse alcohol are at greater risk of experiencing or committing violence, suffering from negative health consequences, and having a shorter lifespan.[7] Alcohol is also the primary substance of abuse for 65 percent of veterans entering treatment centers—nearly twice the rate of civilians. Male veterans are more than twice as likely to be diagnosed with an alcohol use disorder as female veterans.[8]

Drug use. Drug use among veterans can include illicit or prescription drug abuse. Prescription opioids, like Vicodin, may be prescribed to manage service-connected injuries or chronic pain and have the greatest potential to lead to abuse or addiction.[9] Marijuana is the most commonly used drug, with 3.5 percent of veterans reporting use in the last month and 11.1 percent (2.3 million) reporting use in the last year.[10] Even more alarmingly, nearly 11 percent of veterans were admitted to treatment centers for heroin use, with more than 6 percent admitted for cocaine use.[11] Male veterans are twice as likely to develop an addiction to drugs as female veterans.[12]

Mental health. The presence of mental illness and SUD, also known as co-occurring disorders, is especially common in veterans.[13] Mental illnesses (such as depression and anxiety) and PTSD can lead to substance use. These efforts to self-medicate symptoms or manage stress make veterans more prone to developing SUDs.[14] In addition, these mental health diagnoses can result from any combination of factors: genetic predisposition, the stresses of being deployed, exposure to combat and traumatic events, injuries, and the challenges of reintegrating into civilian society.[15] Approximately 37 to 50 percent of veterans who served in Afghanistan and Iraq were diagnosed with at least one mental illness.[16] More alarmingly, between 82 and 93 percent of veterans who served in Afghanistan and Iraq who already had a substance use disorder had at least one co-occurring disorder.[17] Specifically, veterans who have an SUD are three to four times more likely to be diagnosed with depression.[18] Nearly 10 percent of veterans in general have symptoms of anxiety, while about 11 percent have symptoms of depression.[19] What do all of these statistics mean? If you are struggling with any of this, you are not alone. Help is available.

COMMON SYMPTOMS

The most practical observation we can make to help veterans is to list common symptoms of SUD. The most important step in addressing SUD is to recognize it in yourself and to take the first step to getting help. Please keep in mind that these are generalizations, and everyone's situation can be different.

- Feeling that you have to use the substance regularly, daily and even several times a day
- Having intense urges for the substance that block out any other thoughts

- Taking larger amounts of the substance over time
- Making certain that you maintain a supply of the substance
- Spending money on the substance, even if you don't have it
- Not meeting obligations or work responsibilities, or cutting back on social or recreational activities because of substance use
- Continuing use even though you know it is causing problems in your life or causing you or others physical or psychological harm
- Doing things to get the substance that you normally would not do, such as stealing
- Driving or doing other risky activities when you are under the influence
- Failing in your attempt to stop using
- Experiencing withdrawal symptoms when you attempt to stop abusing the substance

Common symptoms of alcohol abuse:
- Being unable to limit the amount of alcohol you consume
- Wanting to cut back on the amount of alcohol you drink but being unable to do so
- Spending a lot of time drinking, getting alcohol, or recovering from alcohol use
- Feeling a strong craving to drink
- Failing to fulfill major obligations at work, school, or home due to repeated alcohol use
- Continuing to drink even though you know it's causing physical, social, work, family, or relationship problems
- Giving up or reducing social or work activities and hobbies to use alcohol
- Using alcohol in situations that are not safe, such as driving or swimming
- Increasing your tolerance for alcohol so you need more to feel its effect, or you have a reduced effect from the same amount

- Experiencing withdrawal symptoms, such as nausea, sweating, or shaking, when you don't drink or drinking to avoid these symptoms[20]

Because alcohol use is more pervasive than drug use, let's focus here for a moment. "Despite the recent studies and impact of alcohol use, 68 percent of active-duty troops said they perceived the military culture of being supportive of drinking, and 42 percent said their supervisor doesn't discourage alcohol use," according to a Health Related Behaviors Survey.[21] If you abused drugs and alcohol or used them moderately before entering the military, there is a strong possibility that you will continue to abuse, or develop dependencies on, drugs and alcohol once you separate from service. In fact, the chance that you will continue these behaviors, or develop an addiction, is only exacerbated and climbs exponentially if you were exposed to a traumatic event during your military service.

HELP AND TREATMENT

While a range of treatment options are available, evidence-based therapies have been extensively studied and shown to be effective at treating SUD. These types of substance abuse treatments can be tailored to a veteran's specific needs by addressing mental health issues, trauma, chronic pain, reintegration into civilian life, homelessness, and social relationships. We have found that in many cases, therapy for underlying and distressing issues is critical to finding a way out of substance abuse. Treatment is provided in a variety of settings and can be accessed through the VA or other facilities. There are 935 treatment programs in the United States that treat veterans, and 107 of these are VA facilities.[22]

Many service members and veterans do not get treatment for substance abuse disorder for a variety of reasons, including limited access to treatment, gaps in insurance coverage, the negative stigma associated with the problem, fear of negative consequences, and a lack of confidential services. In response to the increase of returning veterans and these problems, the military's TRICARE health system has expanded its treatment services, and the VA has been reexamining its approach as well.[23]

If you are suffering from substance use disorder (SUD), we encourage you to get help. Some treatment resources:

- Substance Abuse and Mental Health Services Administration (SAMHSA) maintains a free hotline for immediate assistance, which can be reached at: 800-662-4357; or visit www.samhsa.gov online.
- Your local VA Medical Center has SUD treatment resources. See www.VA.gov.
- Free, national, and twenty-four-hour drug addiction and substance abuse hotline numbers are available on the website www.DrugAbuse.com.
- Crisis line: 800-273-TALK (8255).
- Call or text 988.
- Military OneSource: Call 800-342-9647.

POSTSCRIPT—ROB AND ALEX FREQUENTLY TOAST VETERANS WITH A DRINK, BUT THAT'S NOT THE WHOLE STORY

We believe that we must be thankful for those who have served and those who continue to serve our country, protect our nation, and uphold the ideals of liberty for all. If that means every now and then we have to raise a glass to those who have gone before us and are no longer with us, then we are guilty of being patriots. We feel this is a ritual that defines what we are fighting for. Yet, we understand that our good spirits, no pun intended, are ultimately meant to define moments with a celebration of high achievement or enhance an evening of fellowship among friends. We are also acutely aware that these moments, if they include overindulging, can be shadowed by poor decisions and consequences that ruin good careers, families, and lives. All we are asking is for you to practice good judgment, be safe, and get help if you need it.

VETERANS' VOICES

"When I was in the Navy, my abuse of alcohol and other things continued, and frankly it got worse. The military and my CO, really, were the first ones to let me know that I could get help. But, I have to say that what really triggered me to start to get help and to heal myself from these abuses was the shame I felt in letting my teammates down while I was part of a high security clearance radio operator team. The way I felt they looked at me when I was abusing, the shame and disgust I felt, was what moved me. That was stronger than my addiction. God bless my teammates for this. I ended up getting help. And when I got out, I had to look at my wife and children, and that reinforced my desperate need to stay sober. My wife has been my hero—she is the true warrior in my story. God bless her."

—John Sheehan, former petty officer third class (radioman),
U.S. Navy; currently CEO, Sheehan and Sons Security

"After my depression and drug addiction, things changed for me when I went to the VA, started a 12-step recovery program, got medication, and found people with whom to speak. Then I went to college and met my wife. When I was sitting on the death bed of my mother, she said to me, 'I'm so proud of you.' She's the one that never gave up on me. And she said, 'Don't go back.' She said, 'Stay the beautiful person you is.' So it was in her honor that I could never go back. I couldn't; I would do her an injustice. There's a lot of veterans out there that suffer from mental health drug addiction that need help. And if I can tell them one thing, go to the VA. It saved my life."[24]

—Greg, U.S. Army veteran

"To all the Veterans out there, if you need help, if you see yourself going through these similar motions where you're drinking by yourself, or not taking care of yourself, you're gaining weight, or you find yourself isolated—don't. Let your light shine. There's people out there that care for you, that want to help you. Just open yourself up. Let it come in."[25]

—Stephen, U.S. Navy veteran

"The healing hero, therefore, is the one who finds some creative way out, a way not already known, and does not follow a pattern. Ordinary sick people follow ordinary patterns, but the shaman cannot be cured by the usual methods of healing. He has to find the unique way, the only way that applies to him."

—MARIE-LOUISE VON FRANZ

CHAPTER 6

MORAL INJURY AND PHYSICAL INJURY

"The soldier, above all other people, prays for peace, for he must suffer and bear the deepest wounds and scars of war."
—GENERAL DOUGLAS MACARTHUR

This chapter covers two very different wounds of war, one deep and invisible (moral injury); and one profound and life-altering (physical injury). While the two may seem unrelated, what we have found is that, for some veterans, they share an uncommon appreciation of each other, and the road forward shares some common features. The numbers are not small—more than six hundred thousand Iraq and Afghanistan war veterans have been left partially or totally disabled from physical or psychological wounds.[1] While estimates vary, it has been reported that about 36.8 percent of combat veterans have a form of moral injury,[2] 41 percent of veterans who served in Iraq and Afghanistan are morally injured,[3] and more than 90 percent of veterans with PTSD had at least one severe symptom of moral injury.[4]

MORAL INJURY

The simplest explanation of moral injury is that it is a deeply distressing emotional, psychological, physiological, and even spiritual reaction to having participated in or witnessed an event or events that offended one's moral beliefs or code at a deep level. The individual often feels that they witnessed a great transgression that was beyond their control, and the sense of injury inside that individual develops in the occurrence's aftermath. It is not hard to imagine how the warrior's experience in combat could give rise to these reactions. Killing, harming others, the sense of failure at not having been able to save close comrades or others, freezing in battle, suffering from sexual assault, or witnessing horrific events are just a few of the instances that routinely arise in war and leave the warrior with an injury to their soul and sense of identity. At a deeper level, moral injury is "an affliction of moral conscience, a negative judgment we pass on ourselves in response to violating our core moral values or being contaminated by exposure to evil. This type of injury can make us believe we are unforgiveable," as Dr. Tick, whom we met in chapter 3, notes.[5] Many have described it as a wound of the soul. Per Dr. Tick, it often comes from a sense of betrayal of what is right,[6] and produces a "crisis of faith" in the wounded, who may be "unsure if the Creator or anyone is walking with them, unsure of whether they do good or evil, unable to discover trustworthy answers or companions."[7] In the transition to civilian life, the moral injury suffered while in the military can be exacerbated, making the person feel worthless and unlovable, leading to a state of despair and even depression.[8]

What Moral Injury Looks Like and Common Symptoms

Let's unpack this further to help you identify moral injury, either in yourself or in loved ones. Warriors often carry with them powerful feelings of guilt, shame, disgust, anxiety, and anger in reaction to their military service.[9] Many find it difficult to forgive themselves, which can result in self-sabotaging behavior. For many who are left with a sense of hopelessness in living with these feelings, depression can set in,[10] which often leads to self-isolation and a corresponding worsening of one's condition. A common observation of therapists is that someone suffering from moral injury "seems stuck in stagnant grief over acts they'd committed" or witnessed, as noted by Dr. Brett Litz of the Veterans Affairs Boston Healthcare System.[11] Dr. Litz described the lingering trauma as resulting from mounting guilt and hopelessness, from a sense of what veterans were exposed to in combat, the "totality of inhumanity, the lack of meaning and the participation in grotesque war things" that has left many feeling like pariahs.[12] These feelings and the sense of being stuck in grief can make it difficult for veterans to relate to the people they were before and their families and friends.[13] The very nature of these symptoms makes it hard for many veterans to seek help and talk about these experiences. These reactions can last a long time, and for some, a lifetime.

Many studies have shown a correlation between moral injury and PTSD and an overlap between their symptoms and a resulting increase in suicide. David Brooks told us, "People generally don't suffer high rates of PTSD after natural disasters. Instead, people suffer from PTSD after moral atrocities. Soldiers who've endured the depraved world of combat experience their own symptoms. Trauma is an expulsive cataclysm of the soul."[14] In fact, a successful treatment of PTSD must often first heal the related moral injury.[15]

Common symptoms of moral injury include:

- Persistent negative feelings, including guilt, shame, and remorse about the event that caused the moral injury.
- Disinterest in previously enjoyable activities or difficulty in enjoying activities that one used to do.
- A lack of trust in others.
- A difficulty in connecting to other people out of a sense that the world is a dangerous place and these other people do not appreciate that, with a common reaction of avoiding people.
- Many who suffer from moral injury withdraw from social interaction and society, feeling that they do not fit in or others cannot comprehend what they are going through.

- Feelings of anger and betrayal.
- Self-sabotaging behavior, such as engaging in drunk driving, violence, and irresponsible or illegal acts.
- Turning away from a religion or spirituality; perhaps feeling disconnected from it or even betrayed by it.
- Feeling emotionally numb.
- Reliving the event that gave rise to the moral injury, including being awakened at night or having intrusive thoughts that feel hard to control that take one back to the traumatic event.
- Turning to drugs and alcohol as a way out of feeling and experiencing the trauma again.[16]

Treatment

We do not believe there is a single route to healing from moral injury. Rather, the full range of therapies should be considered. Here is some of the most practical advice we've collected for healing from moral injury:

- *Therapy.* Getting help from a trained therapist is critical. Most therapists will be informed about moral injury; if yours isn't, you should find one who is. Finding the right therapist is necessary.
- *Pastoral guidance.* For those who are spiritual or religious, healing from moral injury is sometimes both complicated and helpful. It can be complicated because moral injury can raise a central, difficult question if one believes in a good God or higher power: Why do bad things happen to good people? It can be beneficial because of the healing power—for those who believe—that comes with forgiving others and seeking forgiveness for oneself and what that means for accepting one's injury.
- *Fellow veteran group discussions.* Having a group of fellow veterans who have also suffered from moral injury has been a source of comfort and healing for many.

- *Developing trustworthy relationships.* More generally, voicing one's pain is a crucial step toward healing it. Discussing moral injury can be a daunting task because it leaves one vulnerable and often with a feeling of isolation. Therefore, when someone who is suffering from moral injury opens up to speak to others, trust is critical. The person listening must be prepared to be emotionally present, even openhearted. A related aspect of that is the value and need for having and building trustworthy relationships. As sharing unfolds over time, the pain of moral injury can lessen.

- *Service.* Many veterans also seek to be of service to others and to make a difference for good, which enables them to experience a sense of worth and value. Erwin McManus observes, "Serving others functions like a compass in the midst of a fog."[17]

- *Follow positive healing practices.* As we have summarized in other chapters, when seeking healing from the wounds of war, there are some general good practices to follow, including:
  - Caring for yourself, with good eating and sleeping habits.
  - Engaging in physical activity, including physical training or sports.
  - Practicing meditation and mindfulness.
  - Exposure to or practicing a form of creative expression such as art, music, theater, or dance.
  - Having the company and companionship of animals, particularly dogs.
  - Being in nature, whether with a walk by the ocean or a forest or taking a hike with friends or fellow veterans.
  - Reconsidering a self-narrative that is positive and puts your injury into a broader framework of how you consider your life story.
  - Hanging on to hope. Find small, good things to do every day, celebrate your victories, and believe that wholeness awaits you.

Here are three final observations about healing from moral injury that take some explaining—and, we'd suggest, some rereading from time to time—since these are points that, from our own life experiences, can't be boiled down to what to do and what not to do.

It is a process that begins with acceptance. Healing from moral injury takes time and involves a process. At some level, it begins with accepting what happened and processing the emotions involved.[18] It is critical but often hard to find acceptance within yourself, especially if you have a tendency to either take on too much responsibility or to blame yourself unnecessarily. If you can get to that place of acceptance, your healing will have begun. Acceptance cannot be programmed or planned for, somewhat like plotting a land navigation route. But it is most important to have healing and wholeness as your target.

The source of suffering is the key to recovery. The very source of our suffering from moral injury is the vulnerability of our hearts. In that knowledge, we have the route to our healing and recovery. Suffering from moral injury is often rooted in a deeply shocking event that caused you to question on a deep, implicit level your expectations about life and the world around you. Underlying this is great hurt to one's heart, conscience, and even soul. What we have found from our own lives, research, and conversations with veterans is that the heart and the soul are more resilient and more indestructible than we seem to recognize in our thoughts, in our heads. The very thing that makes us vulnerable to moral injury is the source of our own healing. Underneath the feelings of guilt, shame, remorse, and despair is ultimately a hurt heart, but a heart that is still beating. In that beating is hope.

Service and wisdom often come from pain. Even at one's darkest hour, we have found some common themes across the terrain of healing for veterans: the simple nobility in how veterans are called to serve one another and our country; the power that lies in that service to help us find some meaning and redemption in our own lives; and how growth and even wisdom come at a high price—as the ancient Greek playwright Aeschylus wrote, "In our sleep, pain which cannot forget falls drop by drop upon the heart until, in our own despair, against our will, comes wisdom through the awful grace of God."[19]

For many—if not all—veterans, the journey to healing from moral injury and other ailments is one based on spiritual beliefs, even appealing to a higher power. Dr. Tick describes this as a "psycho-spiritual" journey. This may not be for you; and perhaps, especially if you suffered a moral injury, you may have felt abandoned by God or a higher power. We won't tell you what to believe, and we recognize that there is more than one path worthy of you and your quest for wholeness.

PHYSICAL INJURY

For the physically injured warrior, there are additional challenges to surmount during the transition to civilian life that few can imagine. Physical injury, depending on its seriousness, cuts deep—into your identity, your sense of self, and what you are capable of. It can provoke disorientation, loss and grief about the life you used to have, anger, and even conjure up a negative self-image and feeling like you've somehow let friends, family, and fellow warriors down—even though this couldn't be further from the truth. This is not, however, the end of the story. It is the beginning.

Six Ingredients to Recovery

In distilling what we've learned from injured veterans, we've identified six ingredients of recovery, though we recognize that the specifics of recovery vary by the individual and are not one-size-fits-all.

1. *Find something real to hang on to.* The early days after your injury and separation from the military are often the most difficult. During this time, you may even question your sanity. When you're in the thick of it, hang on to something that matters to you, something that is an image of strength, something good and worthwhile If you don't think you have anything like that, we bet you can find it. Hold tight to all good things about it as you begin to recover.

2. *Make and pursue a rehabilitation plan.* As you work with your doctors (and physical therapists, if applicable), make a plan for your rehabilitation and pursue it. You don't have to take what doctors say as gospel. As the patient, you are entitled to your opinion about your care. If you think it's relevant, push them for what you feel you need if you are not getting it. You must be your own best advocate. Pay attention to your soul and heart as well as your body.

3. *Find and accept the love and support of family and friends.* That's it. It is simple, the source of love and life. Every injured veteran with whom we spoke noted how important this is.

4. *Connect with fellow injured veterans.* While it may seem that we are all different, in reality, we have much in common with one another. This is especially true for you. Finding a fellow injured veteran, or a group of veterans, whether injured or not, whom you can talk to and listen to, is critical to your healing. Fellow injured veterans are all around you: in the hospital with you, at the VA, and in veterans' groups. Annex 1 of our website, www.heroes-journey.net, contains a list of resources for injured veterans.

5. *Find new purpose.* Every veteran transitioning to civilian life must grapple with the challenge of finding new purpose. For you, that may seem more daunting because of your injury—including if adjusting to your injury means a change in life circumstances. What injured veterans have told us is that they began to realize that their injury was not going to define them as a person, was not going to define or limit their lives and relationships with other people. The injury became one more challenge, one more obstacle course to complete. We don't repeat those words here glibly—as Paralympic athlete and former Navy SEAL Dan Cnossen said, finding new purpose is easier said than done—but rather, we repeat them with awe. In chapters 11 and 12, we'll delve deeper into the process of refinding purpose.

6. *Get in charge of your VA benefits.* As with any veteran, understanding and navigating the Veterans Administration system can be a challenge. But the VA has tremendous resources available to you, and, today, there are also great resources available to the injured veteran from private sources. However, you must be the one to take charge and become your own best advocate to get these benefits and maximize them. We provide a partial list of resources for injured veterans below, with the full version in Annex 1 on our website, www.heroes-journey.net.

We offer these considerations with the greatest humility since we have not been injured while serving. Rather, we hope to serve you, the injured veteran and your family, by collecting and presenting the best observations and practical advice we have found.

THE STORY OF LIEUTENANT DAN CNOSSEN, U.S. NAVY (RET.)— PARALYMPIC CHAMPION

Rob met Dan Cnossen when he was a freshman (plebe) at the Naval Academy and Dan was in his junior year. Rob expresses his thanks: "I can't thank him enough for all his mentorship over the years and working with me on my combat sidestroke in the pool. It was bittersweet when he came to congratulate me and meet my family when I finished SEAL training. I would not see him after that as I checked into SEAL Team 3 and he was assigned to SEAL Team 1 as a platoon commander."

In 2009, Dan was conducting a turnover operation as the incoming SEAL platoon on a night mission in Afghanistan. As the platoon's leader, he moved to take the high ground of the mountainside location before many in his unit, a standard procedure for someone of his rank. Dan and about ten members of his team cleared a hilltop before their assault, but in doing so he stepped on a buried improvised explosive device (IED), which blew away most of his lower legs. He admits his memories of the moment are hard to piece together, "almost like a kaleidoscope" that can "get shaken up and get assembled" in different ways. "I just remember laying there in the dirt wondering if my team-mates were okay because I knew I needed them," he said. "They started to treat me and clear a route to get out of there because it was going to be a race against the clock to get the helicopter back," he explains. "A helicopter was coming. They had to drag me down off the mountain, and I was just in an incredible amount of pain. I was awake during this, trying to hang on." Through sheer determination, Dan's platoonmates managed to bring him to the helicopter, which was already running low on fuel. "It was really, really close," he told us. He was lucky to sur-vive, as he was in the middle of an IED field that contained nine other IEDs daisy-chained together. Saint Michael the archangel must have been looking out for our brother that day, because the initial IED went low-order and did not fully detonate. Dan, who was awarded a Purple Heart and Bronze Star with Valor for his service, said, "Due to these circumstances, I've gone in my mind from thinking it was unlucky to step where I did, to thinking I'm actually really lucky that all of this lined up, and that my teammates were able to get me out of there and get me loaded on the helicopter."

For the next two years, Dan fought for his life, enduring more than forty different surgeries, all while readjusting to being a civilian. It was at this time that he found cross-country skiing and the biathlon. He trained and earned a spot on the 2014 U.S. Paralympic Team. He then returned to graduate school to earn a master's degree from the Ken-nedy School of Government and a master of theological studies from the Divinity School of Harvard University. At the 2018 Paralympic Games, Dan won one gold, four silver, and one bronze medal over a period of eight days, earning him the title of Best Male Athlete of the Games. Dan's story is one of great physical injury and great recovery. Though many would have given up, he found the strength inside, with the love of family by his side, to plot a new course in life. Today, Dan is an inspiration to those around him—and to us. In his encouraging talks to students and others who have suffered, he gives practical les-sons on resilience and grit along with the all-important hope of a bet-ter tomorrow. He lifts up those with whom he speaks. Without Dan's input, we could not have written this chapter.

Resources for Injured Veterans

- BreakLine is an organization that provides education and coaching for veterans, including those who have disabilities, among others.

    Website: www.breaklineeducation.org
- Centers for Independence (CFI) offers disability support services, including job training and placement.

    Phone: 414-937-2020

    Website: www.cfihope.org
- Disabled American Veterans (DAV) is a leader in connecting veterans with employment by hosting job fairs and providing resources. If you have a service-connected disability that you feel has become more debilitating since leaving active duty, or you wish to file a new claim, the DAV can be of assistance and help you with the required medical screening and paperwork.

    Phone: 877-426-2838

    Website: www.dav.org
- The Department of Defense's Operation Warfighter offers a temporary assignment/internship program that matches qualified wounded, ill, and injured service members with nonfunded federal internships.

    Website: www.dhs.gov/homeland-security-careers /operation-warfighter.
- The Disabled Transition Assistance Program (DTAP) is a resource of the Veterans Alliance that provides crucial support to veterans who are transitioning out of the military due to disabilities. DTAP focuses on guiding these veterans through the Vocational Rehabilitation and Employment (VR&E) Program offered by the VA, ensuring they receive the necessary support and information.

    Website: www.va.org/the-dtap-or-the-disabled -transition-assistance-program
- The Disabled Veterans' Outreach Program (DVOP) provides job and training opportunities for veterans with service-connected disabilities, by working with employers, veterans'

organizations, the VA, the Department of Defense, and community-based organizations. There is no single but rather multiple DVOP organizations.

Website: www.benefits.com/glossary/disabled-veteran -outreach-program-dvop/

- Federal Recovery Coordination Program: The FRCP is a joint effort between the Department of Veterans Affairs and the Department of Defense to help provide federal, state, and local benefits, including rehabilitation and reintegration, for the veterans who are "seriously" wounded, ill, or injured.

Website: www.va.gov/vadodhealth/frcp.asp

- Job boards that seek to connect employers with injured veterans:
   o American Association of People with Disabilities (AAPD) Career Center (www.aapd.com/employment/)
   o abilityJOBS (www.abilityjobs.com/)
   o AbilityLinks (www.abilitylinks.org)
   o Association of University Centers on Disabilities (AUCD; www.aucd.org/)
   o disABLEDperson (www.disabledperson.com)
   o Diversity job boards (e.g., www.diversityjobs.com)
   o Getting Hired (www.gettinghired.com)
   o Job Opportunities for Disabled Veterans (JOFDAV; www.jofdav.com)
   o OurAbility Connect (www.ourability.com)
   o Sierra Consultation Services (www.thesierragroup .com/services)
   o Workforce Recruitment Program (WRP; www.wrp .gov/wrp)
- Disabled veterans are eligible for a free National Park Service lifetime access pass.

Phone the U.S. Department of the Interior/USGS, for information: 888-275-8747

www.nps.gov/planyourvisit/veterans-and-gold-star -families-free-access.htm

- Paralyzed Veterans of America: PVA helps paralyzed and disabled veterans regain their independence after injury or diagnosis.
  Phone: 800-424-8200
  Website: www.secure.pva.org
- SoldierStrong is a charitable organization whose mission is to provide revolutionary technology, innovative advancements, and educational opportunities to veterans to better their lives and the lives of their families.
  Phone: 888-898-3235
  Website: www.soldierstrong.org
- The Department of Veterans Affairs' "Careers and Employment" section can help you find work as a vet if you have a service-connected disability.
  Phone: 800-827-1000; 800-698-2411
  Website: www.va.gov/careers-employment/

There are numerous federal, state, and local agencies and also nonprofit companies that provide information and services to those with injuries and disabilities, such as employment networks, the Council of State Administrators of Vocational Rehabilitation National Employment Team, state vocational rehabilitation agencies, and the Employment Resource Referral Directory maintained by the Department of Labor's Office of Federal Contract Compliance Programs.

VETERANS' VOICES

[Two Afghan teenagers on a motorcycle were driving toward a Marine outpost, and the Marines mistook sticks and bundles they were carrying for guns and muzzle flashes for lights bouncing off the motorcycle's chrome. The Marines killed the two Afghanis.]
"I can't forgive myself. And the people who can forgive me are

dead...There's no day—whether it's in the shower or whether it's walking down the street...that I don't think about things that happened over there."[20]

—Timothy Kudo, former U.S. Marine Corps captain; currently a graduate student at New York University

"I know the brothers that I lost would trade places with me in a heartbeat. So, to me, it's an injustice not to live my life to the fullest, not to inspire others. This is a fucking testament that yeah, life's a bitch. If life knocks you down, make sure you land on your back so you can look at it right in the face, get back up, and say, 'What else you got, bitch?'"

—Omar Avila, sergeant, U.S. Army (Ret.); currently CEO, Five Toes

"When you are injured and lying in a hospital bed, you face a choice: feel sorry for yourself and drink the pain away, try to get back to the person you used to be, or open your eyes and finally love life. Become better than you ever were...The more time I spent at the gym, the happier I became. The more I focused on improving myself and giving back, the better I felt. When I left the military, I started teaching corpsmen, Marines, and police officers combat trauma medicine. I later started working for the Elizabeth Hospice Center, which honors the service of veterans with six months or less to live. After thousands of people helped me recover, I found happiness in helping others."

—Redmond Ramos, hospital corpsman third class, U.S. Navy (Ret.); currently a motivational speaker

UNLESS YOU'VE BEEN A SOLDIER

Unless you've been a soldier,
You just won't understand,
The things that we have seen and done,
In the service of our land.
We have trained to live in combat,
To cope with awful sights,
That shouldn't be seen by anyone,
And keep you awake at night.

We don't discuss the wounds we have,
To the body or the mind,
We just put our hurts behind us,
And turn our memories to blind.
We are proud we served our country,
And remember those we lost.
For the freedom that you have today,
They paid the awful cost.

—CLIVE SANDERS, FORMER OFFICER,
BRITISH ARMY

CHAPTER 7

THE SILENT ASSASSIN: PTSD

The gates of hell are open night and day.
Smooth the descent, and easy is the way.
But to return, and view the cheerful skies,
In this the task and mighty labor lies.

—VIRGIL, *THE AENEID*

Along with TBI, post-traumatic stress disorder (PTSD) has been one of the signature wounds suffered by the veterans of this country's wars the last twenty years, though not fully recognized by our country since our founding. So, what exactly is PTSD? In its simplest form, PTSD occurs when veterans continue to suffer symptoms after exposure to traumatic events or stresses has ended.[1] The phenomenon of warriors returning home with profound psychological difficulties is not new. In fact, it is universal across all countries, from ancient times to today—"The wound goes with war," as Dr. Tick has reminded us. We have evidence of PTSD from as far back as 490 BC, when the ancient Greek historian Herodotus told the story of an Athenian warrior returning from the Battle of Marathon who became blind when the soldier standing next to him was killed, though he was not otherwise physically injured. Regrettably, what PTSD is and what it's not, as well as methods of healing from it, have remained little understood by most warriors and even by many medical professionals. But what is new are some promising treatment methods and ways of thinking about PTSD. In this chapter, our goal is to provide education about PTSD, including the latest therapies available and a new way of understanding it more holistically, with the hope of helping veterans and those who love them get the help they deserve. In doing so, we also hope to raise awareness regarding these new treatments, most of which were not available in the Vietnam era, as Dr. Bob Koffman mentioned—the period that first saw the characterization of so-called "post-Vietnam syndrome." We have written this section as fellow travelers who have sought—or wished we had sought—the kind of treatment we summarize below when we underwent our own forms of trauma.[2]

FIRST: A WARNING ORDER

Before we discuss PTSD, let us say first, that if you are suffering, if you have acute symptoms or you can't sleep or function, get yourself to a doctor. We refer to PTSD as the silent assassin for a reason. If you need medication to get yourself stabilized, listen to your doctors. If conventional psychotherapy works, pursue it. If you are not satisfied with what a doctor recommended for reasonable reasons, go get a second opinion.

UNDERSTANDING PTSD

When one witnesses or experiences one or more traumatic events, such as death, violence, the threatening of your life, sexual trauma, moral injury, miscarriage, or intense grief after a loss, the impact of that experience can affect one's senses, reactions, relationships, and, at a deeper level, one's soul. In fact, these kinds of trauma can rewire the brain, affecting one's emotions and physiology and one's response to others and the world around us. PTSD can affect every area of one's life.

On an intuitive level, one way to understand PTSD is that, after a traumatic event has occurred, our innate survival mechanisms are stuck on high alert. If the feeling is unfamiliar to you, imagine you are driving your car wondering about your to-do list for the day, when another car comes out of nowhere and crashes into you; you suddenly slam on the brakes and your cars skid across the intersection and hit a wall. Once you stop, you get out and pull out the other driver, a woman who is bloodied and barely breathing, who whispers to you to "take care of my children; tell them I love them," whereupon she dies in your arms. Up until then, you have been reacting. Later, your body does a reset—you may sweat, your heart rate may spike, and thereafter you cannot get what happened out of your head. You get stuck in a mental loop, reexperiencing those events, and afterward, you cannot get into your car without reliving what happened that day.

After the fact, you feel stress and your sympathetic nervous system, which controls the "fight-or-flight" response, is on overload. All humans have a built-in fight-or-flight response, which is essential to our survival. But it's meant to be a short-term reaction. Our brain and our body are not designed to stay in a hyper-aroused state for any significant length of time. Some describe the cascade of emotions that then follows as a runaway train. This is what the "stress" in the name post-traumatic stress syndrome refers to—meaning the nervous system, brain activity, and bodily reactions are cranked all the way up. PTSD is far beyond what could be considered normal feelings of anxiety or fear. A normal amount of stress, what clinicians identify as "eustress," is beneficial. This type of short-term stress can be motivating. It can help prepare your brain and body for action and improve resilience. With PTSD, as a result of the initiating traumatic event, your arousal response of stress stays disproportionately high, ready for the next "fight" or "flight." In essence, because of the force of the impact of the traumatic event, our bodies recalibrate for a new level of perceived threat and that heightened response stays with us as our new normal state. We also note that ineffectiveness of the "fight-or-flight" response can lead to "freezing" as a third element of reacting.

It is not hard to imagine warriors suffering from PTSD due to their experience in combat, let alone if they have witnessed the deaths of their brothers and sisters or civilian casualties. Take the example of the car accident above and imagine it playing out in front of you but the one who dies is a brother- or sister-in-arms, whom you love as if they were your own blood and with whom you have lived, trained, and fought. Some warriors have been trained or developed the ability to continually adapt to their environment by putting aside their emotional reactions in order to continue the mission—to ignore, override, and push through. Once they come back home, whether after a deployment or as they are separating from the military, it is often then that they get hit with a flood of strong or even overwhelming feelings, flashbacks, and the stress described above. This often happens out of the blue. A warrior is triggered in a way they can't easily anticipate, which is a shocking experience to someone who is used to anticipating and being in control of almost everything in their environment. For those who have served for a long time and have been exposed to continued combat, loss, and suffering, we can imagine the ways their nervous system, brain activity, and bodily reactions remain in a highly aroused state as a semipermanent condition. This takes a toll inside, particularly if they have never been given a healthy way to process what's happened to them—to unlock the box and remove these experiences from their compartment. When the warrior returns, the body and the heart will need to take their time to decompress—and it can't be done on a schedule. The heightened state, reactions, and, at times, fear level, remain long after the events on the battlefield or elsewhere have ended.

In this state, Dr. Koffman explained, the brain's ability to modify the strength of the firing between neurons (referred to as "synaptic plasticity") is compromised because the neurons keep firing in an extreme fashion, more appropriate for situations in which there is a real, ongoing threat of danger, even though the feared object or circumstance is no longer present.[3] The brain's way of communicating by electrical activity (neurochemistry) changes how its neurotransmitters function, such that these pathways change themselves to accommodate the new high-speed rail of communication (neurotransmission). The brain and its blood supply release chemicals and stress hormones on a nearly continuous basis. Once the brain and the nervous system are overactivated beyond a certain threshold, they get stuck in a pattern of extreme response and are unable to drop back to baseline. Some medical literature suggests that patients with PTSD show a reduced ability to downregulate their nervous system and a reduced ability to exert control over an emotionally overactive brain. In other words, the almond-shaped amygdala, deep within the limbic system of the brain, functions as a "quick reaction force" (QRF), ready to engage at a moment's notice.

Dr. Kamran Fallahpour, MD, PhD, licensed clinical psychologist, and director of the Brain Resource Center in New York City, explains that those with PTSD typically show an increased sensitivity to stress, an overgeneralization of fear to external stimuli that in one's normal state would not trigger an exaggerated response. There tends also to be an impaired ability to extinguish fear memories. Conversely, people who are resilient to PTSD, or who recover more quickly from traumatic or stressful experiences, are better able to discern between genuinely fearful and nonfearful stimuli and are also able to display effective ability to extinguish fear memories. Living with PTSD often means living in a chronic fight-or-flight state where one's body and physiology are hijacked by various triggers. The changes in the brain and nervous system reshape both the body and the brain, compromising sufferers' capacities for pleasure, engagement, self-control, and trust, among other things, according to Dr. Bessel van der Kolk in his book *The Body Keeps the Score: Brain, Mind, and Body in the Healing of Trauma*.[4] In fact, this state tends to impair one's ability to cope with life itself.

Common Symptoms of PTSD

We outline below some common, specific symptoms of PTSD. Needless to say, symptoms can vary over time and vary from person to person.[5]

Intrusive Memories
- Recurrent, unwanted distressing memories of the traumatic event
- Reliving the traumatic event as if it were happening again (flashbacks)
- Upsetting dreams or nightmares about the traumatic event
- Severe emotional distress or physical reactions to something that reminds you of the traumatic event

Avoidance
- Trying to avoid thinking or talking about the traumatic event
- Avoiding places, activities, or people that remind you of the traumatic event

Negative Changes in Thinking and Mood
- Negative thoughts about yourself, other people, or the world
- Hopelessness about the future
- Memory problems, including not remembering important aspects of the traumatic event
- Difficulty maintaining close relationships
- Feeling detached from family and friends
- Lack of interest in activities you once enjoyed
- Difficulty experiencing positive emotions
- Feeling emotionally numb

Changes in Physical and Emotional Reactions
- Being easily startled or frightened, particularly with strong reactions to sounds and noise
- Always being on guard for danger
- Self-destructive behavior, such as drinking too much or driving too fast
- Trouble sleeping
- Trouble concentrating
- Irritability, angry outbursts, or aggressive behavior
- Overwhelming guilt or shame[6]

Depending on the nature of their trauma, some individuals with PTSD may experience emotional numbness, as noted above, particularly if their reaction to the traumatic event was to "shut down" in defense. In these cases, in order to "feel alive," the afflicted may expose themselves to extreme and potentially dangerous situations, to try to provoke a sense of feeling.[7] Jake Wood, in his book *Among You: The Extraordinary True Story of a Soldier Broken by War*, said:

You are no longer human, with all those depths and highs and nuances of emotion that define you as a person. There is no feeling anymore, because to feel any emotion would also be to beckon the overwhelming blackness from you. My mind has now locked all this down. And without any control of this self-defense mechanism my subconscious has operated. I do not feel anymore.[8]

Another potential effect of PTSD is repetition compulsion. Fueled by the desire to master or resolve a traumatic experience, an individual might have an unconscious need to reenact or continually review the event. As a result, the individual may be more prone to participate in high-risk or even self-destructive behavior. While mere insight into such a dynamic is often not enough to prevent the individual from engaging in such behaviors, awareness of the dynamic may still be one step in the right direction toward reducing such behavior. In addition, many veterans with PTSD face a temptation to self-medicate with drugs or alcohol just to get a night's rest, which often leads to habitual substance use.

The symptoms we describe above often also arise in the wider context of the challenges of veteran reintegration to civilian society. Many veterans find it hard to be understood as well as to understand aspects of the civilian world around them for several reasons, including the lack of structure, differences in culture (including what many today refer to as the military-civilian divide), the loss of comrades, the loss of purpose, and the large number of new choices to make. This can often lead to a sense of feeling profoundly displaced, as Dr. Tick described,[9] which then may result in a feeling of isolation. When symptoms and negative emotional reactions stack up, there can be deep emotional pain. Not knowing where to turn, some veterans then sense that hope for them is gone. We can tell you that if this describes you, there is hope and inspiration for healing to be found. You are not alone. Please read on.

Diagnosis and Treatment

The diagnosis of trauma and what it means for treatment requires great care since it can be complicated and touch on other ailments, such as TBI, moral injury, and depression. In addition, PTSD should be understood to be a catchall term that is used to describe a wide range of conditions—one size does not fit all.

Before we outline current, conventional treatment options, we will present below some overarching treatment insights from our research and interviews with Drs. Koffman, Fallahpour, and Tick:

- *A silver lining: The source of vulnerability is a potential source of healing.* The source of PTSD can be one key to its successful treatment. The very vulnerability of the brain in its sensitivity to injury is a reflection of the brain's inherent plasticity, meaning it has the potential to rewire its circuits, adapt, evolve, and adjust. The brain's potential to find new pathways to transmit messages to the nervous system is a source of healing and hope.

- *PTSD is not a pathology.* While scientific and medical literature characterizes PTSD as a "psychiatric disorder" and a "pathology," as we discuss below, we urge you to approach it differently. It is a very human response to terribly unhuman circumstances that you were put in the middle of by your service for your country. While it can be serious and its treatment needs to be taken seriously, if you have PTSD symptoms, it doesn't mean you are crazy. It means you should seek help and get stronger as a result.

- *PTSD is a complex diagnosis, and so is its treatment.* A holistic understanding of PTSD involves recognizing the interplay of its physiological, neural, emotional, behavioral, and even spiritual components. Successful treatment involves treating the whole person in each of these facets of their life, which often requires a multipronged approach.

- *Understand comorbidity factors.* One aspect of the complexity of a PTSD diagnosis arises from the existence of other, commonly occurring symptoms (so-called comorbidity factors). Various types of brain injury, including post-concussion syndrome (PCS) and TBI, which we cover in the next chapter, frequently occur among combat veterans. Many symptoms that

PTSD patients suffer from are also experienced by patients with a history of PCS and other types of brain injury. Mood changes, depression, anxiety, irritability and explosiveness, insomnia, sensitivity to noise and light, brain fog, memory deficits, and poor impulse control are among the symptoms that may be experienced by either diagnostic group. Therefore, being mindful of the dynamic between PTSD, PCS, and other ailments is important when seeking treatment.

- *Be an educated patient.* Having an understanding of PTSD and your treatment options is a key component to pursuing—and encouraging or pushing your doctors to devise—a successful treatment plan. Don't be intimidated by the fancy medical talk you may hear, but it is up to you to own and understand it. Only you, often with the help of a spouse, can take responsibility for your own healing.

We summarize below what are regarded as the conventional treatments for PTSD.

Cognitive behavioral therapy (CBT). CBT is a form of talk therapy (including conventional psychotherapy or counseling) that helps individuals learn to identify and change negative thoughts, cognitive distortions, and so-called maladaptive behavior (behavior that interferes with normal life). CBT can also help individuals with PTSD learn coping skills and strategies to better manage their symptoms. Skills training is an important component of such treatment.

Group therapy. Group therapy can provide a safe and supportive environment for individuals to share their experiences and learn coping strategies from others. An experienced group therapist familiar with group dynamics and supportive techniques is recommended in order to benefit from such intervention. Veterans from every war throughout history have found a degree of healing from speaking and listening to one another, and healing to some degree can happen only in community. It is well recognized that veterans have an easier time engaging in group therapy with other veterans because of the implicit trust and credibility in the group. However, talking with nonveterans also has advantages, such as the value of different perspectives, and helps veterans relate to civilians as a general matter.

Medications. Antidepressants and antianxiety medications can help manage and alleviate some PTSD symptoms, such as depression, anxiety, and sleep disturbances. However, some medications have unpleasant side effects and they often do not help the underlying disturbances to the brain and the nervous system. Medication can be a short-term solution to symptom management, and while it can allow a patient to avoid a short-term crisis (such as a prolonged lack of sleep, which can be debilitating and lead to depression and suicide), it does not teach the brain new skills or more adaptive responses to triggers. Relying only on medication without addressing the underlying cause of PTSD doesn't do much but numb the symptoms.

Exposure therapy. This type of therapy involves systematic and gradual exposure to traumatic memories. The hope is that reexperiencing some degree of the underlying source of trauma in a controlled, safe environment may lead to a different result. Exposure therapy can help individuals confront and overcome their fears related to the traumatic experience. Some words of caution here: First, premature exposure to traumatic memories or situations without proper training in self-regulation techniques can lead to re-traumatization. Second, there should be a foundation of trust between patient and provider here, which will ultimately make the therapy safer and more effective. Don't try to do this on your own. An experienced clinician can teach you skills such as relaxation techniques, breathing exercises, guided imagery, and progressive muscle relaxation. These techniques can help strengthen your ability to cope with high levels of stress before you undergo the therapy.

Eye movement desensitization and reprocessing (EMDR). EMDR involves recalling traumatic events while also moving the eyes back and forth or similar techniques that require intentional motor movement during a session in which the trauma is recalled by the patient. Although the exact mechanism behind this treatment is still under investigation, there is some evidence that this type of therapy can help some individuals process traumatic experiences and reduce the intensity of their PTSD symptoms. Research suggests EMDR may involve activating the brain's natural healing processes and reducing the intensity of emotional arousal associated with traumatic memories. Dr. Tick advises that after any EMDR or other session, it is valuable for the patient to speak about their experience, even retelling the story of the traumatic events, as a continuation of the effort to put themselves back together.

Stellate ganglion block (SGB). In this procedure, a local anesthetic is injected next to the stellate ganglion, a collection of the sympathetic nerves located in the neck that help regulate many involuntary functions such as heart rate, blood pressure, and sweating. SGB was originally approved by the FDA as a pain-relieving treatment. However, it has recently been used off-label to treat some symptoms of PTSD, as it's been shown to help regulate an overactive sympathetic nervous system and "reset" the fight-or-flight response to its baseline. This treatment might be a good first step toward obtaining some relief in the most severe cases before following up with other, noninvasive approaches.

Neurofeedback. Neurofeedback uses real-time feedback on brain activity to teach PTSD patients how to regulate their own brain function. A 2016 study published in the journal *Frontiers in Psychiatry* found that neurofeedback was effective in reducing symptoms of PTSD in veterans, with significant improvements in sleep quality, mood, and cognitive function.[10] A 2017 systematic review of the literature on neurofeedback for PTSD found that most studies reported some degree of improvement in PTSD symptoms, though the outcomes were not always consistent across studies due to some study design limitations.[11] In Dr. Fallahpour's clinical work, he has seen consistent improvements in the areas of self-regulation and cognition using these techniques, including symptoms of anxiety, stress over-reactivity, explosiveness, sleep disturbance, and aspects of cognition (such as memory and attention).

Music and sound therapies. Music has the remarkable ability to influence various neural pathways, neurotransmitter systems, and regions of the brain. Studies suggest that carefully designed music interventions can help regulate emotions, reduce stress, and improve cognitive function. If you're someone who enjoys music, you likely already know that, as a general matter, music affects and can help our state of mind. Upbeat music can trigger the release of the neurotransmitter dopamine, eliciting feelings of pleasure and the anticipation of reward. Slower, quieter music can be calming to the nervous system, reducing stress and anxiety and promoting a sense of relaxation and calm. The synchronization of brain waves with a musical beat may improve attention, memory, and problem-solving skills. Music can be used to supplement pain-suppressing mechanisms, can help with motor and movement coordination rehabilitation, and enhance communication and the critical way that the brain balances different activities at the same time.

Combined treatments. Overall, the most effective treatment for PTSD often involves a combination of therapies, and it is important to work with a trained therapist, doctor, or mental health professional to determine the best approach for a patient's specific needs.

Additional Observations About Treatment

Some additional, commonsense treatment suggestions and observations include:

- *Take care of your body and your mind.* Any successful regimen for treatment and healing involves caring for your body and your mind. If you can, work out and train, alone or with others. We recommend some kind of mindfulness practice, such as meditation, yoga, or tai chi, and sports.
- *Engage in healthy behaviors.* We've made this recommendation before and will continue to do so because it's important. Eat well, try to get enough sleep, limit your intake of substances, and avoid dangerous or self-sabotaging risk-taking. Make sure to read the sections "Recognizing and Harnessing Fear" and "Self-Regulation" in chapter 10.
- *Seek out alternative therapies.* If you feel the need to seek alternative therapies to supplement conventional medical treatment, explore them! An example is acupuncture, which Dr. Koffman explained has been beneficial to many veterans with PTSD. Treatments like acupuncture should be used supportively, and not in place of the treatment options we list above.

- *Animal therapy.* For more than thirty thousand years, dogs and other animals have been some of our best companions, including our most healing companions. Alex can attest to the fact that having a relationship with a dog that shares love and affection without condition, that shapes your routine in a healthy way, and teaches you about being present is hard to replace. There are many animal shelters and other animal retreats that serve veterans. Interacting with animals often alleviates stress and supports reintegration back into society.
- *Explore art.* At the National Intrepid Center of Excellence, Dr. Koffman created the Triple A program for veterans— animals, acupuncture, and art. There is a substantial amount of evidence from our lives and clinical research that engaging in art can be healing for the soul.[12] Any kind of art will work—find what interests you the most. It might be music, as we have suggested, visual art, drama, or anything in between that involves expressing yourself. Dr. Tick informs us that there is an ancient and ongoing tradition of "warrior art."
- *Navigate the VA and health-care system.* Taking advantage of what the Department of Veterans Affairs has to offer is critical. Learning to navigate the system and advocating for yourself will take you far. Outside the VA, there are many resources available at private clinics and foundations, such as Dr. Fallahpour's Brain Resource Center in NYC, and the All Secure Foundation, which assists veterans with PTSD and other ailments and provides coaching to individuals and couples. Its cofounders and co-CEOs, Jen and Tom Satterly, have made a world of difference in this terrain.

WHAT THE EXPERTS GET WRONG

Contrary to the American Psychiatric Association, PTSD is not really a "psychiatric disorder,"[13] or at least not a psychiatric disorder on its own. We believe that PTSD should not be diagnosed as an "emotional condition" or a "psychiatric" or "psychological" problem. In addition, many reject the idea that the "D" belongs as part of the acronym at all because they argue convincingly that it is not a "disorder." Dr. Tick observed that the sooner we de-pathologize PTSD, the sooner we will make PTSD more understandable to veterans and their spouses. That understanding may lead to PTSD more readily being regarded as treatable.

So how should PTSD be understood? There is ample evidence from veterans' experiences and medical and clinical research that PTSD is a physiological condition that includes physical, emotional, psychological, behavioral, and, for those who believe in it, spiritual components. Colonel Charles W. Hoge, MD, U.S. Army (Ret.),[14] one of the preeminent doctors in the field, explains, "[PTSD] is a physical condition that affects the entire body and is best understood through the emerging science of stress physiology, which describes how the body reacts to extreme stress," based on the study of nerve functioning and chemical processes in the nervous system.[15] The insight that emerges from the work of Drs. Hoge, Koffman, and Van Der Kolk is that if trauma and PTSD are physiological conditions, with physical, emotional, psychological, behavioral, and, for those who believe in it, spiritual components, then its treatment should mirror that assessment.[16]

In speaking with veterans and their spouses, there is a common visible wincing, a rejection of the characterization of PTSD as a "psychiatric disorder," and a cynicism about doctors who throw pills and medications at them. That approach doesn't do them justice, makes them feel even more broken, and can discourage them from seeking truly effective help. Many veterans also not only resent the idea, but find it confounding and maddening that a bunch of doctors who have never seen a day in uniform or even combat can provide a manual of diagnoses that don't reflect the condition, its causes, or its treatment. In addition, some veterans feel betrayed by the doctors who do not appreciate the military world or the experiences of veterans.

The reactions we describe above are a reality in the veteran community, but it would be a mistake to leave those reactions unexamined for several reasons. First, there is a world of effective, caring doctors, nurses, and therapists who help veterans in general and with PTSD in particular; and there is a world of evolving and valuable medical, scientific, and clinical research. Finding a good doctor is like finding a piece of gold—you hang on to it. Take Alex's advice, based on an analogy to his own profession (as a lawyer): "Most lawyers, like most plumbers, accountants, mechanics, doctors, and therapists, suck. Find the right one and hold on to them like a piece of gold." It would be self-defeating to think they are all pill-prescribing bots. Second, veterans and their spouses must learn the meaning of the diagnoses and treatment options to navigate the VA and get proper treatment. Finally, it would be a mistake for veterans to listen to advice only from, and socialize with, other veterans—to wall themselves off from civilians—because it tends to lead to further isolation and impedes reintegration.

THE WARRIOR'S RETURN

In *Warrior's Return: Restoring the Soul After War,* Dr. Tick proposes a holistic way of understanding veterans' returning to civilian life and healing around three steps (which overlap with Dr. Glick's four stages of reintegration that we reviewed in chapter 3) set in the context of the hero's journey. At its core, Dr. Tick's approach is based on the belief that warriors can "turn war's inevitable wounding and suffering into wisdom and growth that truly brings warriors home and benefits us all." In his words, he offers a "new, holistic, hope-filled and heart-and-soul-centered understanding of war trauma and its healing."[17]

Dr. Tick's approach is based on the following three-step process of reintegrating the warriors back into civilian life.

Step #1: Initiation. In the first step, the returning warriors undergo a new initiation, different from the one they underwent when joining the military, one in which they leave the soldier on the battlefield and grieve the loss of this part of their identity. In this phase, there are the critical steps of physical healing, though Dr. Tick cautions that healing should not be limited to "symptom management, stress reduction, altering brain chemistry or learning mind-body cooperation." Veterans with trauma must tend to their emotional wounds, including despair, anguish, and the loss of faith that many experience. A deeper transformation can begin, one in which veterans recognize the service and sacrifice they made for their society and one another. What can evolve is a new, more mature and wiser person, one who wears the badge of their service and suffering with great pride and purpose.[18]

Step #2: Restoration. Here, veterans are welcomed back to the community as warriors, a term to be understood according to its ethos and sacred duty, a duty to serve others at the highest level of moral and physical courage. Geronimo told us that the warrior's code was a solemn religious matter. In Sitting Bull's thinking, "the warrior is not someone who fights, because no one has the right to take another life. The warrior, for us, is one who sacrifices himself for the good of others. His task is to care for the elderly, the defenseless, those who cannot provide for themselves, and above all, the children, the future of humanity."[19]

It is only by the community engaging in this welcome—with an appreciation of the role and sacrifice of the warrior—that our warriors can be restored in themselves and our community can evolve to what it is meant to be. Dr. Tick outlines dozens of steps communities can take to welcome back and appreciate veterans, including by inviting veterans into schools and community centers to educate our young about war, transforming college campuses into houses of initiation to make them veteran-friendly, creating literary and artistic programs for veterans and the community, and creating a veterans service corps to allow veterans to serve others. Dr. Tick's great insight is that veterans' reintegration into civilian society can be made fully possible and the veterans can fully activate and deploy the special and even sacred things they have learned and become—for the benefit of themselves and our society as a whole—only with the invitation and participation of their communities. This is the third stage of the hero's journey, one in which the warrior returns with the power of the gods available to give back to their community and one that can truly occur only if we welcome our veterans back in a way that recognizes their service, sacrifice, and the sacred meaning of what it means to be a warrior.[20]

Step #3: Return. To fully return, warriors must undergo a series of steps in their journey home, steps that necessarily involve their communities. These involve purification from battle and seeking catharsis to relieve them of emotional burdens (including from psychotherapy); engaging in a discussion if seeking forgiveness is helpful or relevant (such as might be the case with moral injury or whether their return was difficult for family); a search for some measure of solace; accepting their destiny as warriors (including if they felt the burden or invitation of service because their ancestors served); storytelling in community; and even a blessing of their wounds. When combined with the prior steps, feelings of disillusionment, brokenness, and despair can be overcome by a transcendent understanding of meaning and purpose in themselves and connection to community. In reflecting on their own transformation, the hope is that, ultimately, the warriors can understand their wounds as honorable, as sources of strength, wisdom, and growth. In this transformation, veterans can refind energy, motivation, commitments, and love.[21] Lifelong suffering after war then is not inevitable, but becomes the most powerful source of growth, meaning, and honor for us all.

A VETERAN'S VICTORY OVER PTSD

In all of our interviews with veterans, we have come across no more profound account of a journey of a veteran's struggle with PTSD and, ultimately, her victory, than the story of Chief Hospital Corpsman Tammy Archibald, U.S. Navy (Ret.). She said,

> As I took my last steps in uniform and heard the lonely sound of my last service being piped ashore with my family in tow, I felt like a stranger in my own home upon my return. I was no longer the same person that had left, and I struggled with severe separation anxiety, depression, PTSD, and isolation. My health was also negatively affected by all the surgeries and MST (military sexual trauma) I endured during my service. I did not feel prepared to reintegrate into civilian life and felt like an outsider in my own town.
>
> Adjusting to civilian life has been tough to say the least. New schedules, routines, and social expectations confused me, causing me to suffer from chronic insomnia, nightmares, night

sweats, and a feeling of unsafety. I was constantly checking door locks and could not handle large crowds. My nervous system was overwhelmed, and I did not know how to regulate it despite the medication I was taking. My physical and emotional scars affected my day-to-day life. I sought therapy to cope with my chronic pain, PTSD, depression, and anxiety, but it did little to resolve my issues. Instead, I was often prescribed medication to numb my pain. The VA health-care system was a nightmare at times, making it difficult to get appointments and care, especially when the COVID-19 pandemic hit.

Employment was another challenge as I struggled to find civilian jobs that felt meaningful and rewarding. My military experience in the medical field required additional certification or college to be recognized in the civilian sector, which was discouraging. I struggled to find assistance in translating my military skills to civilian opportunities.

My family and friends had grown distant during my time in the military, and rekindling those relationships was challenging. Reestablishing my relationship with my son and now granddaughters was even more of a struggle for me. There were times I would literally cry myself to sleep because I was in so much overwhelm and pain in my mind and body.

I feel like as women we're seen and devalued in a different light because we are women. I'm not saying we need our hands held, but what I am saying is we need to be supported, seen, and heard in the same light and respect as men are! We put our armor on and laced our bootstraps the same way men did! We served our country faithfully and gave the same of ourselves as they did if not more!

I have found new meaning in my work as a healer and naturopath, in my rekindled relationships with my family and my friends. More than anything, I found a new lease on life with the Lord. It allowed me the freedom to let go of everything that I was trying to hold on to, such as who I was in the military, pretending to hold it together when I was internally falling apart, learning to let go and let God take the reins, and learning to be okay with letting others in to help me when I never knew how to trust anyone enough to do so. I have a new lease on life.

RESOURCES FOR TRAUMA, PTSD, AND TBI

We list below some resources for those with trauma, PTSD, and TBI. See Annex 1 on our website, www.heroes-journey.net, for more resources.

- The Avalon Action Alliance is an organization that connects veterans and first responders to care for TBI, PTSD, and substance abuse. The Avalon Action Alliance is affiliated with the Marcus Institute for Brain Health, the Boulder Crest Foundation, the Warrior PATHH Program, and various other programs.

    Phone: 417-812-6035

    Website: www.avalonactionalliance.org
- The Center for BrainHealth is part of the University of Texas at Dallas and is a research institute with cutting-edge programs. Admiral and Mrs. William H. McRaven are its national spokespeople.

    Phone: 972-883-3007

    Website: www.centerforbrainhealth.org
- The Cohen Veterans Network assists veterans in overcoming the challenges of transitioning from active military service to civilian life and beyond. They have clinics that offer specialized therapy for depression, anxiety, PTSD, adjustment issues, anger, grief and loss, transition challenges, and other concerns. Their website advertises marriage counseling, relationship counseling, and help with children's behavioral issues.

    Phone: 844-336-4226

    Website: www.cohenveteransnetwork.org

- Centerstone provides a full range of mental health and substance use disorder services to help you get through the tough times and live your best life.

  Phone: 877-467-3123

  Website: www.centerstone.org/get-help-now

- The Traumatic Brain Injury Center of Excellence (TBICoE): Formerly known as the Defense and Veterans Brain Injury Center, TBICoE is a congressionally mandated collaboration of the Departments of Defense and Veterans Affairs to promote state-of-the-science care from point-of-injury to reintegration for service members, veterans, and their families to prevent and mitigate consequences of mild to severe traumatic brain injury.

  Phone: 800-870-9244

  Website: www.health.mil/Military-Health-Topics /Centers-of-Excellence/Traumatic-Brain-Injury-Center -of-Excellence

- The Home Base Program, operated under the auspices of Massachusetts General Hospital, is dedicated to healing the invisible wounds of war, including PTSD and TBI, for active-duty service members and veterans.

  Phone: 617-724-5202

  Website: www.homebase.org/about-us

- The Marcus Institute for Brain Health offers comprehensive care for the physical, emotional, and cognitive changes that can accompany trauma to the head. They have partnerships with the University of Colorado Hospital, Children's Hospital Colorado, and the University of Colorado Medicine.

  Phone: 303-724-4824

  Website: www.medschool.cuanschutz.edu/mibh

- The National Intrepid Center of Excellence (NICoE) is the headquarters of the Defense Intrepid Network for Traumatic Brain Injury and Brain Health. It is dedicated to improving the lives of patients and families affected by TBI through collaborative efforts with patients, families, referring providers, and researchers.

Phone: 800-600-9332

Website: www.health.mil/Military-Health-Topics /Centers-of-Excellence/NICOE

- The National Brain Injury Information Center provides brain injury support and resources and was established by the Brain Injury Association of America.

Phone: 800-444-6443

Website: www.biausa.org/brain-injury/about-brain -injury/nbiic/contact-nbiic

- The SHARE Military Initiative at Shepherd Center is a comprehensive rehabilitation program that focuses on assessment and treatment for active-duty or separated service members who have served in the U.S. military since September 11, 2001, and who are experiencing symptoms of or have a diagnosis of moderate brain injury or concussions and any co-occurring psychological or behavioral health concerns, including PTSD. SHARE Military Initiative provides hope, assistance, support, and education to service members and their families during their recovery, treatment, and beyond.

Phone: 404-603-4314

Website: www.shepherd.org

- The Veteran Wellness Alliance of the Bush Institute connects high-quality care providers and veteran peer networks to empower veterans to seek treatment.

Phone: 214-200-4300

Website: www.bushcenter.org/publications /veteran-wellness-alliance-best-in-class-peer-based -networks-and-care-providers-addressing-veterans -mental-health-barriers

- The Wounded Warrior Care Network is a partnership between the Wounded Warrior Project and four academic medical centers (Emory Healthcare, Massachusetts General Hospital,

Rush University Medical Center, and UCLA Health), with a focus on PTSD.

Phone: 877-832-6997

Website: www.woundedwarriorproject.org/programs/warrior-care-network

- The Veterans Health Administration offers care for TBI.

Phone: 877-222-VETS (8387)

Website: www.polytrauma.va.gov/understanding-tbi/

- Make the Connection—Effects of Traumatic Brain Injury is not a medical site but, rather, an organization that offers veterans inspirational stories of healing.

Phone: 800-698-2411

Website: www.maketheconnection.net/conditions/traumatic-brain-injury/

VOICES OF VETERANS AND THOSE WHO CARE FOR THEM

"The brave men and women, who serve their country and as a result, live constantly with the war inside them, exist in a world of chaos. But the turmoil they experience isn't who they are; the PTSD invades their minds and bodies."

—M.Sgt. Robert Kroger, U.S. Air Force (Ret.)[22]

"The common therapeutic model that misses the point is that PTSD is primarily a moral, spiritual, and aesthetic disorder—in effect, not a psychological but a soul disorder. All of its aspects concern dimensions of the soul, inasmuch as the soul is the part of us that responds to morality, spirituality, aesthetics and intimacy."

—Reid Mackey, former U.S. Army helicopter crew chief

"Sometimes a soldier returns home and all he can do is share his story in the hopes that somehow, in some way, it helps another soldier make sense of things. And although the stories may not be perfect, sometimes just sharing is enough to make a difference."

—Michael Anthony, author of
Civilianized: A Young Veteran's Memoir[23]

"I am young, I am twenty years old; yet I know nothing of life but despair, death, fear, and fatuous superficiality cast over an abyss of sorrow."

—Paul Baümer, in *All Quiet on the Western Front*,
by Erich Maria Remarque

SENTRY

I look into your soft eyes
as you hold up your tattered shield—
to keep me from seeing
The Beast
fangs dripping...
and you with nowhere to run...
But don't think I can't hear
the desperate howl behind your silence
the crashing of your heart on the jungle floor

It is you I really want to see,
even when it hurts...
I ache to hold your broken heart,
and sing and rock and rest...
So I keep vigil outside your door...
humming the ancient Warrior Song
all night long.

—KATE DAHLSTEDT

CHAPTER 8

TRAUMATIC BRAIN INJURY

"A brain injury may change how a person functions, but it doesn't define who they are."

—UNKNOWN

Before we dive into the details, we first need to say that if you are experiencing symptoms of traumatic brain injury (or TBI), seek help immediately. There are many treatments and resources available today that did not exist even a decade ago. If you have not yet transitioned out of the military but you're planning to do so and have a possible case of TBI, we urge you to see a doctor within the military. For several reasons, the best time to get a diagnosis and begin treatment is at the time of the injury.[1] If you do not, and TBI is not part of your medical file, it will be difficult to have your treatment paid for when you separate.

WHAT IS TBI?

Traumatic brain injury (TBI) and PTSD have become the signature wounds among veterans of the post-9/11 era. Per Patricia Kime and Rebecca Kheel, "While other wars had their associated illnesses—the scarred lungs from mustard gas in World War I, cancers from exposure to Agent Orange in Vietnam, and unexplained symptoms from the 1990–1991 Persian Gulf War—the diagnosis of TBI and PTSD recalled the tremors, dizziness, tinnitus and 'thousand-yard stare' once described as 'shell shock' during WWI and 'combat stress reaction' in World War II."[2] One can only conclude that the signature illnesses of our time, the silent killers of TBI and PTSD, have long affected veterans for generations. However, with the advancement in modern medicine, our silent enemy has been given a name.

In 2003 and 2004, troops began to return from combat in Iraq and Afghanistan with injuries sustained by roadside bombs or improvised explosive devices (IEDs). These devices became a common tactic to destroy our armored vehicles and to disrupt or destroy our troop movements and operations. For many years the Department of Defense (which we also refer to as the DoD) remained focused on the visible injuries, whereas mental deficits went undetected, undiagnosed, and untreated. Sadly, at the same time, suicide rates among veterans began to rise to numbers exceeding rates among the general population, Finally, research has begun to provide an understanding of the condition and clues that link TBI and suicide, yet more work is needed.[3]

TBI was reported in approximately 380,000 service members between 2000 and 2017, and 82.3 percent of these TBIs were classified as mild (mTBI). Due to the widespread use of IEDs and other explosives in more recent military conflicts, blast-related mTBI has emerged as one of the most common types of injury sustained by warfighters, whether through combat or training exercises. There are a range of TBI diagnoses, from mild, as mentioned, to more severe types. In this chapter, we generally do not distinguish between mTBI and TBI of a more serious or severe nature—however, the severity of TBI will often determine the best course of treatment.

Diagnosis of mTBI often requires either a battle buddy or an observer to note a warrior's changed mental status after a concussive or, more likely, a seemingly innocuous sub-concussive event. An alternative involves self-reporting by the individual (often in the thick of battle) of momentary changes in sensorium (i.e., getting their bell rung). Typically, formal diagnosis of TBI is made much later, well after the blast, fall, or fight; and many times, not at all. This is why combat-related mTBI is largely underreported. To further complicate things, individuals who sustain a blast-related mTBI are significantly more likely to develop PTSD from their disrupted nervous system. Undiagnosed, untreated mTBI can lead to chronicity, or "persistent post-concussive symptoms." This occurs when problems with headaches, dizziness, and lapses in concentration and memory last longer than six months.

A difficult aspect of TBI is that it commonly occurs with PTSD, which can exacerbate irritability, among other symptoms. The development of a mood disorder (such as major depression) can mimic memory and concentration changes. Don't forget decreased sleep due to chronic pain, which in itself produces diminished sleep. Realize that the body repairs itself during restorative sleep. Not sleeping reduces healing and thus repair!

COMMON SYMPTOMS OF TBI

For veterans who have been exposed to combat and blast levels as described above, we encourage you to be aware of the following symptoms commonly associated with TBI:

- Headaches
- Anxiety
- Nausea or vomiting
- Fatigue or drowsiness
- Difficulty with speech
- Difficulty sleeping
- Depression
- Lightheadedness
- Memory loss
- Confusion
- Attention issues or distractibility
- Difficulty with balance
- Aggression or anger
- Mood changes
- Sensitivity to light and sounds
- Sensitivity to movement and sensory-processing issues
- Difficulty with decision-making
- Difficulty with emotional regulation, including impairments in self-monitoring and control
- Reduced emotional awareness, disinhibited emotional behavior, and reduced emotional awareness and expression
- Cognitive deficits, including difficulty in conceptualizing and measuring problems
- A disorganized inner state

Many symptoms commonly associated with TBI are nonspecific. They can be the result of many different brain impairments such as stroke, chemically induced damage to the brain from exposure to toxic substances, infection by pathogenic microbes (HIV, bacteria, etc.), primary or secondary (metastatic) brain tumors, and neurodegenerative diseases (such as Parkinson's, Alzheimer's, ALS, Huntington's, etc.), in addition to TBI.

Several institutions are working to better understand TBI with the help of veterans and their families, some of whom have donated the deceased veterans' brains to research. Findings are showing that these warriors had repeated exposure to blast waves, severely damaging the structure of their brains and causing microscopic tears in the brain's tissue, internal lining, and blood vessels.[4] These micro tears cannot be seen or detected during an MRI or a PET scan. "Even with mild injuries, you can see neurochemical changes and troublesome deficits," Dr. Warren Lux, a neurologist who served as medical director of the Defense and Veterans Brain Injury Center, said in an interview with Military.com.[5] Researchers are also finding that having multiple TBIs can have a multiplying effect on suicide risks.

Understanding the symptoms of TBI should also be put in the context of the difficult transition to civilian life for many veterans. "The other thing that is happening with brain injuries," Dr. Lux explained, "is the frontal lobe is very involved . . . The injured lose the ability to monitor themselves, and they lose the ability to understand consequences." Now, factor in that "the sometimes lengthy period of readjustment to civilian life can be particularly fraught for veterans. The sudden upheaval is tied to feelings of grief and loss, physical and mental health problems, employment and financial uncertainty, and adjustment issues. And notably, a marked increase in the risk of suicide. There's a whole set of factors that are impacting these younger service members as they transition out of military service back into civilian life," added epidemiologist Jeffrey Howard. "What these data are saying is that that's exacerbated by these kinds of exposures such as having TBI."[6]

A NOTE FROM ROB:
WHAT C-4 PLASTIC EXPLOSIVES DO

For readers who still can't visualize what any of this means, let me give you a personal example of how far blast overpressure, or blast waves, can be felt. On my last deployment in 2012 to Afghanistan, my platoon was embedded into an Afghan village in the Sangin Valley in Helmand Province to conduct village stability operations, otherwise known as VSP (village stability platform). We lived in the Afghan village for nine months with the same living conditions as the Afghan local populace we were working with and protecting: no running water and no electricity. We needed to be fully embedded to beat the Taliban at their own game by winning the hearts and minds of the locals. As my unit controlled nine contiguous villages around us, the Marines operated to my north and south. Though our respective areas of operations (AO) were well defined, the Taliban had no regard for operational boundaries and would engage my unit or the Marines indiscriminately. When troops were in contact along our borders, my Marine counterparts and I quickly deconflicted and pushed situational awareness to each other when we found ourselves in a gunfight or crossing over into each other's respective AOs. On many occasions the Taliban would engage the Marines and cross through our AO and then traverse the Helmand River to the west bank. This section of the river created a natural barrier—one hundred meters across, thirteen feet deep, a four-knot current, and fifty-five-degree water temperature—for the Taliban and gave them a safe haven west of the river. During one firefight with the Taliban, a Marine was killed in action and the insurgents retreated and traversed the river. My unit conducted an air strike on two of them, eliminating them both, in a tree line along the west riverbank. Despite this air strike and follow-on sniper overwatches that eliminated other insurgents, attacks persisted against my unit and the Marines, causing significant wounded in action from this area in the subsequent weeks and months. After each engagement, the insurgents would traverse the river and go to the same tree line to stash their weapons and then retreat to a nearby village.

We knew we had the capabilities to thwart these attacks. For weeks we developed intel to strike at the heart of the problem to take out the weapons cache. We assessed every insert and egress route and determined our only viable options were a helicopter insert or a swim across. Since there were no supporting elements west of the river, and we wanted to avoid the nearby village to remain clandestine under the cover of darkness, a helicopter insert was ruled out. We were going for a swim.

After two weeks of planning, we were approved to execute. Our approved concept of operation used truck inner tubes that we would inflate using CO_2 cartridges from our dive gear. We created a web bottom on the tubes using one-inch-thick line that would carry one hundred pounds of C-4 explosive and our bomb dog (it was a requirement from our commander that we take the dog). Given the strong current, our recon team inserted 300 meters north up the east riverbank and would use the current to traverse the river. Just like drinking beer on a lazy river, this gave us enough offset to float down the river with gear and explosives and the dog in the inner tubes while the recon/demo team swam beside the inner tubes to get within close proximity to our target. The remainder of the team took up position directly across the target to get eyes on it, and a small contingent pushed south in case the recon/demo team overshot the target or needed to egress in case of being compromised.

After forty-five minutes the tree line was rigged to blow. The recon team exfiled and floated south to our supporting element, only mildly hypothermic (joking; they were cold as shit) and consolidated back to the command-and-control position. With a full head count, we detonated one hundred pounds of explosives and rocked the shit out of that safe haven and the nearby village. As a result, we incapacitated the area and didn't have any significant activity for six months: mission accomplished. When we returned to our VSP in the early morning, our enablers said they felt the overpressure in our operations center. That was two kilometers away as the crow flies.

Aside from explosives, more frequently we are subjected to constant gunfire of all calibers and an assortment of shoulder-fired weapons. My favorite was the Carl Gustaf, an 84 mm recoilless anti-tank weapon. The overpressure on this weapon will rock your world. I'm not talking about the best night of your life out at your favorite bar and you get lucky with a one-night stand. Firing that weapon is a new kind of rocked: The overpressure or blast wave generated by the Gustaf will cause blast- and burn-related injuries to those behind the weapon and is dangerous to thirty meters (meaning it can kill you if you stand within 100 feet behind the weapon when fired) and hazardous from about fifty to seventy-five meters. We were told during training that gunners are allowed to fire only six rounds a day and the assistant gunners can fire only six rounds a day because the overpressure can cause micro tears in our organs. Sadly, safety reports had not been made, and many troops were not informed of this as the war on terror commenced and our arsenals were quickly outfitted with this weapon. It would take years of research to understand the physical and mental toll these weapons had on us.

TREATMENT OF TBI

Because there are often so many overlapping symptoms between PTSD and TBI, effective treatment of TBI relies heavily on an individual's unique symptoms. Your doctor may discuss post-concussion brain dynamics and the regions of the brain that were impacted by the injury. It is important to identify any abnormalities in brain networks, how these changes in brain dynamics impact the nervous system, and how they may impact motor skills (movement), mood regulation (feeling depressed or anxious), and cognition (memory, attention, executive functions, etc.).

For mood regulation issues in the PTSD population, there are a variety of symptoms such as anxiety, depression, volatile mood, agitation, and explosivity. Poor impulse control is a key symptom that is often present in both brain injury and PTSD patients. Cognitive effects like short attention span, brain fog, difficulty with working memory, and executive functions are among the most important skills that are impacted.

Given the complexity of TBI, it is difficult to summarize treatment options. Having said that, there are many forms of conventional treatment available for TBI in general. These include:

- Cognitive therapy to improve memory, attention, perception, and learning and planning skills

- Physical therapy to build physical strength, balance, reflexes, coordination, and flexibility, and to help restore energy levels
- Speech and language therapy to improve the ability to form words, speak aloud, and use other communications skills
- Psychological counseling to help anxiety, depression, and other reactions; to learn coping skills; to help work on relationships and generally improve well-being, which can include medication
- Occupational and vocational counseling to help the patient return to work and to help come up with a way to function and heal effectively at home in practical ways
- Medication to address a variety of symptoms, such as seizures

Depending on the circumstances, surgery may be needed in acute situations to stop brain bleeds, remove blood clots, repair skull fractures, or alleviate inflammation. Any effective treatment regimen for TBI should be holistic. In that regard, many of the therapies that we summarized in chapter 7 about PTSD can also be helpful to those with TBI.

There are many hospitals and doctors that are innovating new treatments for TBI, and with great promise. We highlight just one of them here, Home Base, a nonprofit organization that operates under the auspices of Massachusetts General Hospital in Boston. From Dr. Ronald Hirschberg, medical director of the Home Base Program, we learned that special forces operators are one of the main groups in the active-duty and veteran communities who suffer from TBI. Their jobs take a toll on the body due to physical exertion and blunt force trauma, repetitive orthopedic injury, hard parachute openings and hard landings, combatives, and close and far-ranging explosives, which are all unique occupational hazards of the special forces operator.

The program for these operators at Home Base takes on two main forms: an expeditious assessment program (five-day Comprehensive Brain Health and Trauma program, or ComBHaT); and an intensive treatment program (two-week Intensive Clinical Program, or ICP).

The two-week ICP has been implemented for both PTSD and TBI tracks and is notable for condensing more than a year of therapy within fully loaded days of rehabilitation focused on balance and reflex issues, improving eye tracking ability while following moving objects and while also jumping between objects, and wellness treatments (fitness and yoga, nutrition, resilience programming, and the arts). Part of the protocol Home Base developed includes education and discussion about brain health and getting help from different kinds of providers as well as the significant role that family and friends play in healing.

Given the complexity and variety of brain injuries and comorbidity factors, the brain injuries may or may not be detected on imaging. Having said that, as Dr. Hirschberg points out, the work in diagnostic assessment of blast-related trauma holds promise with current and developing MRI, PET, and other technologies. At the same time, it is clear that conventional clinical evaluation and treatment protocols for symptoms and treatment remain the standards of care.

For a list of resources for TBI, see chapter 7 on PTSD in this book and Annex 1 on our website, www.heroes-journey.net.

A NOTE FROM ROB ON TBI

When I was getting out, I went and got checked for TBI at Balboa Naval Hospital. Not only had I sustained years of blast waves from our arsenal of weapons, but also, I experienced a concussion on my last deployment during a combat operation. From the second I walked in the waiting room, the staff were very intrigued and kept asking me questions. Finally, a doctor said, "We don't see too many of you guys in here." Exactly—because we are afraid of the stigma or, worse, not being able to operate.

VETERANS' VOICES

"I'd say the biggest thing I had to deal with was frustration because I am normally very in control of myself. But with my brain injury, I couldn't speak right, I couldn't act right, and it was something I couldn't control. When I got to the VA, I got a general physician, and I started explaining what I was going through. They lined me up with the right clinics and the right meds to deal with my problems. I started speaking more clearly; I got less frustrated and less angry. Talking the problems out helped more than anything else. Well...swallowing my pride and talking to somebody may be a better way of saying it, and I did and I am the better for it."

—Anonymous veteran[7]

"When I was going through individual therapy, my wife got educated on what to expect. She was educating my son and my daughter. They had certain things that they were expecting and they got educated about the whole thing, even though I could not understand the whole thing."

—Anonymous veteran[8]

"I knew my wife before I joined the Army. After a deployment or two, then she started saying things like: 'I don't even know you anymore. You're not the same person I married'—that kind of thing. And in her defense, I wasn't. [My brain injury and stressors finally reached a boiling point where] not getting help became unsustainable... [After getting help], I am able to go out and meet people again and talk to people and, actually, I feel alive again."

—Brent, Sixth Ranger Training Battalion, 101st Airborne Division[9]

"Battle of Fallujah in November of 2004. That was heavy...
You're going from one heavy environment and nonstop action,
nonstop patrolling, back to a normal way of life [back home].
I felt issues right after that, right when we got back and we're
transitioning back to the States...PTSD, TBI, herniated disk
in upper and lower back, chronic migraines, with multiple...I
got tinnitus. It's nonstop ringing...there were days when I just
wanted to break my car and just drive it off somewhere and
destroy it, just to maybe hurt myself or something. Lots of bad
dreams...These past seven months, I started [cognitive behavioral therapy and worked with a doctor who listened to me] ...
Got a job again [after losing my old one], building gardens for
a local Veterans Center...I'm working on getting better, you
know. My son, I don't want him to grow up to be, you know, isolated himself, I want to be there for him and do those things with
him...go for a walk, you know, exercise. Take your kid out to ice
cream...[that's what I want to do with him]."

—Ryan, former U.S. Marine Corps veteran[10]

"Let us strive on to finish
the work we are in, to bind up
the nation's wounds,
to care for him who shall have
borne the battle and for his
widow and his orphan,
to do all which may achieve
and cherish a just and lasting
peace among ourselves
and with all nations."

—ABRAHAM LINCOLN'S SECOND INAUGURAL
ADDRESS, AND THE OFFICIAL MOTTO
OF THE DEPARTMENT OF VETERANS AFFAIRS

CHAPTER 9

THE NEW TREATMENT FRONTIER: PSYCHEDELICS AND PLANT-BASED REMEDIES

"For the men and women who have stepped up to defend us and have come back wounded in many different ways, it is our sacred obligation to ensure that we don't leave behind any advancements in medical treatments that could benefit them."
—LT. GEN. JACK BERGMAN, U.S. MARINE CORPS (RET.),
currently U.S. representative (Michigan)

In recent years, there has been a notable surge of interest and involvement among veterans in psychedelic-assisted therapy. We believe this comes from the twin sources of many kinds of innovation: both desperation and inspiration. The desperation has come from veterans who have been frustrated by the lack of success of many conventional medical protocols for the treatment of post-traumatic stress disorder (PTSD), major depression, generalized anxiety disorder, and even the neurologic condition most closely associated with these wounds of war, TBI. Veterans have been at the forefront of the effort to find and make available new therapies. The inspiration has come from a growing body of renewed scientific research and cutting-edge clinical work with psychedelics and plant-based remedies. Specifically, several psychedelic compounds are being studied for use and are being used in treating the invisible and hidden wounds of war, principally the ones listed above. Additionally, a handful of preliminary studies suggest that psychedelic-assisted therapy can help with one of the most intractable, consistent, and co-occurring conditions observed in too many veterans, substance use disorder. There is even hope for how the treatment of these conditions can lessen veteran suicide. After research; consulting with experts such as Dr. Bob Koffman, whom we met earlier and who essentially coauthored this chapter; and interviewing veterans involved in this area, such as Jesse Gould of the Heroic Hearts Project, we intend to shed light on this promising avenue for mental health treatment, particularly for those who are seeking alternative therapies. Having said that, we must note that psychedelics remain controversial today within the medical community, and any use of them must take place under carefully prescribed circumstances.

A BRIEF HISTORY OF ALTERNATIVE TREATMENTS

The use of psychedelics is not new. In North America, there is an ancient tradition of plant-based remedies, as summarized in an article in *Notes from the Frontier* called "Hallucinogens & Native Spirituality":

> Anthropologists and historians believe hallucinogens have been used as early as 9,000 B.C. Early cave paintings and pictographs by indigenous people on rocks in North America and other areas of the world are believed to have been inspired partially from hallucinogenic influences. When Spanish Conquistadors and missionary priests came to the New World in the 1500s, they wrote of the use of psychotropic plants by [indigenous groups], especially peyote, morning glory seeds, and mushrooms.[1]

For some native traditions, psychedelic plants and fungi were understood to be sacred family members, and the spiritual use of entheogens (chemical substances derived from plants that produce a non-ordinary state of consciousness) enabled one to see and feel God or the divine within oneself. This knowledge has been kept sacred in light of the fact that Indigenous populations used entheogenic substances for communion with God, divination, and, in keeping with the predominant interest of veterans, healing. Matt Buckley, founder of the No Fallen Heroes Foundation, observed, "You go to Peru or the middle of the Amazon, and these medicine women and men look at you like where [have] you all been? We've been doing this since then, 1000s of years, years to heal our people."[2]

In the modern era, the history of scientific and medical research into psychedelics reveals the great potential these substances have for treatment, their troubled past, and the remaining legal and social constraints on them, including the continued stigma associated with their use. In the 1940s, the Nazis experimented with barbiturates, morphine, and mescaline on imprisoned Jews at the Auschwitz concentration camp. In 1953, the CIA and the U.S. Army, aware of LSD's mind-altering effects, embarked upon Project MK-Ultra, which was an illegal experiment to see if LSD could weaken people and force confessions through brainwashing and psychological torment. During the 1960s, there was a large increase in valuable academic and scientific studies, and psychedelics became associated with their abuse in the countercultural anti-war movement and the drug epidemic. In 1971, the Department of Defense released a report stating that more than half of the armed forces had smoked marijuana; almost a third had used psychedelics such as LSD, mescaline, or psilocybin; and 4.5 percent of service members tested positive for heroin.[3] Based on evidence that service members were returning from Vietnam exposed to unbridled drug use, President Richard Nixon ordered the entire military to begin "Operation Golden Flow," a mandatory urinalysis to check for controlled substances, in 1971.

Despite the fact that several psychedelic drugs have been found to be nonaddictive, with positive safety profiles and the wide range of psychiatric conditions that early researchers identified as potential indications for clinical use, psychedelic drugs have been characterized by the Drug

Enforcement Agency as Schedule 1 controlled substances, meaning they have a high potential for abuse and are "dangerously addictive" with "no accepted" medical use. Our sense from a distance is that the Department of Defense, the Veterans Administration, and the Food and Drug Administration continue to grapple with the troubled history of psychedelics, the restrictions imposed by the Schedule 1 category, and the continuing stigma associated with psychedelic drugs.

PSYCHEDELICS TODAY

The confluence of promising new research, large amounts of investment capital directed to this area, and demand from veterans after two decades of war in Afghanistan and Iraq (as well as civilian needs) have led to an inflection point in this area of study. In 1986, pioneering research institutions like the Multidisciplinary Association for Psychedelic Studies (MAPS), began developing, studying, and promoting the careful use of hallucinogens for mental health, well-being, and connection. Since then, there have been many scientific and medical studies of the use of psychedelics,[4] resulting in several influential books, including *This Is Your Mind on Plants*[5] and *How to Change Your Mind*[6] by Michael Pollan; and *Psychedelic Medicine*[7] by Dr. Richard Louis Miller. Notably, in 2023 the George W. Bush Institute published an article titled "We Need to Explore Psychedelic-Assisted Therapy for Veterans."[8] Several universities, such as the Center for Psychedelic and Consciousness Research at Johns Hopkins, among many others, are studying psychedelics to advance scientific understanding and "their potential for treating mental health disorders, enhancing well-being, and expanding our understanding of consciousness."[9]

Veterans, driven by frustration with the mediocre results from existing treatments and a shared desire to find new and more effective treatments for a wide range of mental and physical health issues, have taken a proactive role in advocating for expanded access to psychedelic therapy. Juliana Mercer, a Marine Corps veteran and now director of Veteran Advocacy and Public Policy at Healing Breakthrough, said:

We were trying everything from meaningful employment to equine or puppy therapy, yoga and meditation, everything you could think of that could help. It was frustrating. Compound that with now almost 20 years of our country, myself and my friends being at war. I found myself in a place where I no longer felt I had a purpose [in treating veterans]...[My own psychedelic treatment] opened me up to a world I had never heard of but also [saw] the possibility and the potential for healing... Anybody that's been involved in trying to solve the veteran suicide epidemic recognizes this as a light at the end of the tunnel.[10]

Veteran-led organizations and advocacy groups have played a pivotal role in raising awareness and supporting research efforts. For example, VETS, run by Amber Capone and her husband, former Navy SEAL Marcus Capone, provides grants, coaching, and resources for veterans to receive psychedelic-assisted treatments in countries where they are unregulated but legal. While VETS is primarily for special operations veterans, other organizations exist to help the military community obtain access to psychedelic therapies for PTSD and TBI, among other debilitating illnesses. Even since the research for this book began, there has been widespread growth in the number of responsible clinics that use ketamine and other psychedelics to help veterans suffering from conventional, treatment-resistant ailments, such as depression, anxiety, PTSD, and TBI, with a corresponding increase in medical and academic studies. We believe this has led to an increased awareness and openness on the part of the VA regarding ketamine as a treatment option, such as discussed in a recent article that the VA published online, "From Resistance to Resilience—A Veteran's Renewal with Ketamine."[11] In our opinion, there is sufficient reason and momentum to push past the stigma associated with psychedelics to pave the way for them to continue to be studied and to be used in a controlled, responsible manner to provide new medical treatments to patients. "There's a risk of doing nothing as veterans are seeking care elsewhere," said Dr. Shannon Remick, a psychologist at the VA, who is leading a study of MDMA as a treatment for PTSD among a group of ten combat vets. She continued, "It's our priority to make sure veterans are safe and getting the best care."[12]

The number of veterans aware of, and who have experienced, psychedelic-assisted therapy is not small. In a soon to-be-published study and the largest of its kind, Dr. Koffman and others surveyed veterans' attitudes toward the use of psychedelics and found that nearly one-half of veterans completing the survey acknowledged having used psychedelics, compared to only about 10 percent of the civilian population. Among the respondents, more than eight in ten reported deriving benefit from their psychedelic use. Although nearly six in ten reported having experienced at least one adverse event, even those who experienced an adverse event viewed them as largely temporary and reported an overall positive experience. In the study, a high percentage of veterans characterized the experience as beneficial.[13]

The shift in public and veteran perception about psychedelics has facilitated more open discussions about alternative treatments for serious mental and physical health issues that conventional therapies have not adequately treated. Through their advocacy, determination, and willingness to share their experiences, veterans are contributing to a broader understanding of how psychedelics can be harnessed to alleviate the profound psychological burdens they often carry. As research advances and regulatory barriers evolve, the integration of psychedelic-assisted therapy into mainstream mental health care may offer new hope for veterans, their spouses, and nonveterans struggling with mental and physical health conditions worldwide. Dr. Leslie Morland, a clinical psychologist at the Veterans Affairs Healthcare system in San Diego, who is studying the possibility that MDMA can enhance couples therapy for marriages strained by PTSD, said, "The VA is in some ways the best place for this type of research to happen...the VA is going to make sure that we have good data that supports the safety and efficacy before they offer it to veterans, as I think is appropriate."[14]

The new willingness to engage in research has coincided with a push to study the use of psychedelics as medicines for the nation's veterans, whose challenges with mental illness and trauma have led to a suicide rate and other ailments that are higher than that of civilians, as we documented earlier.[15] In this regard, there has been a marked increase in recent media reports of federal and state governments' willingness to explore and fund tested psychoactive substances in plants for use in treating veterans and others.[16] For example, the Defense Advanced Research Projects Agency (DARPA) is sponsoring research into the synthesis of new "psychedelic-like drugs" (drugs that have action at the 5-HT2A receptor, to take advantage of desirable mind-repairing effects without the "undesirable side effects" of hallucinations and non-ordinary states of consciousness). Recent legislative and regulatory shifts have made room for increased research into psychedelic therapies. In 2017, the FDA gave MDMA-assisted therapy a Breakthrough Therapy designation, though an advisory panel of the PDA declined to recommend approval for it on June 4, 2024. In 2018, psilocybin was granted the same designation for treatment-resistant depression. Certain jurisdictions have recently decriminalized possession, signaling a changing landscape.[17]

The conventional treatment for PTSD and serious mental illness remains the prescription of pharmaceutical products (meaning drugs). This type of treatment generally has a negative perception among veterans as another pill-prescribing exercise with little positive effect for them. In fact, numerous studies have demonstrated limitations in the effectiveness of these conventional pharmacotherapies for PTSD and other ailments. According to Dr. Hoge, conventional pharmacological treatments for PTSD have only low to moderate efficacy, based on his 2004 study.[18] Likewise, Dr. Maria Steenkamp reported that about two-thirds of individuals who were treated with cognitive behavioral therapy (CBT) or prolonged exposure (PE) therapy, which are the recognized gold standards of intervention therapy in the mainstream medical community, still met the published criteria for PTSD, meaning the treatments were not effective based on the fact that the patient still exhibited symptoms.[19] Alternatively, after only two to three doses, more than two-thirds of subjects undergoing MDMA-assisted therapy for PTSD no longer met the applicable criteria, meaning the therapy was effective. Unlike conventional psychiatric medication, which is typically taken daily for the duration of the illness, some psychedelic-medication "journeys" have proved to be effective after only one session. By contrast, current trauma-focused therapies, such as prolonged exposure therapy, involve the detailed telling and retelling of the "worst day in your life" for the veteran. While effective for some, for others, this can be very provocative in a negative way and, therefore, ineffective, as evidenced by dropout rates of up to 40 percent. However, the dropout rate in the phase 2 and phase 3 clinical trial of MDMA conducted by MAPS was less than 8 percent.[20] In addition, studies have documented that patients continued to receive the benefits of MDMA treatment for more than four years after their treatment, which is another significant result and one superior to many conventional therapies.[21] In 2020, Dr. Alan Davis and others published a study of the beneficial effects of psychedelic treatment for trauma-related psychological and cognitive impairment in special operations forces veterans.[22] In September 2022, MAPS published a phase 3 study evaluating the efficacy and safety of MDMA-assisted therapy compared to placebos, indicating that this therapy reduced PTSD symptoms and functional impairment in a diverse population with moderate to severe PTSD and was generally well tolerated.[23] Recently, the FDA has allowed MAPS to continue offering MDMA for PTSD, though as noted above an FDA advisory panel expressed caution. At the time of this publication, we are not aware of studies that are being conducted within the Department of Defense, though multiple VA sites are exploring the use of MDMA for PTSD. We must acknowledge that at the time of this writing, much research remains to be done, but we also notice that the most experienced and responsible medical professionals who treat veterans are among those investing their time and effort into developing psychedelic protocols because of their great promise.

THE POWER OF PSYCHEDELIC AND PLANT-BASED REMEDIES

Let's get into the specifics: What is psychedelic-assisted therapy and what are the psychedelics used? Psychedelic-assisted therapy refers to a group of therapeutic practices involving psychedelics; entactogens (substances that allow a touching within or reaching inside to retrieve repressed memories); and empathogens (substances that increase a person's feeling of empathy and benevolence toward others as well as feelings of being socially accepted and connected). Psychedelic-assisted therapy involves administering a measured dose of a psychedelic to a properly screened individual, in a highly controlled setting and under the care and guidance of doctors, medical professionals, and also what are sometimes referred to as guides, therapists, or sitters. The importance of being guided by trained doctors and therapists cannot be overstated.

While research is ongoing, the following psychedelics have shown promise in clinical settings:

MDMA (methylenedioxymethamphetamine):
- MDMA-assisted psychotherapy has shown promise in treating PTSD and moral injury.
- Dr. Koffman explained that, distinct from a true psychedelic, MDMA is better characterized as an empathogen, a substance able to produce a sense of oneness, openness, and communication with others, while simultaneously creating a sense of benevolence and even transcendence. These reactions can engender trust in a relationship with a therapist, which then can allow the patient to process traumatic experiences in a more effective manner. Though not yet formally studied, researchers using MDMA-assisted therapy to manage combat-related PTSD anticipate that the empathic self-love and forgiveness MDMA facilitates may in fact be helpful for healing moral injury and PTSD.
- Phase 3 clinical trials have demonstrated significant improvement in PTSD.

Psilocybin (found in certain mushrooms):
- Psilocybin has shown potential in reducing depressive symptoms and anxiety associated with moral injury, PTSD, and TBI. Some say psilocybin can induce profound mystical experiences and a feeling of openness, oneness, and even transcendence, which may promote insight about oneself and healing.

- Clinical trials have demonstrated significant reductions in depressive symptoms and improved well-being in individuals with PTSD and related conditions.
- A Breakthrough Therapy designation was awarded by the FDA to psilocybin for treatment-resistant depression in 2018 and for major depressive disorder in 2019.

LSD (lysergic acid diethylamide):
- Some suggest LSD-assisted psychotherapy may facilitate deep introspection and emotional processing, potentially benefiting individuals with PTSD.
- While research is ongoing, preliminary studies suggest potential therapeutic effects in reducing symptoms of anxiety and depression.

Ketamine:
- Ketamine has been primarily used as anesthesia. Its use as a psychedelic is relatively new.
- Although not a classic psychedelic, ketamine has demonstrated rapid antidepressive effects in controlled settings and carefully controlled dosages. It has the potential to be particularly useful in treating comorbid depression and PTSD in individuals with TBI.
- The FDA has approved ketamine for treatment-resistant depression, which often co-occurs with PTSD.
- While there has been a recent rise in ketamine clinics, veterans are cautioned to follow the advice about proper treatment in the next section of this chapter and not simply walk in for a drug treatment.

Ibogaine:
- Derived from the iboga plant, this psychedelic has shown potential in treating addiction and trauma-related disorders. It may help individuals confront and process past traumas.

- Early studies suggest promise in addiction treatment and trauma recovery, but further research is needed.

DMT (dimethyltryptamine):
- Ayahuasca (a psychoactive beverage containing DMT) ceremonies, guided by experienced shamans, have promoted deep introspection and emotional healing for some. DMT has shown potential in treating PTSD and trauma-related conditions.
- Limited clinical research has explored its therapeutic potential, but anecdotal reports and observational studies indicate positive outcomes.

Some of these therapies have been used in conjunction with functional magnetic resonance imaging (fMRI) and electroencephalography (EEG) to explore possible brain changes associated with their use.

HOW DO PSYCHEDELICS WORK?

Psychedelics are believed to exert their healing effects through interaction with the system of neural networks called the default mode network (DMN). The DMN is responsible for self-referential thinking, such as when one is lost in self-reflection, self-criticism, self-doubt, or frequent symptoms of depression or anxiety. Psychedelics can diminish awareness of the DMN, as a result of which the person experiences relief from these symptoms. One way to think of this effect is that psychedelics open a door of consciousness, allowing therapy to reset disruptive patterns. This is the reason psychedelics have shown improvement in serious mental illnesses such as major depression, generalized anxiety disorder, and highly ruminative conditions like obsessive-compulsive disorder. Dr. Robin Carhart-Harris noted that though the effects of the dose may last only hours, the net result can be a complete reset of one of the most complicated, intriguing, and important organs in the universe— the human brain![24]

OBSERVATIONS ABOUT PROPER TREATMENT

Psychedelic-assisted therapy is not just about taking some new compound and thinking that your problems are solved. The taking of psychedelics should be monitored by trained professionals, after proper screening, and with a whole process built around it. As Jesse Gould observed, "You can have all the epiphanies in the world, but if you're not going to put in the hard work and discipline afterwards, you're probably going to fall back into old patterns." Gould went on to explain that veterans also make use of talk therapy and positive habits like yoga, meditation, and other mindfulness techniques, which we summarize elsewhere, to continue healing.[25]

Dr. Koffman suggests a three-phased approach to psychedelic-assisted therapy: preparation, dosing, and integration.

Preparation. During the preparatory phase, the therapist does intake to confirm the appropriateness of the treatment and seeks to build a trusting, dependable therapeutic relationship with the patient, which forms the foundation for the experience. According to a study led by Dr. Roberta Murphy in 2022, the strength of therapeutic alliance predicts the extent of emotional breakthrough.[26] The length of the preparation phase varies considerably depending on what the patient needs, and can range from a few hours over a few sessions or days or weeks, depending on which protocol is followed. The therapist seeks to educate the patient on the experience, its trajectory, the anticipated effects, and possible side effects. The therapist will often suggest loosely setting the participant's intentions, meaning what the veteran wishes to get out of the experience. Setting the intention is no small thing: Being clear and articulate about what one seeks to get out of the therapy increases the chances of fulfillment, particularly when combined with the sense that psychedelics allow one's own "healing intelligence" to operate. Examples of intended changes include better ways to care for oneself, better lifestyle choices, a deeper understanding of where one is in life, and where to go from here in terms of healing and life direction.

Dosing. During the actual dosing phase, the patient should be allowed to go through the experience in whatever way suits them to allow them to gain insight into and acceptance of their feelings, values, and behavior, called "nondirective therapy." Dr. Koffman encourages those going through it to have a beginner's mind, meaning an open mind, allowing one to more fully be present and enjoy the current moment. This approach may allow for the reset of the DMN and the dissolution of the ego to allow one's heart and instincts rather than a historic mental self-image to contribute to the healing process. Dr. Koffman told us he often pictures his role in the psychedelic experience as the veteran's Sherpa, someone who will help unburden a heavy load, pointing and leading the direction to the top, but allowing the traveler to "dig deep and make the ascent themself" if they wish to "savor the view at the top."

Integration. Following the psychedelic experience, it is important to continue the work with the therapist to integrate the experience into your life. That can be no small feat since the psychedelic experience can include profound visual, auditory, and sensory experiences but also an improved sense of physical movement and effort, according to studies by Dr. David Nichols in 2016[27] and Dr. Samuel Turton in 2014.[28] These experiences can also change mental imagery and modify one's thinking process, among other changes, according to studies by Dr. David Nichols[29] and Dr. Torsten Passie.[30] The therapist and the patient debrief regarding the nature of the experience in several settings. The focus is on what the experience means to the person and how the person can bring the perspectives envisioned in the psychedelic journey into their daily life with renewed meaning, effectiveness, and related behaviors, as described by Dr. Eduardo Schenberg.[31]

Dr. Koffman added an important caution in his description of the process, emphasizing that the importance of the "therapy" component cannot be understated. He continued, "Psychedelics—when used in the proper manner, at the proper dose (with the right preparation), for the appropriate clinical indication, are believed to open doors to new insights and awarenesses. This deep therapeutic work, as described by

Aldous Huxley in his seminal novel *The Doors of Perception*, remains a gateway of guided opportunity. Scientific rigor has yet to identify which specific type or manner of therapy, for which behavioral conditions, and prompted or enabled by which psychedelic, offers the greatest therapeutic efficacy. This partnership between medicine, therapist, and participant allows patients to take with them the benefits of the experience on a permanent basis."

FINAL CONSIDERATIONS ABOUT PSYCHEDELICS

The range of experiences from taking psychedelics is broad. In addition to the positive, there have also been negative experiences with psychedelics, some of which have been severe. We are not endorsing the use of psychedelics for veterans, and this chapter is not meant to give you free license to use them recreationally. Rather, we present information regarding this promising new frontier for the veteran or military spouse who has not had success with conventional forms of medical treatment. Research is ongoing, and while initially positive, these treatments have not yet been universally approved for widespread use and not all treatments have received FDA approval in the United States. As Dr. Koffman emphasized, it is important to note that while promising, psychedelic-assisted therapy is not without risks, and rigorous screening is required to ensure individuals with other serious mental illnesses, such as bipolar disorder or schizophrenia, are excluded from participation.[32]

In years to come, veterans may derive significant benefit from psychedelic-related neuroplasticity (which we described earlier). As a group, because psychedelics are responsible for promoting neuroplasticity and the ability to reset brain circuits, they have given rise to a new psychiatric class of compounds (psychoplastogens). There is good reason to believe that in the future, these psychoplastogens will offer real therapeutic hope for other neurodegenerative diseases as well, such as multiple sclerosis, Parkinson's disease, and other disabling—and common—disorders of the nervous system, including chronic migraines.

VETERANS' VOICES

"[Psychedelics] kind of lets you restart, jump-start your system, clean you out and give a fresh slate. I came home and finally I started to feel hopeful for the future, which I had never remember[ed] feeling, and I was able to laugh and cry and access emotions in a way I never could."

—Phil Sussman, a former U.S. Army captain who was among
the veterans featured in the photo journal *The Twenty-Year War*
as well as the exhibition; currently International Cooperation/
Humanitarian Assistance—Crisis Operations

"The immediate thing I have to tell you is there is a way out; healing absolutely is possible. If you're sitting there in the gray or in the dark, I've been you. I've been lying on a bathroom floor, man, and I have had my dark nights of the soul. And these medicines are potentially life-saving and life-changing. So, the first thing I have to tell you is that healing is possible...You deserve to be healed...

"Let me just tell you that, the five of us [who] went down there [to Mexico] came home completely different human beings, and I healed decades, decades of trauma with psychedelic-assisted therapy...I gotta be honest with the man, it kind of makes me furious that I gotta take a veteran who incurred injury serving this country to another country to heal their traumas."

—Matthew Buckley, former U.S. Navy fighter pilot;
currently CEO of Top Gun Options and Strike
Fighter Financial; as well as CEO and founder of
the No Fallen Heroes Foundation

"I was prescribed antidepressants and countless prescriptions to treat a variety of ailments from PTSD to a mild TBI. I couldn't even count the number of psychiatrists, psychologists, therapists that I sat down with for…ten years, but nothing was getting better. I was getting diagnosed, but I wasn't really getting, in my opinion, the treatment that I personally needed…My life did a 180 in 2017…when I went down to Mexico to do psychedelic treatments. I was [then] at a tipping point where I didn't want to be here anymore. I thought life would be better for my family without me here. Ibogaine turned that around, almost instantly…These things get to the root causes of problems. They get down in your soul and kind of pull out things that you may be struggling with."

—Marcus Capone, former U.S. Navy SEAL; currently founder,
Veterans Exploring Treatment Solutions (VETS)

"We are what we repeatedly do.
Excellence, then, is not
an act but a habit."

—WILL DURANT, *THE STORY OF PHILOSOPHY*
(SUMMARIZING ARISTOTLE)

CHAPTER 10

FINAL PERFORMANCE TIPS

"One day, you'll tell your story of how you overcame what you went through, and it will be someone else's survival guide."

—BRENÉ BROWN

In our discussion of the stages of reintegration and healing the visible and invisible wounds of war in chapters 3 through 8, we listed what we found to be the best practices in each chapter. Now, we make a related but different point: Tackling any challenge requires preparing in advance, training for it, and mastering techniques to help you succeed. So, whether you are seeking additional tools for healing or just to enhance your performance in the transition and in life generally, we have found five essential and overarching techniques that may be valuable to you. They are (1) meditation; (2) recognizing and harnessing fear; (3) creating and maintaining a positive self-narrative; (4) self-regulation; and (5) finding hope. As Dr. Eric Potterat and Alan Eagle explain in *Learned Excellence*, becoming a top performer requires a commitment to learning excellence along the way.[1] That's how we have understood the summary of Aristotle, the ancient Greek philosopher in the quote that precedes this chapter, that excellence is not an act but a matter of developing the habit and practicing excellence.

THE POWER OF MEDITATION

Meditation is not a religion or a cult activity. In fact, it is an essential art practiced by ancient and modern warriors,[2] and it has become an important survival skill for veterans. Meditation is a valuable way to process physical, emotional, and spiritual pain, and to restore your sense of self and power. For those to whom meditation may seem daunting, foreign, or inaccessible, we can assure you that meditation is highly learnable and teachable. Existing utterly in the present moment of meditation has transformative results.

So, what exactly is meditation? There are several kinds, but at its core, meditation is a simple practice of learning to sit for just a few moments in silence, while being mindful of your breath and being present in yourself as much as possible. If you want to try it, sit somewhere that is quiet and peaceful, close your eyes, and breathe, while focusing only on your breath in and out, in a slow, calm manner. Try it for one minute to start. You can then extend the amount of time if you wish. It is the act of creating that moment of silence and, if possible, stillness within yourself that is the meditation.

There is ample evidence about the effectiveness of meditation for returning warriors. According to an article in the *Journal of the American Medical Association*, 61 percent of a transcendental meditation group had clinically significant symptom improvement from PTSD and noted that meditation is as effective as the VA's first-line recommended treatments for PTSD, prolonged exposure and cognitive processing therapies.[3] If the stats don't convince you, please consider this story: A World War II combat veteran began to meditate in his seventies, and afterward he was able to share his wartime experiences with his family for the first time, creating a new period of openness, communication, and love.

If you are curious about meditation, we recommend starting with the meditation programs offered by the David Lynch Foundation (davidlynchfoundation.org); as well as the foundation's Resilient Warriors Program (resilient-warriors.org). Lynch, a film director, has been committed to transcendental meditation for years. We list other meditation resources in Annex 1 on our website, www.heroes-journey.net.[4]

RECOGNIZING AND HARNESSING FEAR

We all experience fear, though often we're unaware of it, and we may not realize how limiting and damaging it can be. Of course, some fear is rational (like the feeling in your gut during combat or running from a bear in the woods), and some is irrational (as in the phrase that "fear" represents "false evidence appearing real"). We need to learn how to experience fear so that it doesn't affect our day-to-day lives. The key is to master fear, not to vanquish it—but to embrace and harness its power so it becomes an asset rather than a liability. We ask three questions to help you recognize and harness fear.

#1: How Do We Recognize Fear?

Fear can manifest in a variety of ways that are well camouflaged. Fear injects itself as anxiety about a job interview ("Am I good enough?"), sometimes mixed with a sense that we are an impostor applying for the job we really want, and we are waiting for someone to notice. It is easy for fear to set in, at times, when leaving the structure and familiarity of military life, particularly if one hasn't unpacked and addressed the reasons one leaves the military and made oneself prepared for the next phase of your life; it certainly arises in veterans in the process of seeking wholeness and healing around the topics discussed in chapters 3–9. The key to recognizing fear is for you to be sufficiently grounded and self-aware to recognize it. That's not easy if your system is used to living with it. What we have found is that if you can recognize the signs of fear, such as a tightness in your gut or shoulders, you can mentally link that feeling with the emotion or thought—such as when you say to yourself, "I am sitting down for an interview and my hands are fidgeting and my stomach feels tighter. Why? Oh, maybe my nerves are acting up."

#2: How Do We Gain?

Military training gives veterans much to learn about fear. Each branch, particularly each branch's special forces units, incorporates fear-control training. We are forced to undergo structured chaos from day one, being placed in scenarios to induce panic and fear. These impulses, if not controlled or harnessed, could lead to critical mistakes on the battlefield, compromise the mission, and lead to serious injury or death. Our impulses were tested during pool competency (known as "pool comp") in the second phase of BUD/S and post-BUD/S; and again when we went through the hooded box drill as part of our Close Quarters Defense training (which has since been removed from the training).[5] Most people experience fear and anxiety at some point in open and deep bodies of water. In pool comp, an instructor harasses the student for approximately twenty minutes. The trainee's mask is ripped off from the start. He is disoriented and his air hoses are knotted. The student has to assess the problem and work through a learned procedure to correctly regain his air supply, as the attacks are repeated over and over. About half the time a trainee is starved for air and taken to his limits. The trainee must overcome the signals to his amygdala of panic and the urge to surface. His frontal lobe must win this battle and overcome this fear. After repeated attacks, and once a trainee determines he cannot unfoul whatever ninja knot the instructor has tied in his air hoses, he must signal to ditch his tanks and bring them over his head to begin working on the problem. If the student determines that he cannot regain his air supply, he places his weight belt over the tanks, turns off his air valve completely, kisses the bottom of the pool, and conducts a free ascent to the surface, being cautious not to ascend faster than his slowest bubble during exhale. Once on the surface, the student will learn if he has passed pool comp.

Early on in the war on terror, Special Operations Command (SOCOM) tasked each of the respective services to grow by 20 percent to meet war demands. This was easier said than done. In an attempt to decrease the number of trainees that were failing pool comp, psychiatrists came up with specialized exercises for us to practice in fearful situations to teach mental toughness. Dr. Eric Potterat, who worked as the head psychologist for the U.S. Navy's Special Warfare Command, devised a four-part mental toughness program to help trainees control fear:

1. *Goal-setting.* Focusing on specific goals can keep the part of the brain that generates fear impulses in check. One way to do this is to take a goal and break it into pieces. If you are not

a consistent runner, you would not run a marathon without training. You'd train and work up to your goal.

2. *Mental rehearsal and visualization.* This involves running through a scenario in your mind, so that when you conduct the evolution in real time, it seems more natural and less stressful. This is very much like the visualization exercises we've mentioned before.

3. *Positive self-talk.* This will focus your thoughts. The average person speaks to themselves at a rate of three hundred to one thousand words per minute. Keeping your self-talk positive helps to override fear signals from the brain.

4. *Arousal control.* With deliberate and slow breathing, you can combat the effects of panic. Long exhales get more oxygen to the brain and will mimic the body's relaxation state. This enhances performance. Box breathing is a simple way to practice arousal control. Breathe in through the nose for four counts, then hold your breath for four counts; breathe out of your nose for four counts, then hold for four counts.

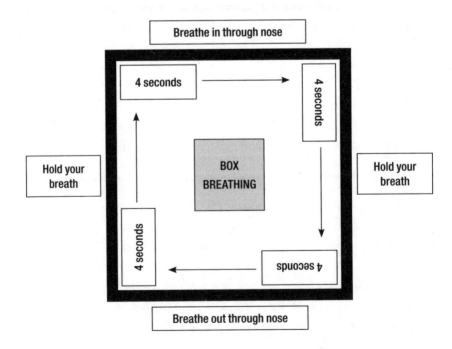

Dr. Potterat and Alan Eagle have expanded on this framework in their book, *Learned Excellence*. They summarize their findings after having studied top performers across all aspects of society, including those in the military, for decades. In short, they conclude that there are five disciplines involved in improving one's performance: (1) having clear values and goals that motivate and sustain you; (2) having a growth mindset that is always learning and providing you with a positive attitude; (3) engaging in a process that you trust and to which you commit; (4) being tolerant and resilient in the face of adversity; and (5) making time for balance and recovery.[6] It's worth reading to learn how these techniques can be applied to improving performance across all sectors in the civilian world, including the transition from the military.

For years, and through extensive training, your mind was trained to become a warrior and rise to any challenge our nation asked of you. Part of that training was to put emotions, including fear, in a box so you could keep on with the mission. Dr. Glick said, "We were trained to treat everything as objects so we could kill and quickly move past what would be a traumatic experience to do our job. It is a survival skill that has to be unlearned. Unfortunately, it bleeds over into other aspects of our lives. We are good at compartmentalizing, but not that good." Rarely does the military teach warriors to unpack that box when the mission or deployment is over. Now, we are telling you to go against your training. Allow your fear to come to the surface and be vulnerable with a trusted friend, family member, significant other, or anyone who will give you a safe place. Next, put yourself first. Be selfish for a moment and allow yourself to heal and face what has been suppressed and compartmentalized by your training.

#3: How Do We Turn Fear on Its Head?

Once you've recognized fear and gotten it under control, how do you harness it? It's simple to say but hard to do. It involves taking the positive momentum and energy from the four-step approach above and reexamining what is underneath that fear. Ask yourself, What caused this fear, whether rational or not? If your fear is that you're not good or worthy enough to get the job, try breaking it down. Take an inventory of the reasons you are great for the job and your areas of challenge or concern. Are you giving too much weight to your challenges? Can you improve in these areas, or do some intelligence gathering to figure out what competitive challenges you really face? Is this a moment to ignore and override the negative voice in your head and push forward with positivity about the great advantages you have? The ultimate goal here is to understand that when you unpack the source underlying the fear reaction, you can identify it, get it under control, and use that knowledge to reposition and reapproach. The only way to conquer what we most fear is to walk into the cave where it is hiding—"The cave you fear to enter holds the treasure you seek," said Joseph Campbell.[7]

CREATING AND MAINTAINING A POSITIVE SELF-NARRATIVE

We all tell ourselves stories about who we are, how we appear to others, what we are capable of doing in our lives, and what we somehow believe we cannot do. Tony Robbins calls this the "blueprint" that we create for our lives. This is done on some unstated internal level, of which few of us are conscious. Our self-narrative, or blueprint, is different from positive self-talk and visualization. The blueprint lays out, usually in an unconscious way, the image and understanding we carry about ourselves and what that implicitly means for how we experience and see the world. It therefore guides us and reveals to us our sense of life's possibilities (whether positive or limiting). By contrast, positive self-talk and visualization are mental tools that we use generally to accomplish specific objectives—I can finish this obstacle course; I am worthy of winning this job; and I can accomplish all of my objectives.

Once you become aware that you are the creator of your own blueprint, you have the power to direct the thoughts and feelings that create it. Here's an example. When you get injured, it is natural to ask yourself why or how it happened. In responding to your own question, you have a choice. You can recognize that what you are experiencing is what is expected from someone who served in combat. This framing, a warrior would say, has in fact helped them to achieve the unimaginable in their road to healing. By contrast, if your story is that you will never recover from chronic injuries, that the government has turned its back on you, you'll find yourself stuck. We say this with full sympathy, understanding that injuries from war, whether visible or not, are real and need to be respected, cared for, and taken seriously. It takes great internal strength to come to a different realization about yourself; to redraw your blueprint. However, doing so can help you with your road to recovery and healing.

Why Self-Narrative Is Significant to Healing

An essential aspect of successful treatment, healing, surmounting challenges, and transforming ourselves in the process involves our ability to modify our self-narrative, to direct our mindset regarding our possibilities in a positive direction. You have the ability to redefine and transform your condition, as Dr. Tick articulated, "into an honorable wound that is a source of strength and growth."[8] How your emotions, psychology, physiology, and spirit are interwoven in the context of recovery is complex, but we do know from experiences in our own lives, through our research, and the great honor of having witnessed this in others, that positive self-narrative plays an essential role in growth and seeking wholeness. The positive change you experience in doing so, often referred to as "post-traumatic growth," helps you to find a renewed sense of strength and personal understanding after experiencing extreme trauma.

A powerful example comes from Jason Redman, a former Navy SEAL, who required dozens of operations and skin grafts to survive and managed to find meaning in his experience. He put a handwritten sign at the door to his hospital room:

ATTENTION TO ALL WHO ENTER HERE

If you are coming into this room with sorrow or to feel sorry for my wounds, go elsewhere. The wounds I received I got in a job I love, doing it for people I love, supporting the freedom of a country I deeply love. I am incredibly tough and will make a full recovery. What is full? That is the absolute utmost physically my body has the ability to recover. Then I will push that about 20 percent further through sheer mental tenacity. This room you are about to enter is a room of fun, optimism and intensive rapid growth. If you are not prepared for that, go elsewhere.

—Lt. Jason Redman, U.S. Navy (Ret.),
currently CEO of Wounded Wear

Dr. Charles Hoge reminds us that a positive or negative self-narrative "actually affects your body chemistry. Having a positive view of yourself is an essential starting place toward navigating the reactions resulting from combat experiences."[9] If you want to take it a step further, then consider following the practice of Dr. Joseph Dispenza, by devoting a part of every day to reframing and reimagining what is possible, shifting your emotions and mindset, which can change the energetic field around you and help you create a new reality for yourself.

SELF-REGULATION

Self-regulation refers to the ability to monitor and manage one's energy state, nervous system, emotions, thoughts, and behavior. This ability is an essential component to dealing with injury, healing, and, even more broadly, how we relate to other people. All of us face situations in which our emotional and physical response to a real or perceived situation is either high (when we get hyper-aroused) or we find ourselves in a down or low state (a state of hypo-arousal). Either state can be appropriate based on what we're experiencing. The primary concern is how to regulate back to a neutral, peaceful, balanced place from which one can respond rationally and appropriately, including to those around you. Regulation helps us understand our own body's process of controlling (or attempting to control) or adjusting our emotional state and expressions, as Dr. Ryan Rana explains. Dr. Rana points to self-regulation as a critical skill that differentiates successful reactions from problematic behaviors in this terrain. He said, "At critical points, each of us chooses to either go toward or away from others that love us. All humans must down regulate. The task is to work with the body's function and do so in a way that leads us to a connected, grounded, healthy peace, balancing how we regulate and, in doing so, being extremely cautious with anything that harms our relationship with our self and others."[10]

Let's take a closer look at self-regulation.

Upregulation

In combat, when faced with real or perceived threats or danger, such as the sound or memory of a gunshot, or strong negative emotions, increased awareness is a necessary survival instinct, though some would say that remaining calm in the chaos is the key to success here. In this state, when hormone levels rise and the firing of nerve cells increases in an anxious, survival mode, it is natural to find oneself in a state of hyper-arousal, or upregulation. Symptoms include difficulty controlling impulses, difficulty in calming down, overreactions, mood swings, sleep struggles, and exhaustion. Staying in an upregulated state is exhausting and unhealthy for us and those around us.

Downregulation

Experiencing low energy and feeling sluggish or unmotivated given the circumstances around you, is referred to as a state of hypo-arousal or downregulation. This can be due to depression, trauma, chronic fatigue syndrome, or feeling disconnected from those around you. Downregulation may also be a reaction to periods of excessive hyper-arousal.

How to Regulate Your Nervous System

The issue posed by upregulation and downregulation is how to shift to a more balanced, peaceful, and appropriate state. The first step in this process is to ascertain whether you are in an up- or a downregulated state by doing an inventory of your reactions. Sitting with yourself (even sitting in silence, in meditation, or just with yourself), taking a time-out, or getting feedback from friends and family are often-used techniques to accomplish this.[11]

There are a few methods of seeking downregulation to decrease your level of arousal. Autoregulation uses an individual's ability to calm themselves (in isolation) through coping skills, breathing, focusing on the task at hand (staying in the present), or even performing through pain toward a goal. In coregulation, one turns toward trusted loved ones to help downregulate. Remember that consistent coregulation is the goal, a state of human relations in which others share your load and know and love the real you. There are also unhealthy forms of coregulation, often referred to as competing attachment, such as drug use, excessive drinking, or sexual activity outside someone's value system that they regret later. These activities provide initial sensations of downregulation, but bring with them many negative emotions, such as guilt, shame, self-loathing, and purposelessness, as well as potential physical consequences.

The techniques to achieve down- and upregulation fall into similar categories of activities, modified for the specific need. These include:

- Getting in touch with your body and self, for example, by deep breathing (including box breathing, which we describe elsewhere);
- listening to music, whether up- or downbeat;
- going to places that center or ground oneself, including nature;
- physical activity, whether calming (such as yoga or tai chi) or invigorating (such as boxing or skiing);
- eating calming or stimulating foods; and
- connecting with others who may enable or accelerate the finding of your balanced center.

Dr. Hoge articulates a central truth regarding veterans: Transitioning home from combat does not mean giving up your internal warrior, but rather learning to dial up or down the warrior responses depending on the situation. He outlines a holistic strategy that involves becoming more aware of your reactions, modulating your reactions, creating a positive self-narrative, and accepting and learning to live with loss.[12]

A NOTE FROM ROB

Military life is filled with adrenaline rushes, victories, and dopamine hits one moment and then, the next, you are faced with hard, life-changing moments, even death. Hitting these highs and lows creates a spectrum that few will ever experience or feel, only amplified by the intensity of the soldier's experience. It is this delta that makes veterans unique, gives us a diversified lens to see the world, and is why people are so intrigued with our life experiences. However, over time veterans can become desensitized to the low points, even emotionally numb, as our training teaches us to "ruck up" and soldier on. This is our survival mechanism in combat. We are told to keep pushing and deal with it later, though we seldom ever do. This served a purpose in the military, but living in this perpetual state is the antithesis of being a warrior and being whole. We become out of balance as we become expert internal pundits, telling ourselves that "it can always be worse." The danger in benchmarking and telling ourselves this is that we forget to ask for help. Time and time again I have watched veterans roll their shoulders back and stand poised and stoic on the outside, when they are actually frail and broken internally, myself included. If you don't fix the internal warrior, and find balance, you will just be adding more stress once you transition, and you will always default inward to what you know: "Ruck up" and soldier on.

FINDING HOPE

There will be times when hope feels far away. Both of us have been there ourselves. There are no magic words that bring in light and return hope. But even in our darkest moments we have a chance to turn a corner where we did not see one before. In these times, focus on what you can control, if only for a moment. Find the one thing you can be grateful for. Gratitude is a powerful source of soothing, an antidote to fear and anger, if only briefly. Shifting away from a sense of desperation can open the door to something else. You can also decide to hold on to the idea that good things can come, that there is reason for optimism. Admiral McRaven reminds us that when confronting darkness, we are asked to reach deep inside ourselves—for ourselves and our loved ones—to be our very best.[13] And today, there is more hope for veterans—from innovative, new therapies and medical research—than ever before.

SERGEANT OMAR AVILA, UNITED STATES ARMY (RET.), ON THE POWER OF HOPE AND INSPIRATION

I [Rob] met Omar ("Crispy") Avila in 2013 when I moved to Dallas and started my transition from the service. Omar survived a two-hundred-pound IED blast and sustained third-degree burns over 75 percent of his body. He has endured 105 surgeries to repair damaged tendons, joints, and severe nerve damage, and had his right leg amputated below the knee. And, while going through all this, he once asked me what I thought he was afraid of the most. I told him I had no idea. He said, "Salad tongs, bro!" Omar can barely use his fingers or his hands, as the tendons were severely cauterized by the burns he sustained. But here is a man who should be dead, and his biggest fear is going to the salad bar. All joking aside, his story of survival is remarkable and what he has done after that is even more so.

Sergeant Avila deployed to Adhamiya, Iraq, near one of Uday Hussein's former palaces, within six months of graduating from the Army's infantry One Station Unit Training (OSUT). On May 14, 2007, eleven months into deployment, he was the gunner in the third vehicle of a five-vehicle convoy when they came under fire from insurgents. As he returned fire with his .50-caliber machine gun, his vehicle hit a bump. More than two hundred pounds of explosives ignited, throwing the Humvee six feet into the air and igniting all the diesel in the back end of the truck.[14] Avila, despite his injuries, rose and resumed shooting at the insurgents with the .50 cal.—until the barrel was so hot that it was melting. He jumped out of the vehicle, breaking both of his femurs, but he pulled out his M4 and continued shooting at rooftops while lying flat on his back. He did this until he ran out of ammunition. After a friend finally dragged him to the lead vehicle in the convoy, Avila found that the driver was on his first day in-country and was screaming in fear. "I did what any NCO would do," Avila said. "I grabbed him, slapped the shit out of him, and said, 'Shut the fuck up, we're getting out of this.'" When a medic gave Avila some water, Avila poured it over his head, allowing all the chemicals from the IED to pour into his eyes, thus leaving him temporarily blind. He was forced to guide the brand-new driver back to the forward operating base (FOB) using landmarks he had memorized.[15]

Omar was awarded the Silver Star and Purple Heart for his actions that day. The injuries Omar sustained in combat were devastating, altering his mobility and lifestyle, and, no doubt, leaving scars inside. Despite the tremendous physical and emotional toll of his injuries, Omar has refused to let adversity define him. Instead, he embarked on an inspiring journey of rehabilitation, pushing himself beyond limits to regain his strength and independence. Then, he became the current world record holder for the World Association of Benchers and Dead Lifters in the Paralympics category. He also started his own consulting firm, Five Toes, and dedicated his life to serving his fellow veterans. Omar now serves as a liaison for Sons of the Flag, helping other wounded warriors through their recovery process. His presence on social media has allowed him to connect with children all over the country who have been bullied for being burned, giving them a role model and a mentor.[16]

More than anything, Avila is a man of relentless positivity, with a hilarious dark sense of humor and a deep appreciation for how lucky he has been. "I know the brothers that I lost would trade places with me in a heartbeat," he said. "So, to me, it's an injustice not to live my life to the fullest, not to inspire others. This is a fucking testament that yeah, life's a bitch. If life knocks you down, make sure you land on your back so you can look at it right in the face, get back up, and say, 'What else you got, bitch?'" Omar Avila's journey serves as a testament to the strength and resilience of the human spirit. Despite the adversities he faced in combat and the wounds he sustained, he continues to inspire others with his unwavering determination and his unwavering commitment to living a purposeful life.

VETERANS' VOICES

"I had a hard few years after the Army. I lost track of my life. Physically and emotionally. Leaving the Army July 2014, the same month my first child was born, was challenging. I was learning to be a civilian and a father at the same time. My partner at the time was younger than me and she was most likely bipolar. It was exceptionally challenging to stay with her after my son was born. We split up when he was six months old and she moved back to El Paso from San Antonio. I dropped out of the Executive MBA program I was attending at the University of Texas at San Antonio. I couldn't afford to stay in the program. After I left, I started a company with my dad and one of his old colleagues in telecom construction."

—Anthony Garcia, former U.S. Army captain
and former mustang (enlisted private first class)

"After I left the Marine Corps, I started college. As I sat in classes with what seemed like children, who were unaware of the world around them, unaware that we were at war and our Marines were dying in combat to give them the peace to be able to go to school, I started to get angry. I wasn't aware of it. It was building inside of me. The structure of my family, my wife, and my focus on getting a college degree helped me. But, at some point, my wife encouraged me to go get help. So, I found a therapist at my local VA, a Vietnam vet who became a therapist helping other veterans. It helped. It helped when he explained to me that 'it's not their fault. They are just a product of their experiences.'"

—Anonymous veteran, former sergeant,
U.S. Marine Corps[17]

"I stood on the window ledge and shut my eyes and said a prayer and was about to jump. I know what got me onto that window ledge, but I also know what got me off that window ledge and why I'm here now. Transcendental Meditation is a humongous portion of the reason why I'm still sitting here now."

—Leshonda Gill, former U.S. Army sergeant[18]

"The journey of the hero is about the courage to seek the depths; the image of creative rebirth; the eternal cycle of change within us; the uncanny discovery that the seeker is the mystery which the seeker seeks to know. The hero's journey is a symbol that binds, in the original sense of the word, two distant ideas, the spiritual quest of the ancients with modern search for identity, always the one, shape-shifting yet marvelously constant story that we find."

—PHIL COUSINEAU

CHAPTER 11

THE HERO'S JOURNEY: A GUIDE TO REFINDING PURPOSE

"I believe we each have what is ours to do. Sometimes we've listened to what we're told for so long that the calling to follow our own path is weak and we'll need time to listen to it."

—CDR. CURT CRONIN, U.S. NAVY (RET.);
cofounder and managing partner, Broadway Strategic
Return Fund; and founder and CEO of Aiki Partners

In this chapter, we'll unpack what it is about returning to civilian life that causes many veterans to feel that they have lost their sense of purpose. Then we'll outline some valuable frameworks for refinding purpose. In the next chapter, you'll hear from a range of veterans who shared their own journeys to refinding purpose.

THE LOSS OF PURPOSE DEFINED

For many veterans, finding a new purpose after their service is the hardest of all the challenges they face. Why is that? There is no one answer that fits every veteran, but we offer the following observations from our interviews with veterans, our research, and our own life experiences.

Having been ingrained with the sense of purpose and mission that comes with serving your country and your teammates, it's difficult to find that same feeling in civilian life.

For many of us, serving in the military was our purpose in life—and we were good at it. We found a family of like-minded people who wanted to serve a higher cause. How do you find the same transcendent cause in the private sector when the focus can be geared toward higher salary, promotion, and routine? Many veterans struggle with this question. We offer some frameworks for solutions later in this chapter.

At a high level, the path to refinding purpose may look like re-forming our identities and, in psychological terms, our ego structure. The quest for a new sense of purpose continues long after we leave the service; we have noticed patterns that reveal opportunities in the search for new or renewed purpose. This is perhaps one of the most important aspects of the return to civilian life, because our sense of purpose and mission animates the rest of what we seek to accomplish in the world and how we relate to other people.

"When people are actively engaged in a cause their lives have more purpose … with a resulting improvement in mental health."
—Sebastian Junger, *Tribe: On Homecoming and Belonging*

Many veterans have written of the addictive nature of combat, particularly the intensity and the camaraderie involved. For some, that experience and its memories will prove to be irreplaceable. However, that mindset may also cause a veteran who has shifted to civilian life to stay in a place that does not permit moving on and truly transitioning. There may be other sides of the coin to explore, as many veterans have discovered. In fact, the image of the difficulty of leaving the intensity of combat, among other aspects of military life, can be an illusion. This is because military life for everyone except for those who dedicate their lives to having a complete military career is a young person's game. The inevitable question often obscured by a sense of loss upon leaving our comrades is that of what we will do next, which would reasonably be to take the very natural next step into civilian life.

In fact, in our discussions with veterans, we have come to realize that the more intense the military training and the stronger the bond with their comrades and service, the more challenging the search for new meaning can be—particularly for those who saw combat.[1] The same can be said for the injured veterans who return home with an utterly different series of physical, financial, marital, emotional, and psychological challenges. All of this change, even in the gentlest of reentries, can cause stress and anxiety and can lead to existential questions about why we are here and what we are meant to do.

GENERAL DAVID H. PETRAEUS ON THE CHALLENGE OF REFINDING PURPOSE

In our interview with General Petraeus, he summed up the challenge of refinding purpose in succinct and wise terms. He highlighted three essential facets of military life that are hard to replicate in civilian life.

1. *Mission larger than self.* This is especially profound for those who have served in combat.
2. *Community.* We lived and served with others, beginning with the oath of service. We were motivated and had the profound privilege of standing next to brothers-in-arms, in service of a mission larger than self together.
3. *Sense of identity.* Those in the military have forged inside them a sense of identity. Uniforms can be a testament to that. The Army has so many identifying features: a patch on your left arm (your current unit); a patch on your right sleeve (your combat unit); hash marks on your lower right sleeve (number of six-month increments in combat). You can see the ribbons and badges on someone's chest and read their accomplishments.

As ribbons accumulate, we become more attuned to all this. In civilian life, we have none of it. We have to start over and build a new résumé.

General Petraeus offered three additional and important observations—things that he confessed he has borne in mind—in our interview with him. First, it is important to alert service members who want to transition that this is going to be difficult. Understand this is going to happen—that one phase of your life is over. Second, he noted, "It may be difficult to replicate the sense of purpose in civilian life that we had in the military. It is not impossible to replicate but difficult to find the level of commitment in the private sector. It will never be what you had in the military, especially in times of war. But it is not impossible to replicate." Finally, he articulated a portfolio approach: "For many of the rest of us, we have found new purpose in a portfolio of activities: family, community, veterans' organizations, and a job that is stimulating, rewarding, and meaningful."

FRAMEWORKS FOR REFINDING PURPOSE

We haven't found a silver bullet approach to refinding purpose. But here we will offer you three different ways of thinking about refinding purpose in civilian life. One approach is practical in nature and comes from Dr. Glick, the next is a way to reconceive of your life, and the third offers an ancient way of finding a sense of purpose from how you fit into your different worlds. These can be used as frameworks for your own reflection on refinding purpose.

Framework #1: Dr. Glick's Four Key Questions

We met Dr. Glick in chapter 3 when he shared his four-stage approach to reintegration to civilian life. Having supported hundreds of his fellow veterans as they faced a range of challenges and reflecting on his own life, he revealed to us the value in asking yourself four basic questions, which can lead to productive reflection and movement toward a new sense of direction and self-definition. Think of this practice as an expansion of visualizing your future.

1. *Who am I?* How will you think of and define yourself now as a civilian? This will no doubt change as your transition evolves.
2. *Where am I going?*
   o   What are your goals?
   o   If you could plot a course to your future, where would you land?
   o   Reframe life and all its post-deployment challenges.
   o   Opportunities will become available to you. Will you take advantage of them? It is important to consider this ahead of time, so you can readily take these opportunities when they are presented to you.
3. *How am I going to get there?*
   o   What will I need to achieve my goals and get where I want to go?
   o   What support systems will I need? It could be family, friends, connection, or resources.
4. *Who am I going with?*
   o   How do those around you fit into your journey?
   o   How do your spouse, children, family, and friends play a role?
   o   Consider that during your transition, your family dynamics may be changing.

These questions are key to the personal reflection necessary for this journey. They also can be very practical prompts to help you build a plan of action. In this relative rare moment, you have a chance to reconcile the past, present, and future chapters of your life.

In considering Dr. Glick's framework, it is clear that there is no single set of questions that fits everyone or that gives you definitive answers. In our interview with General Petraeus, he noted the range of ways veterans do this. For some, they find a single new purpose that replaces what they left behind. Some seek purpose in one new part of their lives. For many of the rest of us, we have found new purpose in a portfolio of activities: family, community, veteran organizations, nonprofits, self-improvement, and a job that is stimulating, rewarding, and meaningful.

The insight from General Petraeus also leads to thinking about the puzzle of refinding purpose differently—from another angle, with the glass half full. That puzzle can be solved by building on one true thing and recognizing that the solution to one puzzle may look a lot different than others. If we are replacing the higher, transcendent purpose we had previously, it may take six or seven different pieces throughout our lives to rebuild an existence with a comparable level of meaning——such as family, continuing our education, developing a job or career, rekindling meaningful friendships, and helping others (especially fellow veterans).

In thinking of Dr. Glick's questions and his four-step reintegration approach, which we summarized in chapter 3, here is a question to consider: If you were motivated in your military service to defend the country and that gave you a transcendent cause, then isn't the country that you fought for worth returning to and building a life in?

A word of caution: If you are constantly comparing your new life with your old life, you won't easily be open to what all of life has to offer you. That would be like constantly comparing your new partner to the previous one, which never leads to happiness. If you remain in a negative state, distracted by things to do, distracted by the materialism of the shoppers at the mall, you will stay there. That'd be you doing that to yourself. There are new opportunities in the life ahead.

Framework #2: The Hero's Journey

This framework offers you a way to think about—to conceive of or to reframe—the story of your own life in a way that can give it great meaning and purpose. It is based on the theory of the hero's journey, which is a way to analyze all great epic tales, popularized by Professor Joseph Campbell. He describes the trajectory of many of our favorite protagonists—an individual is plucked from normal life and called to action; that hero is exposed to transformative experiences and must then return home. You know this trope well; it's found in everything from ancient tales to your favorite movies. The hero's journey isn't an easy walk from point a to b. The hero must undergo challenges and experience deep loss in order to be truly transformed.

"A hero ventures forth," Campbell wrote, "from the world of common day into a region of supernatural wonder: fabulous forces are there encountered, and a decisive victory is won: the hero comes back from this mysterious adventure with the power to bestow boons on his fellow man."[2]

There's probably no better example of the hero's journey than in Homer's *Odyssey*. The warrior king Odysseus spends ten arduous years struggling to return home to his wife, Penelope, and son, Telemachus—after having spent ten years fighting the Battle of Troy. While making his way home to Ithaca, Odysseus battles mythical creatures, the wrath of demigods, natural disasters, and his own temptations. In other words, he battles darkness. He survives these trials and leads his men back by his own courage, resourcefulness, and ability to outwit his opponents, the demigods, and nature.

By the awful grace of suffering, Odysseus is transformed. To overcome the unruly suitors who have taken over his home in an attempt to marry Penelope, Odysseus is given a potion, "nectar of the gods," which is meant to represent the enhanced consciousness and power he earned in battle and on the way home. Upon reclaiming his throne, Odysseus must then acclimatize to living in two worlds, the world of the gods from which he received the "nectar," and the mundane world from which he came and has returned. It is the need to reconcile these two worlds that becomes the final challenge for the hero.

What does all this have to do with you? The hero's journey—just like that of Odysseus—is every warrior's story, as Gen. Stanley McChrystal said when we spoke with him. By making the journey, the individual evolves into a 'hero,' into someone to be worshipped but someone who has mastered extraordinary trials and gives back, as Dr. Tick explained.[3] Enduring that, surviving, and returning home can move us to a higher consciousness, with new power in our souls ... along with all the baggage of combat trauma. In this way, the returning warrior must also grapple with living in two worlds, the military and the civilian. When the difficulty of the transition to civilian life is compounded by physical, emotional, or other injuries, living in both worlds is even more daunting.

So, how do warriors reconcile themselves to returning to the mundane, civilian world, having earned that higher consciousness and power? There are many ways to reframe or reconceive your return. It may be a higher sense of what matters in this life, the value and honor of service to others, how to do a job or build a business, how to relate to others with the highest sense of integrity and excellence, and how to be a better person. Ultimately, you get to define your elixir of the gods.[4]

Framework #3: Finding Meaning in the Hierarchical Assessment

This framework provides a way to understanding how you fit into your different worlds, which in turn may provide a way of finding meaning and purpose. This begins with Rob's time at the Naval Academy. He attended a lecture by Will Guild, master chief special warfare operator, U.S. Navy (Ret.), a former SEAL, who taught ethics and was the first member of the Navy or Marine Corps enlisted ranks ever appointed to teach alongside senior officers in the ethics curriculum. His lecture provided a profound and practical way to conceive of our place and purpose in the world in the context of a hierarchy of purpose and belonging. It's been twenty years, but in Rob's recollection, the lecture paralleled the ancient Greek Stoic philosopher Hierocles and his theory of the circles of concern. "Our first concern was our mind, but beyond this was our concern for our bodies, for our immediate family, then our extended family," Master Chief Guild stated. "Like concentric rings, these circles were followed by our concern for our community, our city, our country, our empire, and our world." The work of philosophy, he said, was to draw this outer concern inward, to learn how to care as much as possible for as many people as possible, to do as much good for them as possible.[5]

The way service members are trained to subjugate their egos and put themselves last is striking. The mantra "team, teammate, self" is relevant here. This aspect of training is what builds highly effective warriors, but now, we need to unpack this training. Now we have to take an emotional risk and be vulnerable by putting ourselves first and talking to someone about our reintegration. This takes an extreme amount of courage and is easier said than done. Many of us joined the military when we were young and malleable. Our transcendent cause to serve our country also put us in environments that were stressful, demanding, violent, and, at times, life-threatening. Just like we were taught to suppress panic and fear, our environment (the military) molded us when our brains were highly responsive to experience and stimulation. To undo this will take hard work and courage to evaluate ourselves.

The following illustration serves to visualize Hierocles's theory of the circles of concern:[6]

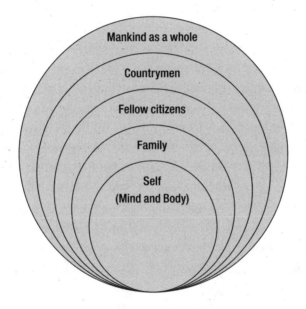

Self: You begin by fully embracing who you are. This sets the foundation to support every level of the hierarchy. Rob's high school English teacher, Christine Cole, once described our lives as rings within a tree. Each year a tree forms new cells arranged in concentric circles called annual rings. These rings tell us how old the tree is and what the weather was like during each year of the tree's life. It's analogous to the physical and mental composition of a person. Preserved inside each of us is the carefree child, the adolescent, and the adult who has embraced achievement and who has been worn by hardship. In a similar way, we can understand how the military changed us, especially through the experience of combat. It's necessary to evaluate where you have been and what you experienced in the military, what skills and character traits you developed, what hopes and dreams you have, and what virtues and shortcomings you struggle with. No matter where you stand in your transition, or in civilian life, giving yourself the permission to inhabit who you are for everything that you are at this moment is fundamental to personal change and growth. But you have to give yourself this permission and have the courage to do the work. Through self-knowledge, we can discover and acknowledge what our reality is, without necessarily being defined by it. Now it is time to exercise one of the greatest gifts we fought for: the choice each of us has about what we make of ourselves.[7]

Family: Some veterans we spoke with said family was the primary reason they sought professional help. Your family is more attuned than most to the changes you went through during your service. Our families are extensions of ourselves. Odds are your family endured along with you many of the hardships of your service, if not more: deployments, separation, uncertainty, injuries, moving, death, and stress, to list some. While you experienced them personally, you were trained to push those feelings aside in order to remain steadfast to support your unit and its mission. Some of us simply had only the military, which served as our surrogate family, and now that is gone. Whatever your situation, we all long for a family unit, an assembly of people who accept and love unconditionally, offer connectedness, give us unity in diversity, support one another, and empower us to achieve and fail without judgment.

Community: Taking and serving one's place in community is an essential way to find purpose. There is no shortage of ways to participate in your community. Chances are you already do—through church activities, nonprofit work, school board participation, volunteering, donation, et cetera. By bringing our attributes forward, we create a shared strength and the connections our communities need. George Bernard Shaw said, "I am of the opinion that my life belongs to the whole community, and as long as I live, it is my privilege to do for it whatever I can. I want to be thoroughly used up when I die, for the harder I work, the more I live."

Citizenship (and nationality): How do we find purpose in belonging as a citizen to our country? Admiral William H. McRaven, then commander of the U.S. Special Operations Command, delivered an inspiring address to the West Point Class of 2015, "A Sailor's Perspective on the United States Army."[8] Admiral McRaven spoke of our purpose in its most essential way. We took an oath, he said, to support and defend the nation, not the institution. Not the Army, not the corps, not the division, not the brigade, not the battalion, not the company, not the platoon, and not the squad, but the nation. It does not matter our branch of service, rank, or MOS. We have all served, and still serve, the Constitution. That was our why. What function we served in the military, how we supported each other and where we served came later. It has made us citizens of this great nation, and it must continue to make us serve in the capacity as a veteran. What we can take from Admiral McRaven's speech is that we all belong to a country, and in return we have rights and protection that we fought to uphold as service members and still uphold as citizens today. You might consider yourself to be a "citizen soldier," "one who is prepared both for civilian leadership in their profession and for military leadership in times of nation need." The taking of this oath, the actions that stand behind it, and the service to our country give each veteran great meaning and identity.

Global: In this ring, we become aware of the wider world and our place in it. Our roles on a collective scale can be understood to be in service of the maintenance of peace and against the evil in the world, to be in the pursuit of freedom and all it can mean—the power of the choice to define ourselves, to enjoy free will and the chance to experience everything that makes us human. Now, you have a chance to act as a citizen of the world, sharing a place of belonging as a part of a global whole. Living a life in service of freedom, respect for one another, and peace across the boundary lines of nations—or however you define and live your own values—allows you to make a wider contribution, to honor the humanity in others on a global level.

Universe: This is for the deep thinkers. How do you play a part in space and time in a universe that is still expanding? Why are we here? Where are we going? If you keep asking these questions or wonder what it is like riding next to a light beam as Einstein did in his general theory of relativity, then this level of purpose is for you. Some will say that these are questions we are not meant to understand, and that the answers are reserved for a higher power. In Hierocles's own words, "It is the province of him (her) who strives to conduct himself (herself) properly in each of these connections to collect, in a certain respect, the circles, as it were, to one centre, and always to endeavor earnestly to transfer himself from the comprehending circles to the several particulars which they comprehend."[9] Simply, the universe encompasses all these other areas of concern, just as they all encompass the universe.

VETERANS' VOICES

"One of the most difficult adjustments to make upon leaving the military is the sudden loss of purpose, combined with a loss of camaraderie and the innate sense that you were working together for a common good. The mission is one that is worth fighting for and even worth dying for, fueling everything you do. When this purpose is taken away and you are left to define your own ultimate purpose and motivation, it can be devastating. After I left, raising and providing for a family became my priority, and my new job became the vehicle for me to do so. As predictable as this sounds—even as I write it now—I remember how hollow it felt at times at my job. To be working with pay as the primary motivator was very hard to get used to. In the civilian world, there was suddenly no overarching good that we were all working toward anymore. It took me awhile to refind my sense of purpose. I began to think about basic principles—what my company did, how I did my job and led and provided for others and the other parts of my life that give me great meaning."

—Cdr. Joshua Klein, U.S. Navy (Ret.); currently professor of business, Savannah College of Art and Design

"I kept five things in mind that served to structure how I thought about refinding my sense of purpose: I maintained a passion to serve others, I focused on and searched out new passions, I continued to look for opportunities to be a part of something greater than myself, I viewed business as another operation to win and be the best at, and I always hungered to learn and grow."

—Bronston Carroll, former U.S. Navy lieutenant;
currently cofounder and COO of Magazine Jukebox

"For those that got out of the military before retirement, why not explore those reasons why you left. Understanding and facing those reasons why people leave the military when it is a career so filled with purpose might help others put into focus their reasons for leaving and how those reasons might help define purpose moving forward with their lives. It has been helpful to me to realize that purpose comes from within and is a uniquely individual journey."

—Siobhan Crawford, former lieutenant, U.S. Navy;
currently civilian contractor, Department of Defense

"Never was so much owed

by so many to so few."

—WINSTON CHURCHILL

CHAPTER 12

VETERANS' PERSPECTIVES ON REFINDING PURPOSE

"Gradually it becomes clear. I will go back. I will find the kind of girl of whom I once dreamed. I will learn to look at life through uncynical eyes, to have faith, to know love. I will learn to work in peace as in war. And finally—finally, like countless others, I will learn to live again."

—AUDIE MURPHY, FORMER FIRST LIEUTENANT,
U.S. Army, from his memoir, *To Hell and Back*[1]

In this chapter, we offer a variety of ways to consider and pursue a new purpose upon transitioning, told primarily through the stories of veterans and of our own lives. In learning the stories of other veterans' struggles, we find the greatest source of inspiration, as well as clues for success and some practical takeaways. We take this approach because there is no single solution to refinding your purpose.

TEAM RUBICON: A STORY OF SERVICE AND REDEMPTION
AFTER THE MARINE CORPS

Jake Wood asked a fundamental question after he left the Marine Corps, "What happens to a soldier after combat?" In his memoir *Once a Warrior: How One Veteran Found a New Mission Closer to Home*, he presents a new kind of hope and redemption for the returning warrior. He describes a range of reactions that are common to many veterans: having a sense that your mission has been stripped of you, and with that your community and sense of identity. Your energy drops, as does your sense of place and purpose, "sinking like a battleship to the bottom of a harbor." On top of that, the veteran's reaction to the outside world, our society, begins to confound them, as if they have returned to an alien place.[2]

Sitting in his living room one day and watching a natural disaster with a terrible toll on human life, Wood's Marine Corps training and heart kicked in. He felt he had to do something to help the human beings he saw suffering. At a deeper level, this was also a central, pivotal moment in his life. It caused him to reframe the meaning of what it is to be a veteran. "What if instead of allowing our sons and daughters to simply fade away," he asks, "we asked them to come home and build a legacy that would strengthen the foundation of our nation? Our communities face no shortage of problems, ranging from social division to income inequality to an increasing onslaught of natural disasters."[3] He gave life to the idea of the hero's journey—that the returning veteran has a rare moment of opportunity, to take all of what they learned and all of what made them grow as people and turn it into a potent source of good that is uplifting for those around them.

In the opportunity for service all around us, he found hope in that battle. Wood explains: "We can reignite a sense of purpose in our veterans by providing them with a new mission that rivals their wartime sense of duty. In the decade since I've left the Marine Corps, I have seen countless men and women become better versions of themselves by serving with Team Rubicon in disaster zones around the world and here at home. Through this continued service, they have found within themselves an immutable sense of purpose and a tightly knit tribe."[4] Wood founded, and today is CEO of, Team Rubicon, a nonprofit company that provides disaster relief.

GENERAL WASHINGTON'S FAREWELL

On December 4, 1783, nine days after the last British soldiers left American soil following the peace treaty with Britain, George Washington invited the officers of the Continental Army to join him in the Long Room of Fraunces Tavern in New York City to bid them farewell. Colonel Benjamin Tallmadge recalled the evening's events:

> The time now drew near when General Washington intended to leave this part of the country for his beloved retreat at Mt. Vernon. On Tuesday the 4th of December it was made known to the officers then in New York that General Washington intended to commence his journey on that day.
>
> At 12 o'clock the officers repaired to Fraunces Tavern in Pearl Street where General Washington had appointed to meet them and to take his final leave of them. We had been assembled but a few moments when his excellency entered the room. His emotions were too strong to be concealed which seemed to be reciprocated by every officer present. After partaking of a slight refreshment in almost breathless silence the General filled his glass with wine and turning to the officers said, "With a heart full of love and gratitude I now take leave of you. I most devoutly wish that your latter days may be as prosperous and happy as your former ones have been glorious and honorable."
>
> After the officers had taken a glass of wine General Washington said "I cannot come to each of you but shall feel obliged if each of you will come and take me by the hand." General Knox being nearest to him turned to the Commander-in-chief who, suffused in tears, was incapable of utterance but grasped his hand when they embraced each other in silence. In the same affectionate manner, every officer in the room marched up and parted with his general in chief. Such a scene of sorrow and

weeping I had never before witnessed and fondly hope I may never be called to witness again.[5]

It is not hard to imagine the meaning and emotions of that evening and what it meant for those present to find new purpose in their lives. We can imagine how each man may have turned to the next, soberly embraced in silence, and quietly taken his leave, carrying with him the sacrifices and inexplicable bonds formed during war.

The story of General Washington's farewell is meaningful on many levels. It represents one of the first speeches to our country's first veterans. It also is of deeply personal significance to Rob, since his ancestor Dayton Irelan served in the Continental Army and fought with those present that night.

It is feasible that when the army was disbanded, Dayton felt the loss of an identity after finding an indescribable national pride, helping to win our country's independence and standing among his brothers,

George Washington Says Farewell to His Officers at Fraunces Tavern, New York, Dec 4th, 1783
Source: Chicago History Museum, USA, Copyright © Chicago History Museum/Bridgeman Images

whose bonds he would never feel in the same way again. In the days to come, it is also conceivable that he suffered from the price of many years of combat, seeing 1 percent of the population perish in war. Perhaps, I am projecting my own feelings onto this historical scene and making his experience too grandiose for the simplicity of life in the 1700s—though I suspect that every veteran I know would have the same reaction. More than likely, Dayton returned to his family's farm and lived out his days providing for his family. Whatever mental distress existed was buried deep down where no one would know of his suffering, fear, loss, and emotional detachment from the "civilian" world. My hope is that he was surrounded by loved ones, found a new purpose in life, and quietly reflected on the sacrifices he and his fellow brothers had made, giving his fellow citizens the freedom to build the foundation for a new homeland.

Though my family played a small part in our nation's storied history, just as many families can trace their lineage to the establishment and preservation of our country through military service, it gives me and my family great pride that our forefathers answered the call and served a higher purpose. This sense of duty and selflessness drove a long line of ancestors, my mother and father, and me to serve our country.

Rob described to Alex how this history filled him with pride, humility to have shouldered Dayton's legacy, a sense of duty and selflessness, and a connection with him and his other descendants who served our country in the military. Rob confessed, "A revelation that all of my mentors, and my coauthor, Alex, in writing this book have bestowed on me is to pay it forward to educate the warriors still serving, the ones standing the watch, ready to go into harm's way, who will one day join the long line of veterans."

RETURNING TO AN UNKIND PLACE

In his books and in his documentary trilogy, Sebastian Junger has shed significant light on the difficulty many veterans experience when transitioning out of the military.[6] In Junger's view, the transition is challenging for the veteran not because of some inherent dysfunction or difficulty within, but because of the society to which he or she returns.

In 2007–8, Junger embedded with a U.S. Army infantry platoon in Afghanistan. During this time, the soldiers deployed for six months, living in primitive huts without running water, unable to change their clothes for months at a time, not eating hot meals, under constant threat of attack by the numerically superior Taliban, and facing frequent combat. These forward operating bases in Korangal Valley saw about 20 percent of all combat and casualties in Afghanistan at that time. And yet, an intensely close-knit brotherhood was formed. The soldiers experienced a sense of common purpose and sacrifice and devotion to one another. On a spiritual or existential level, when the only thing that matters is the survival of the brothers to your left and right, there is a clarity that comes, an essential aspect of what matters in life. When you are willing, day and night, to sacrifice yourself for your brothers and vice versa, there is a shared sense of purpose, devotion, and love that is hard to find in regular civilian life. This experience touches a primordial aspect of the human condition.

If you come from a close-knit community, you know well the security and meaning that come from sharing life so closely with others. On a psychological level, these experiences must be understood in light of the expanded awareness, even expanded consciousness, that occurs for some in combat under extreme stress and risk, particularly with the rush of adrenaline. There is nothing like feeling as if time and space are slowing down when one undergoes an extraordinary life moment—what some refer to as a flow state—which happens to some in combat. Living after having taken such great risks, having experienced such things in a community, as well as the trauma of combat, can result in a euphoria at having survived. These experiences are made more complex and unimaginable by the tragedy of the situation, from the worst parts of war and the inevitable grief of losing comrades. That tragedy, in the eyes of these service members, cements some understanding of why they were there, particularly when their loss is honored for the higher cause they were serving that infuses one's sense of mission, purpose, and sacrifice.

None of the above is meant to romanticize war. Rather, it is to explain what makes some aspects of the experience of combat veterans resonate with an essential aspect of their humanity, and it is to explain the contrast with that when they come back home. When the warriors return, they leave behind their tribe and a series of intense shared experiences. Often, they return to a fractured, alienated, and materialistic society. The modern comforts of life that we enjoy and often take for granted provide a sharp contrast to the simplicity and primitive surroundings of deployment. A regular job rarely replicates the brotherhood and sense of belonging we experienced while in the military. Other than our fellow veterans, few understand us and what we went through, in all of its highs and lows. The fractiousness of our current political climate exacerbates the sense of alienation, particularly since that would never have been tolerated in the military. The sense of loss and, at times, even the question of whether the country to which we returned was worth the sacrifice, amplify the contrast of the meaning and purpose of our experience when together while deployed and when back in the country. The fact that veterans are not wholeheartedly welcomed back and appreciated by the public, as they were during and after World War II, exacerbates the difficulty of the transition.

So, it is no wonder that when a former soldier from an infantry platoon was asked at a polite New York City dinner party the question of what he missed from the war, he responded, "Ma'am, I miss almost all of it."[7]

INSPIRATION FROM CAPTAIN DEREK HERRERA

Captain Derek Herrera and his team of Marines were on patrol in the Helmand Province, Afghanistan, on June 14, 2012, and came under heavy fire.[8] During the firefight, while he was on the roof of a building directing his team, he was shot in the spine and instantly paralyzed from the chest down; his left lung collapsed as well. Derek continued to support his team, communicating information about enemy positions and encouraging and assisting teammates, who rendered aid to keep him alive while awaiting the medevac helicopter. As a small team (ten Americans with ten Afghan partners) and two Marine Raiders were critically injured, they faced seemingly insurmountable odds against a large enemy force that was raining gunfire down on them. If you want an image of heroism while under enemy fire, this would be one such image. Due to the selflessness and heroism of his team, Derek and Sgt. Rick Briere, who was shot through the neck, survived and were able to recover from the engagement. These team members were later recognized for their bravery and awarded multiple Bronze Stars, Silver Stars, and one Navy Cross.

When he returned to the U.S., Derek spent six months in rehabilitation at a VA hospital with his wife, Maura, by his side. Following his injury, Derek, with the support of his wife and family, became determined to walk again. "Initially, I thought very positively about the recovery process, but as the weeks dragged on, I hit the realization that my situation was probably going to be more permanent than I initially thought," he said. Still, despite that realization, he refused to give up and, in the process, discovered his new purpose in life. As he learned more about medical research and technology, he became intrigued— by its potential not only to help him, but to help others with disabilities, including his fellow injured veterans. At that time, Derek also heard about his classmates and friends applying to business schools. He applied and was accepted to the UCLA Anderson School of Management's Executive MBA program. While there, he continued to refine his next mission and recalls speaking to a classmate who suggested he become a stockbroker because he would make tons of money. Derek asked his classmate, "Why?" and his reply was again "You would make tons of money!" What this experience helped Derek realize was that he needed a career, a profession, that would align any profit incentive with purpose. He quickly found this in the medical device industry, where any new product's success is directly correlated to the impact it has for patients. With his mind made up, Derek started his first medical device company, Spinal Singularity, in 2015 and is now the founder and CEO of Bright Uro, the third medical device company he has founded and led since graduating from UCLA.

"In most respects, I would say that getting shot and paralyzed is a wholly negative event. Conversely, the path I have traveled has been absolutely incredible. I am not the least bit sad, bitter, or angry. I feel content, excited, and anxious because I still have the opportunity to achieve goals I have set for myself. Every day is an opportunity for me to do something lasting and meaningful. Every day I think about those who made the ultimate sacrifice and no longer have the opportunities that I do. The past few years have not been easy, but I have found a new cause that I am as passionate about pursuing as I was while leading Marines and sailors in the special operations community. I get up every day excited. I get out of bed knowing the problems I am trying to solve and the impact I hope to have on people's lives. I have this opportunity because of everyone who helped me become a Marine special operations officer, the men who saved my life by risking their lives, and those who have been there to support me every step of the way since I was injured. It is because of them that I am alive and it is because of them that I continue to fight every day to create positive change."

In our conversations with him and in what we have read about him, Derek speaks in inspiring tones about the prospects of technology for amputees and those who have been paralyzed. He speaks about how he can make a difference. "In the next ten years, the technology will be functional and will replace wheelchairs similar to the way prosthetic technology has helped amputees," Derek said. "There will be so much progress with technology that it's not a matter of *if* they'll walk again, but rather a matter of when." To continue to give back, Derek has served on the boards of multiple nonprofit organizations including the Paralyzed Veterans of America Research Foundation, the Marine Raider Foundation, the American Technion Society, and MedTechVets (a company that helps veterans bridge between military service and their next career).

We also sensed the great gratitude Derek carries with him. He wears a bronze bracelet bearing the names of his fallen comrades, not only to honor their memory but to remind him how fortunate he is to be alive. That's the message he wants to communicate to other veterans, particularly those who may be starting their journey with a life-changing spinal cord injury or other disability. At some point, he hopes his fellow disabled veterans will discover that while life will be different, it can still be lived to the fullest. "The question will become, 'How do I expand my business'; or 'How do I lead these people where I'm working'; or 'How can I help someone else today?'" Derek said. "All of the same passions and purposes we had on active duty can be channeled into something meaningful today, and if you're not taking advantage of that, it's a disservice to yourself and others in the veteran community." Derek mentioned an adage from the literature that many of his teammates still use today and that he believes helps to embody this principle: "When in Doubt, Focus Out," meaning it's never a bad option to think about helping others and that, through this work, you can find new purpose and discover so much joy.

Derek's story is inspiring on many levels. In the most difficult of moments, he asked himself, "Of all the things I could do in life, *is there something that only I can do?*" He reflected on how having been in the military, having become an engineer, having a business school education, being a wounded veteran, and having a desire to serve all joined together. From that, he created companies that design products to make people's lives better. This was a journey in which he himself was deeply invested. Notwithstanding the difficulties, he is the foremost example of the virtuous cycle of fulfillment and self-actualization after and during great challenge. We are also struck by Derek's wife and how she stood by him, and the power of their marriage and love. The role of spouses and what they go through in a veteran's transition, which we discuss in chapter 16, cannot be overestimated in its importance and poignancy.

Our discussions with Derek revealed one of the most humble, genuine, ambitious, courageous, and giving people we have had the privilege of knowing. And he is a profound example of one of the stories we have seen unfold in the civilian lives of many veterans: that in seeking to serve others and make his life better, he found new purpose and meaning in his life.

WORDS OF WISDOM FROM GENERAL STANLEY MCCHRYSTAL: FOCUS ON KEY ISSUES TO REFIND PURPOSE

In our interview with General McChrystal, he shared many practical points, including this one: In trying to refind purpose, ask yourself who you are, what you stand for, and how you can add value to businesses. This may take time to develop. Create an inventory of skills and life experiences that may be useful in practical terms to a company. Part of this requires problem-solving—in that you need to figure out how to live and succeed in the new world you are entering. Fight the war you are in by learning the business, by studying it and its people and culture and what drives its success. You went to school to prepare for and master your new operations in the military. Now, do the same thing in civilian life with your new missions. Set yourself up for success again, in a new mission in a new world.

- Realize that you will have to work hard. For some senior officers, this is a turnoff after what they did in the military because they expect they won't have to work so hard to re-create themselves after a successful career.
- Success is not owed to you. You have to show up prepared to earn it every day, every assignment.
- Allow yourself to be successful again.
- *Do you want to have one job, or a portfolio of activities (be part of a team)?*

OBSERVATIONS FROM COMMANDER DAN BOZUNG

In his book, *This Civilian Sh*t Is Hard,* and our discussions with him, Dan Bozung offers an unvarnished and often humorous take on the transition. "Don't expect to find the same qualities in the private sector that made your military experience unique and memorable," he wrote. "Some veterans moonlight as volunteer firefighters or EMTs in an attempt to recapture that same sense of purpose and adventure. But such activities rarely provide any lasting satisfaction."[9]

Dan tells a compelling, evocative story: "I turned to the Navy Reserves. After six years' hard time in a corporate cubicle, I volunteered to deploy. On my final night at sea after moonlighting as the Air Boss on USS *Ponce,* I gathered on the signal bridge for cigars with officers from a dozen nations. We had just successfully completed the largest counter-mine exercise in U.S. Fifth Fleet history. I'd come to feel a real sense of brotherhood with these officers, and, for the first time in my Navy experience, didn't want the ship to pull in. The very thought of shedding my flight suit and returning to my cubicle sank me into a deep depression. As I took a pull on my Cohiba and admired the continuous blanket of stars that stretched from one corner of the empty horizon to the other, I thought, 'Why can't I have this in the private sector?' Because this doesn't exist. And you shouldn't waste a nanosecond of your time trying to find it."[10]

Dan's explanation of the difficulty resonates with other veterans' voices: "The military provides a convenient, one-stop shop for every human need along Maslow's hierarchy. From food to community, from shelter to self-actualization, life in the service offers a very complete existence. It's like being in the mafia. Who were my friends back in my squadron days? Guys from my squadron. What did I do with my free time back in my squadron days? Hang out with guys from my squadron. From where did I derive a sense of purpose, belonging, and achievement back in the squadron days? From all the cool shit I got to do while deployed to various godforsaken places with guys from my squadron."[11]

Finally, Dan echoed the portfolio approach of General Petraeus: "Some civilian jobs may check some of the same boxes, but most won't. You may need a hobby. You may need to do volunteer work. You may need to make new friends. Whatever the case, remember you need to build a new life, not just to find a new job."[12]

LESSONS LEARNED FROM REMI ADELEKE

Remi Adeleke, a former Navy SEAL and teammate of Rob's, spoke with us about the lessons he learned:

> I learned many lessons that I put to good use when I got out. First, the military's way of teaching me to prepare for missions made me think I needed to be prepared for my next one when I got out. I didn't want to work a job that I didn't like in order to pay the bills. I finished my bachelor's degree while on active duty and started my master's degree while I was in, so I could

have education to fall back on. I saved tons of money and built a cushion, which gave me time to figure out what I wanted to do. I ended up using the money to start two companies.

Second, be open to opportunities that you didn't think about or plan for. Don't be afraid of failing. I relied on what the military taught me: teamwork, communication, perseverance, and critical thinking.

Third, I found a new purpose by serving. While working at my job, I worked with prisoners, nonprofits focused on human trafficking, inner-city youth camps, and inner-city schools.

Finally, I took advantage of the mental calluses that I built up while being in the military and going overseas to war. These harden you, prepare you, and strengthen you mentally. A lot of service members use these principles in their work after the military, but they forget to use them with their family. The military taught us to be present and good communicators and sometimes we forget to do that with our spouse and kids.

WISDOM FROM VETERANS

After hundreds of interviews, we saw patterns and clues emerge across the stories of challenge and success we collected. From these patterns and our own lives, we offer the following words of encouragement and advice that have proved helpful to other transitioning veterans:

- *Give yourself time.* Finding new purpose takes time. Think of it as a challenge to build new habits and strengths. That does not happen all of a sudden, but rather is a process that, with the right preparation, mindset, commitment, and work, shows results over time.
- *Never, ever quit.* When adversity and discouragement hit, just keep moving forward. There is nothing wrong with taking a break, but don't let that become an excuse.
- *All that glitters is not gold.* Be cautious about pursuing jobs that seem to offer big pay divorced from any sense of goals

and purpose that you find important. Don't be fooled by cool-sounding civilian job titles or the allure of fellow veterans claiming they are making the big bucks. There's nothing wrong with making good money, but that tends to come when one is first aligned in the right place, in the right job.

- *Find courage daily.* If you need motivation to find that courage, it is all around you, there for the asking. Just look at the stories of Capt. Derek Herrera, U.S. Marine Corps (Ret.); Lt. Dan Cnossen, U.S. Navy (Ret.); and Sgt. Omar Avila, U.S. Army (Ret.). Find courage and purpose from living by honoring those who are no longer with us. Live in a way that honors their lives and sacrifice.

- *Be stoic.* You can find solace from the ancient Stoics in many of their affirmations. For example, Marcus Aurelius said, "Choose not to be harmed—and you won't feel harmed. Don't feel harmed—and you haven't been."

- *Celebrate each success along the way.* Even the smallest success is a reason for celebration. You'll have many of these along the way, so revel in each one.

- *Engage in service and volunteering.* Find purpose from helping others. As Rear Adm. Katherine McCabe, U.S. Navy (Ret.), said, "Volunteering is essential. Veterans have skills that our communities need, and there are organizations out there for every interest. When we make this a priority, it pays off many times over. Volunteering fills our need to serve, fills an actual need in the community, builds your network, and fortifies our resiliency at a time when a lot is changing. If you can only spare an hour a month, do it."

- *Challenges bring fulfillment.* The challenge of finding a new purpose can itself be a thrilling and fulfilling adventure. As Cdr. Curt Cronin, U.S. Navy (Ret.), observed: "What if instead of guilting ourselves over failure, we asked ourselves what would make this challenge more exciting and compelling that I can't wait to create and build on these ideas?"

- *Be aware of different aspects of purpose and identity.* As you refind your mission as a civilian, be aware that it can be made more complex based on your own identity and circumstance. Your racial, sexual, or gender identity may impact your transition to civilian life. Most veterans tell us that what they share together is a hell of a lot more important than these distinctions, but we also want to honor these distinctions. For many, having what makes one different and what are essential aspects of one's identity are necessary pieces to the puzzle in refinding purpose. Self-identity plays a role, and we urge you to take that into account for yourself if it's relevant.
- *Speak with others.* Communicating about refinding purpose is very important. Getting different perspectives on what matters, how to think about this new sphere of life, and hearing stories of purpose redefined, successfully or unsuccessfully, can really be helpful. Nothing beats engaging in conversation with fellow veterans and former teammates about these things—and anything else.
- *Find a mentor.* In this aspect of your transition—which most likely will unfold over time—a mentor might be a helpful guide to you. The fact of your service may give you more in common with fellow veterans than your differences separate you, and mentorship provided by someone who, besides being a fellow veteran, sees you and understands certain aspects of your identity is valuable. A female veteran who is about to or has recently left service may find benefit in mentorship from another female veteran, and so on. If you identify as a member of a group, it's worthwhile to develop a relationship with someone who knows your world.

VETERANS' VOICES

"After I left the Army, I was reading one night in my apartment Malcom Gladwell's *Outliers*. I came across a section that shook me. I realized I was successful because of the people I met. I wasn't a self-made man. I had help every step of the way. He mentioned the term *connector* as a type of person that seems to know just about everyone. I realized at that time I had two connectors in my life. One helped me realize my professional capability, the other helped me find my purpose after the Army. My purpose is supporting my fellow veterans in helping them find meaningful careers after the Army and not settle for what their rank says they should transition to. I also feel very strongly about community engagement and supporting companies like the Mission Continues."

—Anthony Garcia, former U.S. Army captain
and former mustang (enlisted private first class)

"Have I found new purpose? I may be an outlier on this because I'm back active now. Obviously the military isn't for everyone. And sometimes people don't even realize the military is for them until they're out. But if purpose is what you're looking for, you can find it in thousands of career paths and directions both civilian and military. I didn't realize when I got out that the military would always be home, but it turns out it was. I was lucky enough to discover my passion is service to others, hence why I decided to go back. And even if I couldn't have gone back, I would have kept pressing to continue my service in some other shape or form. I would tell anyone getting out, let your passion guide you and you'll ultimately find your purpose."

—S.Sgt. Josh Pelto, U.S. Air Force

"My life was once marked by unimaginable hardship. I tragically lost both of my parents suddenly, endured the painful turmoil of a bitter divorce, and then I lost custody of my children because I was labeled as having combat-related PTSD. I was hurtled into a dark abyss of homelessness and despair, where I grappled with the darkest corners of my own mind and multiple suicide attempts.

"But, in my darkest moments, I found the strength to turn my life around.

"I sought help, confronted my own trauma, and slowly began to rebuild my life from the ground up. Then, I discovered my purpose: to help others who had faced similar challenges. This path led me to creating Grace After Fire, an organization dedicated to supporting women veterans. I not only found my calling but also the means to make a profound impact on the lives of countless women veterans who, like myself, had faced adversity.

"I hope, in my story, that there is a reminder for others, that even in our darkest hours, there is always a glimmer of hope and the potential for remarkable transformation."

—Tana Plescher, former U.S. Navy; currently founder and CEO of Grace After Fire

"The most painful thing during the transition was that I had a massive void. I literally felt empty. My purpose was gone. My buddies were on active duty or moved back to their home state. I felt as if I had lost my identity. I felt unaccomplished. The void does not care about your rank, time in service, rating or MOS, SOCOM versus conventional. Transition is difficult for everyone. It also hits everyone differently and you must understand this. The process of filling the void with purposeful, positive, and healthy tools can be painful, and it can take years for some folks, which it did for me. I didn't feel holistically right until, maybe, five years ago, nearly nine years after ETS. Life is always moving, so transition is actually transitioning, an active verb (or noun), an ongoing process."

—Dustin Bennight, former U.S. Navy seaman apprentice

"Some people live an entire
lifetime and wonder if they have
ever made a difference in
the world, but the Marines
don't have that problem."

—PRESIDENT RONALD REAGAN

CHAPTER 13

PRACTICAL STEPS IN LOOKING FOR A JOB

"When you look for a job, bring all of your tactical skills to bear. Target your job search, conduct a full mission analysis. Be proactive, assertive. Set the conditions for the job search, set the conditions for your future success."

—CAPT. DEREK HERRERA, U.S. MARINE CORPS (RET.),
currently founder and CEO, Bright Uro

In previous chapters, we dealt with some heady topics. Now, we're going to get down to brass tacks and discuss concrete steps to take when preparing to find a job. To start, some of the key skills we discussed in chapter 10 (positive self-talk, visualization, and developing an empowering self-narrative) can be game changers for the veteran's pursuit of the right job and career.

Before you begin, we recommend you involve your spouse or partner in your planning, pursuit, and decision-making. General Stanley McChrystal shared as much with us, and, given what your family will experience alongside you as you shift to civilian life, we believe this is important.

MINDSET

To better understand the mindset of a civilian applicant and how to speak with employers, we turned to Dr. Josh Cotton, a renowned expert and coach to the U.S. military and countless veterans.[1]

Dr. Cotton's key takeaways:

- You must understand your audience and competition. Communication is about the receiver, not the sender. Dr. Cotton said, "Vets are no different than business leaders. We deal with the same problems. The jargon, methods, and culture are different; however, none of that is relevant if you can do the job or not. That is why it is a communication problem."

- "We think this is about us. It's not. This is not about you, it's about them." All of your communication should be about the company.

- Not all vets are the same and all screeners are not the same. For every step of the interview process, you should be prepared to convince every person who interviews you. Don't assume your résumé or qualifications were passed along from your previous interview. Be on top of your game every interview.

- In building trust and rapport with an interviewer, ask them questions about their views, such as what they value in a candidate or their own observations about what makes a candidate successful.

- A company's human resources department may want to treat everyone the same, even if you are all different. Their goal is to find the best-qualified and available applicant. Don't be offended by this. Instead, try reframing it: How will you differentiate yourself to appear as an attractive applicant? You can present yourself, with modesty and integrity, in a way that expresses who you are and what you bring to the table.

- Be careful about letting your guard down. There are times for informality and more personal honesty. Use these sensibly.
- Remember that you should expect competition. So, don't give an employer a reason to shoot you down or to be fearful of you as a former warrior. Come in looking the part and your best.
- As a veteran, you may need to initially start with a role that's beneath your qualifications. It is okay to get started and work your way up.

"Remember that people are unique. This is a psychological principle where we are like leaves on a tree and snowflakes: We're fingerprints, none of us repeat. So, each of us has our own combination of positive and negative features and no one's got A-plus in every category. Realize yours; play to your strengths," Dr. Cotton said.

Finally, know that the interview process can take time. You'll know you're doing well if an initial phone interview leads to an in-person interview request, and then after that, interviews with higher-ups or the people you may work with. There are many small steps to a job offer.

With a truly effective mindset, you'll be able to anticipate your competition. Some key points:

- They have bombed and succeeded at entry-level interviews in their career.
- They have spoken to friends and family in preparation and have tried to gain inside knowledge of the company and position for which they are interviewing. They are after action.
- They have multiple touch points. If they hear something about the company, they look for additional viewpoints. For example, do you believe a single news story, or do you look for multiple sources?
- They read news articles about the company.
- They could possibly have friends or family at the company.
- They leverage their network to give them any advantage in the applicant process.

BUILDING YOUR RÉSUMÉ

Depending on how long you were enlisted, it's probably been awhile since you've had to put a résumé together, interview, or do any of the things involved in searching for a job. Preparing your résumé is a critical part of finding employment. Here are our best tips:

Your Résumé Should Be Easy to Read

- Organize your résumé according to education, experience, and personal information. Depending on your target audience, it may make sense to include a career or job objective. If you have several different career objectives, consider making several different versions of your résumé.
- The visual presentation of your résumé is as important as its content. Don't overcrowd your résumé. Instead, use one-inch margins all around to give the page some blank space. Choose a font style that is crisp and clean-looking, and a simple layout.
- Unless you have a lot of experience and accomplishments, you should shoot to keep your résumé to one page. But don't hesitate to list whatever is necessary to illustrate your story and relevant to the job.
- Be ready to provide references—at least three to five. Have them ready in a separate document, but do not include them on your résumé.
- See Annex 4 on our website, www.heroes-journey.net, for sample cover letters, and thank-you notes for employers.

Write to the Future—Think of Translatable Skills

A résumé lists past positions and accomplishments, but if you think about it, you can summarize them in a way that will allow the employer to easily see that you have all the skills and experience needed for your future job. For example, instead of listing your military awards and accolades, integrate your military achievements into an accomplishment statement. If you were Noncommissioned Officer of the Year, you might present it like this:

> Recognized as #1 of 200 managers in the organization after leading team to exceed production standards by 20 percent and achieving equipment availability rates 10 percent above expectations.

This is not about misrepresenting yourself or being insincere. You'll need to translate your experience in a way that will be relevant for employers.

Write for the New Employer, Not Your Former Commander

Your résumé needs to speak the language of the audience you are sending it to—your new employer. You will demonstrate your military experience aplenty just by your military job experience. Specific things to avoid:

- Avoid military acronyms and limit military jargon. They may sound impressive to you, but a civilian employer will simply not follow or appreciate them.
- One good website to help with translating your military experience into transferable, civilian skills is the O*NET Resource Center (www.onetcenter.org/database.html; under the crosswalk option). This is an extensive database of worker attributes and characteristics.
- Avoid references to some aspects of your military accomplishments, like listing body counts—believe it or not, we have seen this on résumés.
- Oplign has a free online Global Employment Intelligence Platform, called Vetlign, for military and veteran job seekers. This platform solves the translation and identification issue by automatically identifying jobs you should be looking at based on your military experience (www.Vetlign.com).

Explain and Sell Yourself

Think about how to take your experience and prior successes and explain them in a way that will be inviting for employers. Dr. Cotton has some important and blunt reminders here: You need to ensure that whoever reads your résumé recognizes a pattern of success and excellence—not just a series of jobs. There is a difference between describing an accomplishment and conveying it in terms that the reader will appreciate. Put another way, don't just list facts, but instead show accomplishments in concrete terms. For example, consider the difference between the following two versions of the same point:

Managed fleet of military vehicles.

or:

Managed fleet of military vehicles valued in excess of $225 million and achieved 100 percent operational readiness scores for two consecutive years.

Proofread the Hell Out of It

A disorganized résumé full of spelling and grammatical errors and other sloppy mistakes does not inspire confidence. First impressions last a long time—and your résumé will be the first impression you give to an employer. Get help in proofing—have a buddy read yours and you do the same for them.

Remember What's on Your Résumé

If it is listed on your résumé, you better remember it and be ready to discuss it in detail!

Résumés Serve Many Purposes

Think of a résumé as (1) a way to get a job interview; (2) a list of things to discuss when you get the interview; (3) a networking tool; and (4) a basis upon which to negotiate a good compensation when you land the new job.

Does Your Résumé Need Reworking?

If you are not getting interview requests, the odds are that your résumé is the problem. Consider getting some feedback on it and revise it.

Look for Resources

If you're starting from square one, there are many resources online to help you write a résumé:

- HireHeroesUSA (www.hire heroesusa.org)
- TopResume (www.topresume.com)
- Novorésumé (www.novoresume.com)
- Military OneSource (www.militaryonesource.mil/resources /tools/myseco-resume-builder/)
- ResumeGenius (www.resumegenius.com/resume-builder/app /how-to-start)
- Become, "Resume Guide" (www.learnhowtobecome.org/career -resource-center/how-to-create-resume/)
- Military.com, "Top 10 Veteran Resume Mistakes" (www.mili tary.com/veteran-jobs/career-advice/top-10-military-resume -mistakes.html)

NETWORKING

Networking can seem contrary to the way veterans have been trained to solve problems but is absolutely critical in the civilian world. Captain Derek Herrera, U.S. Marine Corps (Ret.), suggests, "In the military, we are discouraged strongly from going outside our chain of command. In finding a job and solving problems once you have a job in the civilian world, you are sometimes only as good as your network."

Networking refers to simply getting out to meet people to develop new relationships, to talk with them about your job interests, to get valuable information to aid in your job search, and to learn about the market for the job you are seeking. Some tips for successful networking:

- *Get advice.* Talk to friends, other veterans, old teachers and coaches, family friends, and just about anyone that could be a good resource. Ask them if they can recommend someone else you should talk to. Some of these conversations will inevitably turn into lifelong relationships.

- *Prepare in advance.* Before any meeting, research the person and their industry, consider what questions you want to ask, and what you want to get out of the meeting. The better prepared you are, the better you will seem to others and the more you will get out of the meetings. All of this is practice for preparing for your eventual job interviews.

- *Find veterans' organizations that help.* There are many organizations that support veterans in their transition to civilian jobs. One such organization is MedTechVets, founded by Capt. Derek Herrera, which helps veterans "bridge between their military service and their next purposeful career," with career transition and mentorship programs, among other things. Annex 1 on our website, www.heroes-journey.net, contains more helpful organizations.

- *The better your questions, the better the meeting.* When networking, be ready to ask what the person's job is like, what made them want it, how they got it, and what they plan to do next. As Lt. Cdr. Chris Grillo, U.S. Navy, said, "The better my questions about what I was looking for, the more I got out of these coffees I would have with people."

- *First impressions count.* Even though networking can be informal, remember that the impression you convey to others lasts a long time. Put yourself together physically and mentally before any meeting.

- *Anticipate.* Think a few steps ahead: Where would I like this meeting over a cup of coffee to go? How can this discussion lead to other people to meet or additional information to acquire?

- *Follow up.* Always send a thank-you note, whether by email (if necessary) or letter (handwritten notes are preferred). Being grateful and humble has no downside. Find ways to follow up with the people with whom you have met—promptly send any information you promised to them and find ways to continue to develop your relationship. You may be able to be a networking contact for them some day.

- *Find a mentor.* There are many advisors, advocates, and mentors—folks who have walked this path—available to you. When the student is ready, the master appears. Mentorship can be particularly important for members of marginalized groups; it's important to be guided by someone who understands your experience. There are many organized veterans' organizations that can provide mentors also, such as Heroes Linked (www.hereoeslinked.org).

- *Mind the company you keep.* Surround yourself with those who will keep you balanced and humble and who share your values. One of the recurring lessons we have learned from our interviews with veterans and our own lives is that if you don't share fundamental values with the people with whom you work and your employer, you won't thrive or even perform well. If you don't do these things and you end up disappointed, then you have no sympathy from us.

- *Be disciplined in your process.* Keep a written list of contacts, meeting dates, information you received, next steps, and follow-up and thank-you notes sent. Update as needed and use this to keep yourself accountable and to keep moving forward.

- *Rinse and repeat.* The networking process takes time and can be repetitive—the closer you get to the job you want, the more you may want to use what you've learned so far and refine your conversations.

- *Pay it back.* In reaching out to get help, ideas, and support, if the opportunity arises, help someone else going through the same thing in turn. Buddy check: Every veteran should be helping someone transition.

A NOTE FROM ROB: CAUTIONARY OBSERVATIONS ABOUT NETWORKING

For many of the veterans we spoke to, getting a meeting was not a problem—it was the *outcome* of the meeting that was the issue. This is a major life step, and finding the right advocate for you is just as important as the decision to leave the military. At first, I was no different. I wanted to cast the widest net to see what opportunities were out there. I sent hundreds of emails and made just as many calls. I had no direction and just wanted to see what stuck to the wall. Everyone would take my calls or schedule a meeting or introduce me to someone they thought could help me. This responsiveness gave me the false sense that finding my path was going to be easy when all it did was waste a lot of time. But, at every meeting, the conversation eventually turned to questions about combat, or what my training was like. When I had a chance to ask my questions about the company, or the industry, I got the same response, "I don't know what we would do with you," or "We don't have anything for you, but let me connect you to a friend that might." It happened over and over and over, like I was stuck in the movie *Groundhog Day*. The mistake I made was in allowing this to happen and not owning the meetings or driving them toward the outcomes I wanted. I have heard this same story many times from veterans. Even General McChrystal dealt with this. He said, "In figuring out what to do next, network, but be prepared to be passed off and be treated like a show pony. People will want to meet with you the more senior you are, but they may not really be interested in helping you. Talk to friends and former comrades."

Second, I, along with many other service members, never learned to understand the value of a network while serving. We may be good at networking within our own unit and immediate command structure. Some of us are lucky early on in our careers to work in a joint environment among services. However, establishing rapport in your unit, in interservice, or among any echelon is almost forced. We need to be able to work alongside every service, rank, and MOS to accomplish the mission. We need to disseminate information, have shared knowledge, and thought leadership to maintain superiority on and off the battlefield. But do we every really network in the military for our own benefit? Not really, because too much self-promotion contradicts what we stand for. We are taught "Team, Teammate, and Self." Here, we're speaking about a level of networking that will raise and build your profile, one that will build your confidence, get you access to job opportunities, and advance your station for career advancement and personal growth.

I was surprised and somewhat unprepared for the degree of networking I observed at the Wall Street investment bank I joined. Every week, there would be a networking coffee hour. There, junior analysts would approach senior managing directors and partners just to meet them. With my background in the SEAL teams, I was not prepared for that and found it odd. And yet, this was part of my own transition and it was encouraged.

Last, I would like to pass along the helpful advice of one of my mentors whom I mentioned earlier, Rich Gray, chief client officer at Engaged Capital:

> There is an extensive community of successful corporate executives that are military veterans. I have yet to meet any of these men and women not willing to be a resource, mentor, or whenever possible, an employer for fellow veterans looking to transition to a career in the corporate world. Additionally, there are nonveteran executives (like myself) that are totally committed to serving in a similar role. Most veterans fail to recognize that their military experience is their "superpower," and not some irrelevant skill set for the corporate world. These executives will help prepare you to present yourself in the best light when engaging with the corporate world. Additionally, they will often make other valuable introductions for you to other executives. Unfortunately, there is no contact database yet to easily source and connect with this community of corporate executives. So how does one get connected with this community? It is not as difficult as you might think if you commit to networking. Networking is essential to getting connected to this executive community, and the network you build will be your most valuable asset throughout your entire second career. With forty years now in the corporate world, I have observed that most successful executives will partially attribute their success to luck:
>
> o "I was lucky enough to be in the right place at the right time."

    o   "As luck would have it, when I called they just happened to be looking for someone with my skill set."

    o   "I've been lucky enough to have worked for a boss that also became a mentor to me."

It's not luck, it's networking! You can create your own luck. The best investment you can make in yourself is to dedicate at least an hour a week to building and maintaining your network.

As you embark on your second career, start networking with other veterans, family, and friends already in the corporate world. You will be surprised how quickly you will get connected with the subset of the executive community dedicated and willing to be a resource to you, our heroes!

DEVELOP YOUR ONLINE PRESENCE

There's no getting around the fact that one's online presence is how we get noticed and how we communicate. As of this writing, the social media landscape includes Facebook, Instagram, and X; however, LinkedIn is the number one resource used by employers and in every business community. You must make this tool your greatest asset for creating a positive virtual image of yourself to use for networking and to learn about people and employers. Think of creating an online presence as running a digital military campaign to win the fight for a job. Some good tips for your LinkedIn profile:

- Stay positive.
- Pause, proofread, and think before hitting send.
- Engage, Engage, Engage.
- Build a relationship/connection before an "ask" or "request."
- Post about your transition experiences.
- You get out of it what you put into it.
- You are your brand.[2]

Let's stop and consider this word "brand," which has come to mean the image you develop and have on social media based on how you present yourself. We can offer a few tips for creating your online presence or improving what's already out there. First and foremost, be authentic. You're not creating a persona, which is a facade. People need to see your true values, skills, passions, and beliefs. Second, know your target audience. You don't need to be liked by everyone, just the people who are going to help you transition, promote you, or help you find the right job. Third, optimize your social media so whoever visits your various profiles will understand who you truly are. We make our judgments within the first few seconds of experience based on the knowledge that we have accumulated over our lifetimes, as Malcolm Gladwell wrote in *Blink*.[3] To put this plainly, we are judged and sized up within three seconds of meeting someone new, based on that person's life experiences. Fourth and finally, have a content strategy. To reach your target audience and build your online community you may want to reference Google's Keyword Planner, BuzzSumo, and AnswerThePublic. These are all great tools for doing keyword research and discovering popular topics.

Be conscious of the images and content you post about yourself. A prospective employer may look at your social media, and if you have any objectionable content, they may consider it a reputational risk. This type of first impression counts just as much as in-person meetings.

THE JOB SEARCH

Finding the right job will involve a process of educating yourself about the possibilities, investigating them, networking, and learning from the pursuit. Engaging in finding a job takes hard work and dreaming, recall that hope is what's in a fortune cookie and not a strategy.

SOME PRACTICAL CAREER ADVICE FROM
GENERAL STANLEY MCCHRYSTAL

General McChrystal found himself out of a job as a four-star general in 2010. He had to quickly adjust and reorient his life and family. From that moment and with support and sage advice from some fellow retired general officers, General McChrystal gave us these poignant words of wisdom for fellow veterans:

1. Be prepared for initial emotional stress as you make the transition and search for a job. This can come from normal life circumstances, such as moving houses or even locations, children moving in with you, the cat getting sick, which, in the context of heightened concern about your transition, may take on added stress.

2. People will want to meet with you the more senior you are, but they may not really be interested in helping you.

   In trying to refind purpose, ask yourself what you are and how you can add value to businesses. It may take time to develop this. Develop an inventory of skills and life experiences that may be useful in practical terms to a company.

3. Realize what you don't know about the job market and treat learning about it as a new mission. Live in and figure out how to succeed in the new world you are entering—fight the war you are in. Learn the business; study it and its people and culture and what drives success. Set yourself up for success again, in a new world and a new mission.

4. Realize that you are starting over. This means:

   o Having to work hard. Some senior officers may find this a turnoff if they expect that the recognition they received in their prior military career will automatically carry over into a civilian job.

   o By contrast, realize that you have every right to be successful again—provided you earn it.

   o Determine how much money you and your family require for basic needs.

General McChrystal also shared advice he received from fellow generals—who recommended focusing on a few key questions:

- Where would you like to live?
- What industry and what kind of company would you see yourself working at and succeeding?

- Do you (and your spouse) understand how to handle your finances? Do you have a financial plan?
- Are you comfortable discussing compensation with your potential employer? Do you know how to ask for what you're worth?

SOME PRACTICAL ADVICE FROM GENERAL DAVID H. PETRAEUS, U.S. ARMY (RET.)

When we interviewed General Petraeus, he made one major observation about how veterans should think about finding a job after they join the civilian world: Invest in a career, not just a job. He discussed the benefits of finding a job that offers a career path, as something in which you can invest all of your energy and work focus, a place where you can lead, train, and mentor junior staff and serve those senior to you, and a place that offers advancement and opportunity.

Let's pause here to consider the story of an admiral that came to us firsthand. He had excelled in the military, and after separating, he sought a job at a major consulting firm. He excelled again and became head of its New York City office. From this vantage point, he was successful in hiring personnel (many veterans—because, as he put it, he knew implicitly the rigor of their training, their leadership skills, their ability to work together and subjugate their egos), building a team that worked as one for the benefit of clients and won and grew significant client relationships. He expressed how the job was fulfilling to him in part because of the prestige it rightfully reflected and also because of what he added in service to clients. He looked upon his company logo with pride. General Petraeus made a similar observation—whenever he travels, he'll make sure that the bag with his company's name and logo is facing out, as he is proud to be a member of an exceptional firm. He feels that his company makes a positive difference in the world and that he is making a contribution to it—all similar to, though admittedly different from, how he felt about wearing his uniform and the honors he wore on it.

INTERVIEWING, FOLLOWING UP, AND SECURING THE JOB

There are three key steps to getting the job you want: interviewing, following up, and securing the job.

Interviewing

It is likely that nothing you experienced in the military will have prepared you for job interviews. The landscape has changed since you went into the service. Here are our top tips for navigating an interview in today's job market:

- *Prepare in advance.* Prepare for each interview as if it was the one key discussion that will lead to your future job. This means learning everything you can about the job, the employer, and its future prospects for you.

- *Seek out the friendlies.* Like on recon, find out if there are veterans at the company with which you are seeking a job and interviewing. They may provide a valuable source of insight, intelligence, and support.

- *Build rapport with your interviewers.* One way to build a successful new relationship with someone, including with a job interviewer, is to build rapport—a relationship of trust and credibility. Find genuine ways to connect with your interviewer. If you share things in common, mention them. Listen carefully to them. Follow and be respectful of their cues and respond in kind.

- *Look the part.* There's an old adage: "Dress for the job you want." Put yourself together as though you've already received the offer. You want to project an image to show you are clear on the work environment and are aligned with your future employer. If you don't know what to wear, don't wing it; get some intelligence about the terrain you will walk into— ask friends, the recruiter, or the HR department (if there is one). Even if you are interviewing for a job that won't require typical business clothes, dress in professional-looking attire, which will show that you take the job seriously.

- *Do you wear that suit or does it wear you?* It is important to look the part, but also to dress in a way that fits you, that makes you feel comfortable, if not great. As someone who has coached veterans and also interviewed them as a banker and a lawyer, Alex remarks that "it's all too painful to watch folks who wear clothes in the job setting that just remind them how uncomfortable they are." If you focus on the right job, culture, and people first, then the right clothes that will be in sync with you and the job will come more easily. If you resent what you feel you have been forced to wear, that will come through in the interview. There's a way to mediate the needs of the work world and what makes sense for you.

- *Got tattoos?* If you have visible tattoos on your arms or legs, consider wearing a long-sleeved shirt and slacks, plus a coat and tie (depending on what's appropriate), because some employers may find tattoos off-putting. You may be proud of your tattoos and feel offended that someone else might find them offensive, but if you don't know how your prospective employer feels, it's best to hedge your bets until you do. Some won't care about the tattoos and will hopefully consider only your skills. But you can remove the risk of any negative judgment by covering them for the interview.

- *The interview starts as soon as you walk in the door.* Many companies, even universities and graduate schools, will take into account how you interact with everyone you met in the office on the day of your interview. You never know who is watching or reporting to the hiring manager, so be aware of your body language and demeanor from the moment you approach the interview location.

- *Be prepared to reframe your military experience for the new job.* In the same way you may have reframed your military experience on your résumé, be prepared to discuss how that experience will be helpful on the job. There is a good chance you learned accountability, leadership, and innovation in a variety of ways during your military service, which will also be valuable in the civilian work environment.

- o *A positive example:* Replace "I managed a fleet of military vehicles" with the more robust statement: "I managed a fleet of military vehicles valued in excess of $225 million and achieved 100 percent operational readiness scores for two consecutive years."

- o *A negative example:* During an interview with a Marine veteran for a manufacturing job, he was asked, "What was your job in the military?" When he answered, "Machine gunner," the interviewer replied, "We don't need many of those." Instead of turning it around, the veteran got up and walked out.[4]

- *Prepare possible interview questions and your answers.* Think of your résumé as the basis of your interview discussion. Be prepared to present short answers that explain every part of your résumé and beyond. Do not assume the person interviewing you will know anything about the military, including acronyms, military jargon, and chain of command. Practice answering these questions with your friends or in front of a mirror. The following are some sample questions you might be asked in an interview. Think through these and prepare engaging answers:
  - o How would you describe yourself?
  - o What did you do in the military?
  - o How will that be helpful in this job?
  - o Give me three reasons why we should hire you.
  - o Where do you want to be careerwise in ten years?
  - o What are your ambitions?
  - o What are your strengths and weaknesses?
  - o Are you in a reserve unit and will that interfere with doing this job?
  - o What do you like to do in your spare time?

o   How do you deal with stress?

o   Do you work well under pressure?

o   Was there a time when you failed?

o   What is the worst situation you have ever been in?

o   When have you shown leadership skills? When were you a follower?

o   Have you ever had a disagreement with a coworker? How did you deal with it?

Be on guard for inappropriate or even illegal questions, some of which we've listed below:

o   Have you ever killed anyone—how many?

o   Did you receive an honorable discharge?

o   Do you have any disabilities?

o   Are you a U.S. citizen?

o   How old are you?

o   Are you married?

o   How many kids do you have?

o   What is your religion?

o   Who did you vote for in the last election?

o   Have you ever been arrested?

o   Are you pregnant or do you plan on becoming pregnant?

If you find yourself unable to respond to a question, here are some possible answers to keep in your back pocket in case of need:

o   "Wow, that's a tough question. Would you mind if we came back to that?"

o   "I'd like to tell you about why I think I could be a great addition to your company and what I've done in the military that could bring great value."

o   "That's not one I am really comfortable answering. I'd like to tell you why I am here today and how I know I can help your company."

You don't want your interview to be the place you hear a question for the first time, or to get stumped and not know how to answer something. Google "top interview questions" and develop some responses. Practice at least thirty of these questions with family and friends.

- *Research the company.* Learn what you can about the company's culture and values, as well as the competencies the company is looking for in its candidates. This is sometimes visible in the job description or in the statement of the company's values. If this is how the company thinks, you will be scored against their standards when it comes to these competencies.

- *Google your interviewer's name if you know it.* Look for anything you may have in common.

- *Prepare your own questions and topics of discussion.* Recall the advice of Capt. Derek Herrera, U.S. Marine Corps (Ret.), to set the conditions for your job search as if you are in control. Prepare questions—what would you like to know about the job? Likewise, you get to pick your stories—so choose those that best represent you but remember to link the story back to the position you're interviewing for. How does that story enhance your potential?

- *Keep a positive, humble, and confident attitude and stay true to your values.* A friend of ours was interviewing for a junior-level associate position at a notable private equity firm. The head of the firm, in the final round of interviews, said to him, "Well, we are down to five candidates, you and four others. The other four, who also served in the military, are all Rhodes scholars who graduated at the top of their class. You did not. What's your response?" Our friend said, "Well, sir, I will just have to work harder than everyone else." He got the job. He did work harder than everyone else and eventually became the president of the firm. Later, he learned that what the head of the firm told him was not true—the other candidates were not Rhodes scholars and had not served.

- *Remember that veterans come from a culture of honesty.* At times, the civilian world can gray the lines and it is hard for us to understand the way civilians sometimes speak in a job interview. We are not advocating that you lie, but remember your competition—they will say they are the best at what they do for one reason or another and often that statement is inflated. Yes, this is unfair to you, but "fair" is just a word in the dictionary. There is a way to convey your strengths and achievements and what you have to offer that is direct, polite, understated, and clear. Learning to sell yourself is hard for many of us, but you have to learn to toot your own horn a little.

- *Your military experience gives you strong traits for any job.* In preparing for job interviews and how to talk about yourself, consider the many strong traits and skills you gained from your military experience. We list several common ones below under "Skills Transition." In reviewing these, we encourage you to reflect on them, consider how to integrate them into your sense of self in interviewing for a civilian job, and even how to integrate them into your sense of self more broadly (what we refer to in chapter 10 as your self-narrative). You should also be aware of the negative images and myths that some civilians have about veterans—also summarized below under "Skills Transition."

- *Consider using PAR.* It may be valuable to speak about your accomplishments. Veterans tend to be terrible at this. A useful way to think about this is to use the acronym PAR: What was the *problem*; what *actions* did you take; and what were the *results*? This approach will help you bridge your military experience to their organization and enable them to determine if you are the right fit for the company.

Final Interviewing Tips

- One of the most common complaints from recruiters at Fortune 500 companies is that it is hard to relate to veterans. They seem uptight, don't relax, and cannot relate. Adjust as needed for your audience and respond to the question in a way that the interviewer can relate to and be comfortable with. Adjust your degree of formality, ease, humor, and connection as needed.

- *What do you do when an interviewer will not let you talk?* How do you get them engaged? Remember, recruiters are not psychologists. They did not sign up to hear people's problems. They are human. Let them talk and let that build the relationship, trust, and credibility between you. They could be giving you an avenue to find common ground that will help win the job.

  If your interviewer says something like, "Hey, thanks for taking the time and it is really interesting to learn about your background. We have a half hour for today and I've got five questions that I want to cover. At the end I'll try to leave room for any questions you might have." This means you have five minutes per question. Be mindful of this when scheduling your interview; politely ask if there is a specific time allotted so you can be aware of any time constraints and adjust your answers accordingly. Feeling like you've got a strict time limit can be unnerving, especially if you don't expect it.

- *Using jargon can be a human divider.* Write and speak as though you are speaking to a civilian friend or your grandmother. You want to use technical or specific military jargon only in a peer-to-peer interview.

- *Monitor yourself.* Try not to do all the talking.

- *What if the interview sucked? What if you were rejected?* Don't get down on yourself—turn it into a teachable moment. A bad interview or a rejection may be the learning opportunity you can take with you to get the next job. Pick yourself up and reflect on what you think went wrong and how you might improve next time. Perhaps the role or the company is not a fit—that happens to the best of us.

- *Reflect.* Did you like the interview? If not, figure out why and use that information to plot your next course. Reflecting on the interview will usually give you good, actionable information about what to do next.

- *Follow-up and thank-you notes.* This is an important part of the interview process and there are a few ways to handle it. It is a matter of politeness, thanking the interviewer and the company, and hopefully staying top of mind with them. For example, if you felt the interview went very well and you like the company, perhaps consider sending something special, like a challenge coin from your unit along with a thank-you note. Sometimes, a thank-you note is sufficient—by email is acceptable, but a handwritten note can be a nice touch and is preferred. See a sample in Annex 4 on our website, www .heroes-journey.net.

Securing the Job

The job you want won't just fall in your lap. Between the end of the final interview and when you hear if you are getting an offer, you may need to take some additional steps. Survey the situation and the factors at play, create a plan, then execute on the plan. In doing so, consider the law of proportionality. For example, if we are in combat and have an armed insurgent, we are not supposed to drop a thousand-pound bomb on him; it's not a proportional response to the threat. Similarly, you don't need to go overboard in your pursuit of the job if the job does not require or call for it. You need to make the judgment call here about whether and to what degree to follow up in your attempt to secure the job.

SOME TIPS ON SALARY NEGOTIATION

You've been offered the job. Congratulations! It's important to be sure you're being paid fairly and in accordance with your skills and experience. Unless the job offers a fixed salary for which there is no negotiation, you will have the opportunity to negotiate your salary. We have heard from many veterans that the idea of negotiating salary is a foreign, uncomfortable, and even distasteful exercise. In the military, everyone is paid the same and it is not discussed. In the civilian world, salary negotiation is generally an expected part of the hiring process. You can do it effectively and with your honor intact. Commander Dan Bozung, U.S. Navy (Ret.), digs into this in his insightful (and hilarious) article "Angry Dan's Guide to Military-Civilian Transitions," which he shared with us (www.danbozung.com/guide). Here are his main takeaways:

- *Know market values.* "The job you seek has a certain market value, and you have a certain market value. The better informed you are of both, the quicker you will arrive at a deal both you and your prospective employer can feel good about." As Alex points out, every seat on the trading floor has a value—you need to figure out yours.

- *Know your comps.* One way to approximate your market value is to look at what the position pays at other companies— called "comparables." "Once you have a range, then consider whether relevant factors should play a role in moving it up or down: the industry, geography, size of the company, and whether the company is private or public."

- *Do company research.* You need to know if your intended workplace is flexible about salary negotiation or not. Large, well-established companies may have a structured, inflexible approach to salaries; smaller companies may be more flexible. Try to find out where the company you are interviewing with falls on that spectrum.

- *Analyze and be prepared to present your case.* If it's relevant, figure out a range of the possible salary and analyze where you can or should fit within that range. "The key determinant of your potential value to an organization is the amount of directly relevant experience you bring to the role."

- *Recall the employer's perspective.* "They want someone with long experience in the same industry, who knows the industry and who has effectively confronted and overcome all the same challenges the hiring organization might face. That reduces the organization's risk. Bad hires are costly, and the company wants to avoid them just as much as you."

A warning: Every industry and company is different, and the key to mastering a salary negotiation is in understanding this, with preparation in advance. Do research and get the inside view from smart networking. This applies to every job, whether you are paid by the hour, on commission, or salaried.

Rear Admiral Katherine McCabe, U.S. Navy (Ret.), told us, "Don't undervalue your first career, financially speaking. Accept a lower salary only if you choose to, as a trade for something you value more, such as flexibility, location, or other benefit. But, maybe as important as that is, the best person to determine how you define success is you."

SKILLS TRANSITION

In the military, you had the opportunity to learn many skills that are directly transferable to civilian life and a new job. In the right role, you can take advantage of these. The best place to begin is by completing an inventory of your skills, including those you picked up before you joined the military.

- *Leadership.* "Leadership is always in demand and a transferable skill in all industries," says Bronston Carroll, former Navy lieutenant. True leadership is almost always in short supply, including in civilian jobs. The quiet, confident leader who emerges at work is worth their weight in gold to any company.
- *Bias for action.* Veterans seize initiative. For the right company, at the right time, that's what management depends on from its employees. Word to the wise: Be sure the moment is right, because overly aggressive behavior can also be off-putting.
- *Discipline.* The discipline you learned and mastered across all areas of military life will be of incredible value in the civilian job market. Being the first one in, the last one out, the best

organized, and the most committed to the discipline of work while remaining goal-oriented will take you far.

- *Coolness under pressure.* Reloading your rifle, giving commands to your team to launch a counteroffensive, and taking care of your men while under intense enemy fire requires coolness under pressure. The same goes for countless other military jobs, from equipment maintenance to kitchen duty. The military environment is intense, and you had to learn to stay calm and do your job consistently. That ability is useful in many circumstances, including at a civilian job while others are losing their heads over a problem.
- *Credibility, trustworthiness, and loyalty.* During your service, you developed a way to work with others that came from a place of integrity and proven competence that built your reputation of credibility. You are trustworthy. You are loyal to colleagues, especially when the chips are down. These qualities are true assets in any workplace.
- *Reputation.* Our currency in the military was our reputation. You have left the military with character. That is what matters.
- *Good attitude, work ethic, and a team player.* Attitude is everything. Nothing replaces a solid work ethic. We know people are our greatest assets in any organization. Rob suggests, "Some will rank experience as next in importance, but I heard a partner at Goldman Sachs say it is your attitude and I agree. It makes sense—in the SEAL teams we train to lead, and in the absence of leadership, we step up no matter the circumstances or situation." Subjugate the ego. We do this by doing the hard things daily and leading from the front.
- *Accountability.* Exude a sense of duty and accountability. This includes the drive to follow through on assignments, particularly under stressful and difficult circumstances.
- *Problem-solving skills and adaptability.* Being able to solve problems in a practical—tactical—manner will resonate with your reputation as a former service member. Likewise, being

able to adapt to changing work, market, and customer circumstances are hallmarks of success.

- *Strategic thinking and lateral problem-solving.* Many veterans have had to learn to think strategically, several steps ahead of the enemy and several steps ahead in terms of issues not apparent if one's focus is only the problem set that has popped up on your email. The ability to engage in lateral problem-solving—using indirect and creative approaches to come up with solutions that are not immediately obvious—is another hallmark of the best of our veterans.

- *Humility.* No reasonable good boss or coworker will ever recriminate you for hard work and humility. In fact, these things will only endear you to them and make them want to keep you there.

- *Life experience.* Former Navy lieutenant Bronston Carroll says, "New skills can be obtained, but the life lessons and experiences learned in the military are what's invaluable and hard to obtain otherwise."

- *Communication.* Communication is everything we do in the military. We learn it at a basic level, to be effective and to survive. Think about past instances in which you learned to communicate effectively and how that can translate in the civilian world.

Jordan Peterson, author and psychologist, said, "There isn't anything you can possibly do that makes you more competent in everything you do than to learn how to communicate."[5] In communicating, it is important to demilitarize your vocabulary. Remember the famous line from the 1967 classic movie *Cool Hand Luke*? "What we've got here is failure to communicate." You don't want that.

At the same time, it is important to realize that when you join a new company, you may have to contend with negative images or myths that civilians have about veterans. These include the image that veterans wait for orders before acting, don't respect nonveterans, and have all suffered trauma.

A NOTE FROM ROB ON COMMUNICATION

Communication is essential to everything we do in the military. We are taught to overcommunicate, both horizontally among our peers and vertically through the chain of command. This often doesn't transition well when it comes to talking about our accomplishments in résumés and job interviews.

I can be reserved, and at times I have struggled with communication. The first phase of SEAL training was no different. The day started off like most days in Coronado, California: The sun was up, it was just cool enough to need a jacket, and the ocean and the horizon merged into a distant haze that eventually burned off. And of course, it would not be SEAL training without getting into the ocean, or, as James Joyce referred to it in *Ulysses*, "the sea, the snot-green sea, the scrotum-tightening sea."

Why not spend this day with 141 of your closest friends at the time carrying a two-hundred-pound boat on your heads through the surf? We were conducting boat races, where the instructors would come up with a series of steps that had to be meticulously followed to win the race. If you won the race, the instructors might allow you to sit out the next race and rest, setting you up to continue to win because you are rested. The great adage of BUD/S: "It pays to be a winner." Each six-man boat crew carried the heavy boats on their heads. All of the boat crews were assembled in numerical order, standing at attention. I could see out of my periphery as the boat crews, one at a time, were told to hit the surf. Of course, the man behind this exercise was none other than Instructor FISH (at least that's what we'll call him here—he was certainly one fit, intelligent, scary human, so the acronym is fitting). I was just out of earshot and could not hear what he was saying to the leaders until he was speaking to another boat crew right next to mine.

Then it was too late—he was right in front of me, definitely standing in my personal space, with a megaphone.

Instructor Fish: *Lieutenant Sarver! We are going to play mental Rochambeau. Loser gets wet and sandy. You go first.*

Me: *Hooya Instructor Fish.*
Instructor Fish: *Well, sir…go!*

You know "Rochambeau" as the game of paper, rock, scissors. However, the weekend before, my roommate, Lt. Brendan Looney, and I were sitting at home channel-flipping and *South Park* came on. That afternoon we learned a whole new version of Rochambeau. One of the main characters in the show, Cartman, developed his own twist of the game, which involved both players kicking each other in the testicles until only one was left standing. I knew that Instructor Fish was putting me on the spot, using a childhood game that I may have had a good association with to put me on the defensive.

Instructor Fish: *Sir, what did you pick?*
Instructor Fish: *Hey idiot, do you know what Rochambeau is?*
Me: *Hooya Instructor Fish.*
Instructor Fish: *We are going to try this one more time, you mental midget…MENTAL ROCHAMBEAU, you go first…GO!*

I thought maybe if I closed my eyes, he would see that I was trying hard and leave me alone. So, I closed my eyes for a few beats and then opened them.

Instructor Fish: *Well, sir, what did you choose?*

Slightly still confused by the game, I responded with the most logical response I could think of…

Me: *Instructor Fish, I mentally kicked you in the nuts first…I win! (Inner monologue: NAILED IT!)*

I thought to myself: *Why is he dropping the megaphone? Oh shit, he looks pissed. Yep, that is definitely a vein popping on the side of his head.* In between him yelling "HIT THE SURF!" he called me everything I imagined was possible. *How rude*, I thought as I ran to the surf to get wet and sandy. Later, I learned that he had to hide behind the students to uncontrollably laugh at my response.

Today, Instructor Fish is a good friend and mentor, a command master chief at a SEAL team, and I would serve alongside him in any capacity. Cartman did not do me any favors that day, but it was a rather small, yet humorous, lesson in communication and alignment. Who would have thought one word would ruin such a great day on the beach? This can occur when we go to job interviews, too. We speak a totally different language. After being out for eleven years now, I can honestly say if a civilian is sitting at a table with a bunch of active-duty military folks, or recently transitioned veterans, and they are having an in-depth conversation, the civilian may not understand the military folks and the other way around in equal measures—except that if the civilian is the one doing the job hiring, then, on this terrain, that's what you got to solve for.

THE EMPLOYER'S PERSPECTIVE—WHAT YOU NEED TO KNOW

Bernard R. Horn, president of Polaris Capital Management, is committed to hiring veterans. Here are a few thoughts he shared with us:

At our company (a firm that invests in publicly traded equities worldwide), we have hired several veterans over the years. We have benefited from the work ethic of the veterans and especially from certain skills that were highly complementary to the existing team. The ability of the veteran to observe and assimilate was strong. Further, the work ethic was quite exemplary in terms of self-educating in the business/investment subject matter. We benefited from the team-building effort that helped us adopt some SEAL team-building techniques; this helped our existing staff. One reason for our recent hire was that the intelligence gathering program in the military experience was analogous to how we need to evaluate companies. This skill set was adapted to our needs successfully. Further, some of the domain expertise in health care, defense, and other industries complemented our existing team knowledge base. So, this is another point of advice in coaching veterans in how to select the next role. Can their skills be additive to the new organization?

That does not mean we have not had to provide some extra time as the veterans have had to deal with the various physical and mental recoveries as they transitioned. I expected a multiyear decompression period which turned out to be accurate. We recognize that this can seem quite lenient to other members of the organization. But, at our company, we support folks from all walks of life, whether it's single parents, those with other needs, and veterans undergoing the transition to civilian life after they have served and defended us. Leadership in the organization can help set an example of tolerance and understanding that is very important. The productivity is so above and beyond that this makes up for any time invested in the decompression process.

Regardless of what skills and experience you think you have, consider what employers need, their perspective on what they are looking for in employees, and also the perception they may form of you as a veteran. This requires a serious reevaluation of how you appear and behave in the civilian work environment. There are many positive *and* negative impressions with which to contend. If you are able to rethink or reframe how your military experience gave you skills, a bearing, and a mindset with which to tackle work's challenges in a civilian environment—and you are able to project that in whatever way makes sense for you—you will likely be viewed as a tremendous asset by your employer. By contrast, be prepared that not all of what made you a success before in the military will work well in a new job environment. In fact, in some cases, this may be the opposite, though you will have extraordinary skills and experience. Consider the following:

- *To be successful, you must make your employer feel safe in your presence and confident in you.* If you have already had a successful military career, you may wonder why you have to do this all over again. It's because you're starting all over again.
- *Outwardly reflect your great military skills, bearing, and mindset.* Doing so will help you gain credibility and reputational points. Some practical tips to keep in mind:
  o Be easy to work with and make your colleagues' and bosses' jobs easier.
  o Be trainable and adaptable to the civilian work environment. Learn quickly and put that knowledge to work.

o   Find opportunities to let yourself—and your military-originated skills—shine.

o   Be aware of some negative stereotypes about veterans (they can be overly hierarchical, behave as if they only act when following orders, don't fit in, etc.) and be conscious of how you come across. Be the opposite of those stereotypes—in the context of what your colleagues and employer need.

- *Be prepared to shed a part of your military identity.* We're not suggesting you need to become a new person—and many good aspects of your identity that were derived from your military life will be key and foundational to your success. We are saying that if you want to be part of a civilian company, you need to be able to be a part of that company in a way that is comfortable for you and them.

- *Are you intimidating?* Veterans can come across as intimidating. It is important to demilitarize and soften our tone. So, while your new employer may have hired you, in part, because of your military background, that organization and its people may not understand or appreciate the world you have come from and you may not be aware of how you appear to them.

- *Are your indifferent?* Veterans can also come across as indifferent to the demands of the job and what it takes to be successful. One hedge fund manager commented about a former special operations warrior: "He was cool, he was a former special forces operator, but he didn't seem to respond to what we and I needed as if it mattered to him. Nothing fazed him—and I mean that in a negative way." The coolness under pressure and stoicism that some veterans carry can give off a negative impression.

- *Be prepared to start over.* The idea of having to start over in a new career after a successful one in the military, one in which you may have risen in rank and responsibility, comes with the territory when becoming a civilian. However, if you perform on the job, you may well advance and leapfrog ahead if you land in the right place, at the right job, with a culture that values who you are and where you have come from.

- *Do you have veteran's entitlement syndrome?* From your perspective, you may have a lifetime of accomplishments, leadership ability, combat experience, and more—all from your time in the military. From an employer's perspective, some may acknowledge that and ask, "Okay, I appreciate your service, but can I plug you into my organization and can you be productive on day one or are you resting on your laurels, with a lot of attitude?" If you carry a sense of entitlement into your interviews or new job and don't have the skill set and mindset to add value from the start, then you won't leave a good impression.
- *Your military experience won't matter if you cannot make a contribution to your new job.* You have a few months to rest on your military accomplishments before you need to start adding value. At some point, your employer will no longer care about your past military experience and that may become a liability in terms of how you are perceived—you don't want to appear as the veteran that is stuck in the past. Specific pointers:
  - Have you earned your seat? Every job has a description, requirements, and standards. Have you mastered them?
  - Your goal is to add more value to your customers and clients than anyone else. This also includes internal clients, like your boss.
  - Have you taken advantage of what the company has to offer in opportunities, in assignments, in new training?
  - Have you taken the initiative to find mentors and engage in leadership?
- *Do not expect employers to appreciate rank and experience differences among veterans.* Your sense of prior accomplishment and the fact that you may have had a higher rank or seen more combat than other veterans may not distinguish you in the eyes of an employer. You may have been hired in part because of your prior rank and experience, but you should not expect that these things will carry you through the new job. Some companies hire veterans but are insensitive in their recognition of

the actual experience of veterans, including prior differences in rank and experience. Be prepared for that.

- *You're only as good as your last movie.* Contrary to the last point, be prepared for employers not to care about your military accomplishments. Rob recalls: "I like what my dad told me growing up: 'You are only as good as your last eval.'" Alex recalls what his Wall Street bosses said: "You are only as good as your last movie." You may have gotten hired in part because of your military experience and accomplishments, and you may have spent a lot of time in the interview discussing it. But that may well become irrelevant on the first day of your job, when you have to start performing. Be prepared for that. And see the upside: that you have a new chance, at a new job, and a fresh start.

- *Find a new balance in how you present yourself.* Alex has spent his entire career in the private sector as a banker and a lawyer and, having gotten to know many veterans, can spot a mile away the different caricatures of veterans seeking entry into the private sector. Forgive the stereotypes:
  o The veteran who walks into an interview defining himself by his tactical past and speaking in jargon— that person is backward-looking.
  o The veteran who is trying too hard to fit into the corporate world with unnecessary slickness.
  o The veteran who knows who they are and is balancing where they come from (radiating confidence in a decent way; command of the situation and ease) with an understanding of what the job entails (why we are here, what this kind of a teammate looks like, and how to engage in the job effectively).

Finding your own voice and presence, taking the best of what your life in the military gave you and learning the new job and its people and culture, per General McChrystal, is not only the way to succeed, but it is a way to live comfortably within your own skin, as who you are.

- *Are you a team player or a lone wolf who cannot delegate?* Depending on your company and your specific job, knowing when to work alone and when to collaborate can be the difference between being perceived as an effective team player or as a lone wolf who doesn't work well with others. If your experience in the military as a teammate, as someone that knows how to work with others, helped you win the job, you will need to deliver on that. If you stand out because you are the only veteran in the organization or your area at work, bringing positive qualities to work that your civilian colleagues will likely associate with your having been in the armed services will enhance your reputation. The opposite is also true: If you are the only veteran around and you don't trust anyone and work alone, your civilian colleagues may attribute that to a negative view of the military and veterans. We hate to say it, but it's better to be forewarned.

VETERANS' VOICES

"I learned to join business networking groups that didn't have veterans because I needed to be uncomfortable meeting other good people. Most of us vets know how to lead, but we don't know how to network, how to market, or how to 'sell' ourselves. I was so hesitant to talk much about my military experiences and colleagues kept yelling at me: 'Mike, that's what makes you unique—work with it!' If I hadn't joined one of those groups, I would not have met the woman who I connected with and who introduced me to a book strategist, who got me an agent in NYC, which led to my first book being published. We are now working on the second book."

—Rear Adm. Michael Giorgione, U.S. Navy (Ret.);
and currently CEO, LeanFM Technologies

"When you leave the military, no one tells you that you will be starting over and that it will be difficult. That is a disservice to veterans. In a capitalist system, you have to add value to get paid. That is a big adjustment to those who grew up in the military. There will be many who will have a cup of coffee with you, but few will really help or become friends. It will be difficult to replicate the bonds when entering civilian life. And yet, there is great value in community in going through the transition. You may be in search of a new overriding mission in this life of finding new purpose and helping others, of serving a transcendent cause.

"I had to learn a new language and how to communicate in the business world. I knew how to do that in the military and to be effective. When I got out, it was as if I was using the same language in the conversation but I was not really communicating and understanding. That is why I went to business school."

—Cdr. Curt Cronin, U.S. Navy (Ret.); cofounder and managing partner, Broadway Strategic Fund and founder and CEO of Aiki Partners

"I recall putting together my first résumé and giving it to one of my professors for their comments. I had included all of my military citations, awards, and medals, divisions I had been responsible for and the various jobs I had executed. After reading it, she said to me 'This all looks very impressive and I'm sure it is, but I have no idea what any of it means.' You need to translate your military past for your future employer.

"Also know that you are better prepared, have more drive, discipline, and sense of purpose than almost any of your civilian peers, so don't be afraid of the civilian world. In order to succeed in it and get started, however, you will also need to be able to translate what you did in the military into things that are valuable to your employer. Once you figure that out and what it is they are looking for, you will get the job and excel at it."

—Cdr. Joshua Klein, U.S. Navy (Ret.); currently professor of business, Savannah College of Art and Design

"The military trains you to communicate only in your chain of command. In my start-up businesses, when solving problems, I was only as good as my network when I had to solve a problem that I couldn't fix. I found that if I reached out to someone in the network of contacts I had, I was almost always going to find a solution and a path forward."

—Capt. Derek Herrera, U.S. Marine Corps (Ret.); currently founder and CEO, Bright Uro

"You expect people in business to be competent, but they are not always. The business world doesn't do training like the military. It focuses on the bottom line and doesn't put a lot of work into developing people.

"Authority is different. You order someone in the military, but you can't use that same tone in a business setting. And they can say no, or ignore you and nothing happens. Your military skills are often valued, but you may still have to work on making them user-friendly."

—M.Sgt. Eileen Cobb, U.S. Air Force (Ret.)

"Probably the biggest skill I have been able to translate is chain of command, and from the day I left the Army I have been able to handle constructive criticism and improve my skill set. I have used my ability to take and implement orders to help transition into the civilian world. And, when I was in the military our survival relied on our abilities to put our differences aside for the good of the mission. Not everyone got along and we had individuals from every walk of life. We found a way to work together and complete the mission."

—Jesse Sargent, former U.S. Army staff sergeant

"Civilians will never truly understand what it was like from the stories of your experiences on active duty and that's okay. But what they do understand or can see is your actions, the way you carry yourself, the way you treat people, and how you make people feel. Characteristics we have but are not limited to: being loyal, team-oriented, solution-driven, efficient, gritty, and methodical."

—Dustin Bennight, former U.S. Navy seaman apprentice

"Baseball is 99 percent mental.
The other half is physical."

—YOGI BERRA

CHAPTER 14

SMALL STEPS TO SUCCESS

"Well-being is realized by small steps, but it is no small thing...
focus on the smallest thing you can do right now."

—ZENO, STOIC PHILOSOPHER

If the experiences of hundreds of veterans who contributed to this book are representative, your full transition likely will not happen immediately. Even if you land your dream job right away, you should take a holistic view of your transition, meaning, there may be many components to it—like going back to school, finding a job, readjusting to civilian culture, reacquainting yourself with your spouse and family (if relevant), healing physical and emotional trauma, finding new purpose, and so much more. For many veterans, it takes several steps to come to a good place. That necessarily entails failures, whether large or small, or just not immediately finding what you want. From those moments—if you reflect on what happened, learn, adapt, and handle it the right way—you can reposition yourself and attempt again. Every one of these moments, whether positive or negative, is a step forward. We recommend celebrating each one of them.

In this chapter, we share observations from veterans about the need to anticipate that success, however measured, will likely take several steps. In short, Rome wasn't built in a day, but there can be many successes along the way for you, and these should motivate and energize you to keep going.

In 2012, Rob traveled to New York City for a week of job networking. His father's godson, Kurt Polk, a Virginia Military Institute graduate and former captain in the Air Force, was at the time CEO of Rainier Mutual Funds and he was gracious enough to set up interviews for Rob. He had Rob stay with one of his good friends, George Mosby, another Virginia Military Institute graduate, so he could enjoy the city at night. In between late-night dinners, visits to bars, and the occasional shouts of "NAILED IT!" Rob made some good introductions and decided to pursue finance.

We have had our NAILED IT! moments in the military and in business. You hit the target and got your objective, dropped ordinance perfectly, won the gunfight, got promoted, passed the uniform inspection with high praise from a superior officer, aced the presentation, or raised money for your new endeavor.

How do you find your NAILED IT! moment now? Life is a series of successes and failures...So, Rob sometimes hears himself saying, "Find a healthy hobby. Dopamine hit." And then with his own sense of humor, Rob adds to himself "curb drinking!"

A NOTE FROM ROB

On my last deployment in Afghanistan in 2012, I served as a detachment commander in charge of a village stability platform (VSP). We had been performing extremely well in our area of operation and had met moderate resistance, unlike previous units during the surge into Helmand, Afghanistan, in 2009 and 2010.

One of our missions was to recruit, train, and equip an Afghan Local Police (ALP) force. The strategy was to secure the local villages and deter the Taliban, while connecting the ALP into the district security, then district to regional security, and then national security, creating a codified national police force. Once training was complete, the ALP were armed with AK-47s. It was a slow process. Our predecessors had managed to output only six ALP forces in eight months when we turned over. However, by the time we left, we had put fifty-four in place.

Near the end of our time in Sangin Valley, Helmand Province, the ALP came to our camp unannounced. On our security cameras, we could see the ALP lifting one member off the truck and placing him down outside our eastern entrance, where our helicopters would land. Immediately, we thought a gunfight had commenced. Rushing to the gate, I was accompanied by my two medics, a joint tactical air controller (JTAC), and an interpreter. Immediately, the medics began assessing the wounded ALP member on the ground as I started to question the other ALP force members as to what happened. At first observation, the wounded man's clothing was covered in blood, he was screaming, and he looked like he was bleeding out. As my medics checked his vitals, we learned that two of them were friends and had gotten into a verbal altercation, which ended with one of the ALP members shooting his friend in the leg with his AK-47. The bullet traveled through both legs, creating four gunshot wounds.

Part of our training curriculum for the ALP was to teach them how to apply tourniquets, which we had issued to the ALP at the end of training. We were pleased to learn from the Afghan interpreter that his fellow police officers had saved the wounded man's life by applying two tourniquets to his legs, which were hidden by his *ghara*. As I was continuing to speak with the ALP and the interpreter, the medics began to cut the bloody garb off to assess the wounds, and the JTAC began to call for a medevac helicopter. Suddenly, I heard a burst of laughter from my medics. "No way!" one of them said. "Holy shit! No wonder he's screaming—they caught part of his nut sack in the tourniquet!" We had a hard time keeping a straight face trying to call in the medevac. I told the guys to reapply the tourniquet correctly. "No one is ever going to believe this," one of them said. I should mention that we were able to get the wounded man some medical attention, and he survived, but none of us will ever forget the sight of that tourniquet...and that poor dude's squished balls.

So, what's the moral of the story? Well, I'm not sure there is one, but it was a helluva story. Perhaps, you could take away that we had one small success in teaching the ALP how to apply a tourniquet...shooting a buddy, not so much. But we suppose one can say that, yes—it can always be worse—you might literally get your nuts caught in a tourniquet. Joking aside, we can't rely on other people to fix us. We are trained in combat, self-aid, and aid for our buddies. But sometimes our buddies get it wrong.

VETERANS' OBSERVATIONS

Throughout the process of transitioning, it is important to remember several vital aspects of this journey. Here's a collection of wisdom we've gathered from our discussions with veterans:

- *Celebrate your small victories.* This will give you energy and a sense of accomplishment to keep on moving.
- *Remember that this is a journey.* It will take time to get your bearings, find a home, land a job, maybe even start a family. You may find that your first job isn't all that you expected or needed, or your first employer may feel the same about you. Part of this is a process of acquiring new skills and retooling. Many of us, whether veterans or not, take awhile before we find a job or a career in an industry that suits us.
- *Expect failure.* Don't be afraid to fail at your first job. Rarely have we seen a veteran stay in the same career once they have left the military unless they had some prior experience in that industry. As Admiral McRaven wrote in his "Make Your Bed" speech, you will fail, and you will fail often. It is not failure, however, if you learn from each event and you pick yourself up, keep moving and never quit.
- *Expect moments of discouragement.* Beyond job failure, veterans from every war have felt disappointment and discouragement from a hoped-for homecoming. This was most notably experienced by Vietnam veterans, but those who came back from the wars in Iraq and Afghanistan connect with it, too. This can lead to despair, demoralization, anger, estrangement, and isolation. We may have processed these emotions upon our initial reentry to civilian life, but that doesn't mean they won't reemerge from time to time.[1] It's the nature of the process. What is important is what you do next.

- *We can improve every day.* We should have the intention—every day—to work on ourselves, focusing our energy on personal growth and growing those around us. Many of us forget that being a warrior is being a person who, when confronted with any obstacle, manages to be successful and persevere. Our training taught us to be agile, to observe our surroundings, analyze the problem in front of us, and take action. We'll need these skills as we face the many challenges of transition.
- *Commit to your new path.* For some veterans, it is critical to commit to the process of starting a new life after the military. It's one thing to maintain friendships with your buddies; it's another to live in a backward-looking state, living in a tactical mindset (carrying a weapon, scanning the room, wearing tactical gear, etc.), and not trying to fully make a go of it in your current situation.
- *Be willing to say no.* In any aspect of your life, including a job, be prepared to turn down things that don't make sense to you. The ability to pass on new assignments when you can't handle more work is important.
- *Take a break.* Take a break and find small challenges that can be celebrated. With brothers and sisters, go to the ocean, climb a mountain, go on a hike, or compete in a race.
- *Serve others.* Serving others, whether veteran or nonveteran, can help us find a moment away from the daily grind, do some good, add some fulfillment, and give us a sense of continuing purpose. Erwin McManus remarked that service can be a compass when we are in a fog.
- *Beware of transition fatigue.* As we've discovered, the transition to civilian life has many stages and hurdles. It can bring uncertainty, frustration, anger, and fatigue. The choices involved can seem overwhelming. If these things hit you, take a break and regroup—tomorrow is a new day.
- *Beware of frequent changes.* Frequently changing jobs or relationships can be a sign that you are not making decisions with

all of the information available to you—that you are rushing in and leaving a situation that may be working for the (often unrealistic) hope that the grass is somehow greener elsewhere. Commander Dan Bozung, U.S. Navy (Ret.), has some insight on this:

"No matter how complete your due diligence, you simply cannot know what an organization is truly like until you're in it. And once you're on the inside, you may not like what you find. From toxic work environments to fraudulent, even criminal, behavior on the part of company leaders, you would be amazed at how the organization for which you go to work differs from the one to which you were recruited. If you find yourself in such a circumstance, you have a choice: gut it out or punch out. It's a personal decision with many considerations. On the one hand, life is short. On the other, you don't want a résumé that evidences too much job-hopping and paints you as a flake. But while you certainly don't want to make a habit of false starts, I'd say one or two is generally acceptable."

- *Define your own path.* Only you can define what success and happiness look like for you. Living according to others' standards is a fool's errand, which yields little real dividends. Thinking that someone else has it made because they have a cool civilian job title or were awarded more medals than you while in the military is a distracting waste of time that gets you off the main objective—what will you do with your own life? Judging human books by their outside covers is usually just inaccurate—someone you believe has the picture-perfect life has their own tough road to home. We are constantly being given the chance to reexamine where we are in our lives, and many of us have a voice in our heads continually questioning our situation. You don't exactly have to give the middle finger to the world—perhaps a lesson Rob and Alex admit to having attempted to learn a few times—but you can live by your own standards and dreams.

VETERANS' VOICES

"I advise vets in transition that you don't hit a home run the first time up—just focus on a clean hit and getting on base. Don't be reckless but land the first job knowing that it will teach you many things and that you may very likely move on after one to two years. Most colleagues I know have changed jobs two or three times within ten years, and a few spent twenty years just with their first firm.

"Depending on financial need, many vets may have to get a consistent paycheck just to support the family, and this often means they are doing things that don't give them purpose. My wife and parents were my best supporters and harshest critics. They are nervous for you and nervous for the family. These are trying times. This is why I recommend that in the first few years, just get on base and learn about things. Be patient; give yourself some time."

—Rear Adm. Michael Giorgione, U.S. Navy (Ret.);
currently CEO, LeanFM Technologies

"The three rules I have often rattled off were Get the Job Done (there are a lot of 'jobs' we do); Take Care of People (the obvious and less obvious); and Have Fun (usually caveated by 'Don't get me in trouble with the JAGs') . . . *We really do need to laugh a little every day, but most especially on the tough days.* A veteran can readily recall doing truly unappealing work in some horrendous environment, usually weeks on end, and somehow finding a way to crack a joke. This is especially helpful in families who can get wrapped up in waiting for (fill in the blank) to feel like they can start living again."

—Rear Adm. Katherine McCabe, U.S. Navy (Ret.);
currently human resources professional, LitCon Group

"When I got into business school, I assumed everything would just take care of itself. I was wrong. In fact, I wrote a book about it called *This Civilian Sh*t is Hard: From the Cockpit, Cubicle, and Beyond.*"

—Cdr. Dan Bozung, U.S. Navy (Ret.);
currently U.S. Navy Reserves

"I hooked up with recruiters and they set me up with several interviews: Olin Brass (St. Louis); Home Depot (Schaumburg, IL); David Weekly Homes (San Antonio, TX). I got offered jobs at every place and they all met my salary requirements but... I couldn't do it. I told myself I didn't leave the infantry to take some half-ass job that frankly sounded boring. I told myself I am going to pursue companies I never thought I could work at: Google, Tesla, Goldman Sachs, and various other tech and financial companies. I wasn't the least bit successful. I went with my backup option, the Executive MBA program at the University of Texas at San Antonio."

—Anthony Garcia, former U.S. Army captain
and mustang (enlisted private first class)

"I was working on the trading floor of one of the large investment banks in New York City. A senior trader in my group was having a rough day—the guy was stressing over a large trade he was worried about. I am not sure what got into me, but I went up to him and said 'Relax. This is not real risk. Real risk is when you lead men into combat and you are at risk of getting killed.' At first, he was pissed at me, and then he calmed down and thanked me for my perspective. I didn't realize it at the time, but my stock with him rose that morning."

—Anonymous veteran, former sergeant, U.S. Marine Corps

"So live your life that the fear of death can never
enter your heart. Trouble no one about their religion;
respect others in their view, and demand that they
respect yours. Love your life, perfect your life,
beautify all things in your life. Seek to make your
life long and its purpose in the service of your people.
Prepare a noble death song for the day when
you go over the great divide.
Always give a word or a sign of salute when meeting or
passing a friend, even a stranger, when in a lonely place.
Show respect to all people and grovel to none.
When you arise in the morning give thanks for the food
and for the joy of living. If you see no reason for
giving thanks, the fault lies only in yourself.
Abuse no one and no thing, for abuse turns the
wise ones to fools and robs the spirit of its vision.
When it comes your time to die, be not like those
whose hearts are filled with the fear of death,
so that when their time comes they weep and pray
for a little more time to live their lives over again
in a different way. Sing your death song and die
like a hero going home."

—TECUMSEH, SHAWNEE CHIEF AND WARRIOR

CHAPTER 15

BE A WARRIOR INSIDE THE WIRE AS MUCH AS OUTSIDE

"What I have found is that the assumption that civilian life is somehow easier than the military is confusing for veterans. And, it often leads to mission failure on so-called easier ground. In many ways, the heroic courage which is required in combat is actually the easier of the choices than what my friend Jordan Hall calls infinitesimal courage, that is, the courage to make the infinite number of small decisions that are individually seemingly inconsequential, but which compound into the greatest impact of our lives after we leave the military."

—CDR. CURT CRONIN, U.S. NAVY (RET.);
cofounder and managing partner, Broadway Strategic
Fund; and founder and CEO of Aiki Partners

As Commander Cronin says above, the idea that civilian life is somehow easier than the military is flat-out wrong for many veterans. It is just a different terrain, with different challenges and stressors, but also joys, fulfillment, and opportunities. There won't be bullets flying at you—unless you join the local police department—and you won't be running into burning buildings—unless you become a firefighter. But make no mistake that reentering civilian life, getting married, investing in and maintaining your marriage, starting a family, building a career, and keeping yourself together in mind and body isn't a piece of cake. Yet, all that you have learned to become a warrior, if repurposed, can energize your transition to a different life, one of great joy, happiness, fulfillment, purpose, and contribution.

Being a warrior inside the wire, as Rob confesses about his own transition, is about finding, and maintaining, balance in one's life. A balanced life considers all aspects: personal and family relationships, work, fitness, health, and emotional well-bring, to name just a few. It is very easy for individuals, especially service members, to get knocked off-balance and become consumed with our profession. This is only exacerbated by trauma. Living an unbalanced life can give us the figurative sense of spiraling downward and losing control, kind of like an emotional vertigo. This break from our true self can make us cause harm to ourselves and those around us to varying degrees. By contrast, finding your center and grounding yourself in these essential aspects of life as a civilian can become your own true north, your own inner sense, direction, and calling.

In this chapter, we discuss what it means to be a warrior on civilian terrain, summarize the lessons learned from veterans, and hear their stories about what it takes to develop an action-oriented mindset to be successful in civilian life. In doing so, two central themes flow throughout. First, to be an effective civilian warrior, we must fight just as hard at it (inside the wire) as we did when in the military (outside the wire). By fighting, we mean giving it everything you've got and putting yourself out there for what matters in your life at great risk, not combat or physical violence. Second, the transition to civilian life represents an opportunity to bring together, integrate, and balance all the parts of yourself and all the values and lessons learned from your military experience in service of your new life and the things for which you stand.

A NOTE FROM ROB

I have been off-balance many times—sometimes self-inflicted and other times just from being in the wrong place at the wrong time. A moment when I did some self-inflicted damage came when I was attending San Diego State University in the newly formed Naval Special Warfare language program.

Lieutenant Brendan Looney and I checked into SEAL Team 3 and I was deployed within four days of graduating. Brendan got married and deployed the next day to meet me in Fallujah. We did the last half of deployment together and returned from Iraq in 2008. This would be the last time I would spend any extended amount of time with Brendan. We both were placed into separate platoons and pursued different training, and, tragically, Brendan died on our 2010 deployment when a helicopter crashed during insert. Nine soldiers and sailors died that day.

In 2008, there was a push for SEALs to do a language qualification. Special Operations Command was spending an enormous amount of money on interpreters and there was a push for more special operations forces, not just Green Berets, to be language-qualified. During the infancy of the program for Naval Special Warfare Command, we did not have a set curriculum or a schoolhouse. I was in the second rotation of guys. Lieutenant Dan Cnossen, whom we wrote about earlier, had just finished Arabic before me. I elected to learn Farsi.

The course was designed to complete an entire year of language education in two months. The class size was small—there were only three SEALs to two instructors in the Farsi curriculum. The classes, which lasted six to seven hours a day, with homework at night, were held at San Diego State University. Before we enrolled, Naval Special Warfare Command told us to wear civilian clothes, with beards being allowed. Basically, we were told to just blend into the student body, not draw attention to ourselves, and not make NSW look bad. We received faculty passes to the gym and parking. Not a bad gig for two months.

After five years of military college and active duty for a little over four years at this point, this was our time to fit in and live life and make up for lost time. As if completing BUD/S and deployments wasn't enough, we felt the need for something more. We needed a challenge that would allow us to have common ground with our fellow man. Something we could relate to for the rest of our lives. We needed to find balance in our lives and walk back our warrior mindset and be normal for a change. Where else does a young man find this calling other than rushing a fraternity and connecting with the college, its students, and school spirit?

As three of us contemplated our plan, our actions took the shape of a plot device from a movie or cartoon. We began by weighing the pros and cons with our shoulder angel and shoulder devil. The angel representing good conscience and accompanied by the devil, who represents temptation. Obviously, starting a fraternity, like the characters played by Vince Vaughn, Luke Wilson, and Will Ferrell did in the movie *Old School*, would have been replete with risk, as would rushing an existing fraternity. But we couldn't just do nothing—that would go against our training as men of action. The inner conflict weighed on us. Wait, let's be honest—who was I kidding? None of us contemplated a damn thing. All our shoulder devils were in cahoots high-fiving each other. *DO IT!* We decided rushing an existing frat was the best way to go. *Animal House*, here we come! With our decision made, we carried ourselves like we had just solved world hunger and walked straight to student services to register. *What could go wrong?*

We didn't take into consideration that Big Brother is always watching. It turns out our names had been flagged in the school directory with a special code, which prompted the faculty at the student activities center to notify the dean's office and inquire what the code was. This in turn prompted the office to call our command to let them know we had tried to sign up for rush week. Dammit! Soon, our phones began to ring and on the other end of the line was our command, yelling at us, of course, and telling us to come in the next morning. Well, let's just say that we put ourselves in the wrong place at the wrong time. A lesson we learned the hard way, even if we then laughed about it. We would have to find balance in our lives some other way outside of a fraternity.

WHAT DOES IT MEAN TO BE A CIVILIAN WARRIOR?

To talk about ways to be a civilian warrior begs the question: What does it mean to be a warrior? We have taken this for granted up until now because we have assumed a warrior is anyone who joins the military, wears a uniform, and raises their hand to make an oath to defend the country and the Constitution. But, to understand what it means to take one's military experience and harness it to be a warrior in civilian life, we must first put some definition around what it means to be a warrior in the first place. For that, there are many descriptions, each of which overlaps with the others. To be clear, we are not lionizing warriors or somehow forgetting the living hell that is war—rather, we are presenting genuine, positive, and also sober images of the warrior so the returning service member can hold on to the best of their military experience and holistic alternatives in service of their transition to civilian life.

Sacred sacrifice for the good of others. Many have recognized that the Native American warrior ideal embodies a unique spirituality, one that carries with it stories, images, principles, and practices for protection, nurturing, guidance, a moral code, healing, and devotion to those in our community.[1] We are struck by the profound sense of transcendent cause couched in Sitting Bull's words, which we quoted earlier, about the responsibility of the warrior and how Geronimo referred to warriorhood as a solemn matter. They evoke the nobility in one's sacrifice in service of others and the sober burden warriors carry with them when they return.

The Western warrior archetype. In the Western tradition, from ancient Greece and Rome to modern day, the warrior is a person who lives according to a code of honor and a higher calling, with "devotion, courage, strategic thinking, leadership action, service and sacrifice,"[2] for the purpose of standing on the wall of our society, in defense of our country, our people, and our higher ideals including those memorialized in our Constitution. Within this code is a commitment that the warriors are willing to sacrifice themselves for us. That purpose animates the life and actions of the warrior. Becoming a warrior involves a necessary, fundamental initiation into service, including mastering all the essential skills of their profession and implicit sense of duty to those around them. It is both the outward, public persona and the inner spirit, and it opens a pathway through life.[3] What we describe here is the archetype of the warrior, one many societies have thought of and sought after as an ideal.

The modern gladiator. Tony Robbins speaks about a twist on the image of the modern gladiator, one that he has utilized to motivate himself when having a difficult time: "You have to be here because you have a mission, a vision bigger than yourself, something you want to outlast you [in service of others around you]. That's the only thing that keeps you going during the dark nights of the soul, when it feels like nothing is working and you've given it your all. It's what makes you work so hard when there's nothing left inside you, and it's what makes you find something more. It's a place for gladiators not for dabbling wannabes. When you enter a warrior state, you're undefeatable. You refuse to give up. You won't accept limitations. You break through the most challenging obstacles with intensity, unending focus, and grit—no matter what. And when you completely revitalize your body, mind, and spirit, you'll start every day in a warrior mindset and be on fire to live out your biggest dreams and passions."[4]

The peaceful warrior. There have been several books that express what it means to be a peaceful warrior, from Dan Millman's *Way of the Peaceful Warrior*[5] to Paulo Coelho's *Warrior of the Light: A Manual*[6] to Erwin Raphael McManus's *The Way of the Warrior: An Ancient Path to Inner Peace.*[7] In his book, McManus's central theme is that a warrior, whether military or civilian, must first know inner peace before they can be ready for battle. The battle for the warrior is the one fought inside, a battle for peace over war, light over darkness, and ultimately to become the person we are meant to be. To understand the depth of this work, it is worth summarizing the code of the warrior that McManus describes:

- The warrior fights only for peace because that is the only real basis to live within ourselves in the way we are meant to be. It requires the courage to walk into our own darkness; from that the warrior develops the peace of mind that comes from realizing they can always find the light even in the greatest darkness of difficulty.

- The warrior seeks to become invisible, meaning the warrior serves not for their own glory but for others.
- The warrior finds honor in service.
- The warrior frees their mind from fear, doubt, and hate, which allows them to take advantage of things unseen, of the ability to conjure endless possibilities in service of hope and love.
- The warrior owns defeat, meaning the honor of the warrior is not built on victory but the nobility of battle.
- The warrior has learned to harness their strength and replenish their energy to fuel their soul and life mission.
- The warrior becomes one with all things because there is infinite power in standing in their pain and vulnerability, evoking the Native American warrior ethos that the warrior bears their wounds well, their scars carrying a beauty that only sacrifice for others can create.

HARNESSING THE GREAT POWER OF BEING A CIVILIAN WARRIOR

If you carry within yourself the essential elements of being a warrior—whether you reach any of the ideals described above or your own version of them—you will have great power and meaning inside you. We are not talking about walking around in tactical gear, checking out the exits to a restaurant, or eyeing potential threats on the subway. We refer to a more profound ethos, one that can energize your return home and transition to a new life. We have found inspiration in many places in our lives for this ethos. When many of you went off to deployment in combat zones, you dedicated your missions to defend your country and family. Now that you are back, the fight to seek your own healing and perhaps the healing of those around you, refind purpose, and be the best husband, wife, son, daughter, and father is a real one—something that many veterans have told us needs and deserves as much courage, dedication, and discipline to accomplish as the missions and operations in uncertain hostile, scary territory. Many veterans return to their spouses and families feeling unprepared to integrate fully back into their roles as spouses and parents. This is understandable, but there is only one thing to do: Train for it. The only person responsible for your emotional well-being, your healing (if needed), your success at your job, and your success at home—is you. You must take the steps necessary to accomplish all of this.

Being back home also gives the veteran a chance to redefine what it means to have been a warrior—and how we can be one in a different, civilian context. Surely that is what is involved in "beat[ing] their swords into plowshares," as is written in the book of Isaiah (2:4). In that, it is also a repurposing, reimagining, updating, or re-forming of our mission and definition of self. It can feel like there is a seemingly endless series of obstacles and challenges, in response to which we have the chance to be a factor in the success, happiness, and fulfillment of transitioning. In *This Civilian Sh*t Is Hard*, Dan Bozung makes several important points:

- Regardless of whether you chose to separate from the military or that choice was made for you, be at peace with it. If you can find peace with it, you have a better chance of moving on successfully. And the reverse is true—if you are always looking back to your days in the military—you will make the transition more difficult and perhaps less likely to be successful.
- Know and remember why you left the military. It will help you down the road.
- Don't compare your new life with your old life. The military is an entirely different environment, and one cannot really compare civilian life with military life. If you are frequently saying to yourself, "This just doesn't measure up," then you're living your life looking backward.
- Assess and use all of what you learned from your military experience for your new civilian life.

Coming to grips with how the veteran chooses to embody what it means to be a civilian warrior is an essential aspect of how veterans can—or have the chance to—redefine themselves once they put down their swords and take up the plows in their lives. But we hope that you never forget the power you have inside you from your military life and what that means for how you can translate that into being a civilian warrior. We need you. "The Warrior archetype is built into us and awakens as part of our psychospiritual development...It is meant to inspire and empower us throughout [our lives]. Without our inner warriors, we are incomplete and weakened. Our society and we are more complete and mature to the degree that we successfully embrace and develop our inner warrior and the moral and protective outer role meant to serve the best in society." Beyond that, "No society is healthy without a healthy, functioning elder warrior class leading the way into a future of hope, responsibility, true security, and peacemaking based on the transformational wisdom and healing gained from [the] ordeal [of combat and war]."[8]

OBSERVATIONS FROM COMMAND SGT. MAJ. TOM SATTERLY, U.S. ARMY (RET.)

Tom Satterly fought some of this country's most fearsome enemies over the course of twenty years and hundreds of missions, one of which was portrayed in the movie *Black Hawk Down*, where he led Delta Force operators in the Battle of Mogadishu.[9] Yet, the enemy that cost him three marriages and ruined his health physically and psychologically was PTSD. It nearly led him to commit suicide, but for the lifeline thrown to him by an extraordinary woman, Jen, whom he ended up marrying.[10] He suffered terror, survivor's guilt, depression, and substance abuse. Tom's long road back is a powerful story of the search for healing after warrior trauma. Veterans sometimes believe they will have to compromise their standards in their new life, new job, and the people around them. They create a story in their heads that civilian life is without standards of courage, high moral ground, or ambition as in the military. Yes, there are big differences, and the transition is difficult, but that is a faulty illusion. As Cdr. Dan Bozung says, you have the chance to surround yourself with A-level players at work and in your life in general. For those with ambition and a sense of self-worth, be careful about associating with B-level players—they will drag you down and compromise your standards, whether civilian or veteran. Challenge yourself to engage with those at the top of their game. In fact, there are civilians who are still as hard-charging and ambitious and living lives with as much integrity and honor as they had while in the military. Devotion to work, family, and country as a civilian has its own dignity and worth. Your military service may have been special, even unique, to you, but that does not mean that others do not have their own lives of service, devotion, and meaning—and that can be useful for you to observe.

Having a healthy mindset about your transition to civilian life is a key and an overarching factor in transition success, happiness, and fulfillment, Tom remarked to us in our discussions with him. It allowed him to serve many veterans and their spouses. Their All Secure Foundation provides resources for special operations forces veterans and their spouses for help with PTSD and TBI, workshop retreats, couples' sessions, and other support.[11] Tom's book, *All Secure: A Special Operations Soldier's Fight to Survive on the Battlefield and the Homefront* and Jen's book, *Arsenal of Hope*, have made a profound difference in the lives of veterans and military spouses. We include his observations here because, while they touch on many aspects of this book, they also sound an alarm bell for veterans and articulate their need to fight inside the wire at home, just as much as they did outside the wire while serving and in combat.

Here are the main lessons Tom shared with us:

- *Become aware of yourself and take responsibility.* The first and most important step for many veterans having a difficult time in transition is to find some degree of self-awareness. Stop pointing fingers at others, at external events. Many veterans, Tom observed, will not accept this kind of self-awareness and self-responsibility. As a result, they are their own worst enemy and the impediment to their healing, which is the beginning of any successful transition to civilian life.
- *Ask for help—you have to want to heal.* Many veterans don't know how to ask for help, as it's not been a part of their training or

their own DNA. They often suffer in isolation. But you must want to get help. Getting help is not a weakness, but a desire to improve and to get stronger.

- *You can find joy, hope, and happiness again.* Tom's path since entering civilian life has, it seemed to us, been a journey of healing and purpose, particularly in his mission at the All Secure Foundation. What struck us, however, was his answer to the question we asked dozens of veterans, "How did you refind purpose in your life?" With simplicity and clarity, he said: "One can always find joy, hope, and happiness again."

- *Did you train for this?* In his biography and in interviews about his combat experience, Tom frequently tells stories of harrowing situations for which the lesson is that one must train for it—like how to reload your weapon and keep engaged under intense enemy fire. At couples' workshops, Tom recounted being asked frequently by active-duty personnel and veterans questions such as: "How in the world am I supposed to know how to deal with this, as a husband or father?" His answer is: "Well, did you train for this? If not, you'd better start now." If we are to succeed inside the wire in unknown terrain, we must train for it, just as we did for combat outside the wire.

- *Commit to getting to know your spouse and family again.* When you come back, you will have an opportunity to get to know your spouse and family again and perhaps in a different way. Your relationships at home may need tending to and repair; it's up to you how you do that. Tom will acknowledge that it was his wife Jen who saved his life, and in a way that moved us, he has committed to being the best husband and father he can and to serving others going through similar difficulties.

- *Keep going.* The training that Tom received as a member of Delta Force remains with him now in his mission of helping other veterans. His mantra to others, when having difficulty in the transition, is to "just keep going."

VETERANS' VOICES

"We need to learn how to sell ourselves and that includes being confident and bold enough to put ourselves out there and take care of ourselves first—something we're not used to. You have to trust that this is okay and that you need to do this in order to better take care of others. Put your oxygen mask on first before you help others with theirs, just like they say in the airlines."

—Rear Adm. Michael Giorgione, U.S. Navy (Ret.);
currently CEO, LeanFM Technologies

"My wife and daughter are awesome. Their message to me through multiple transitions has consistently been 'I trust you. Just don't screw this up.'"

—Commander Dan Bozung, U.S. Navy (Ret.);
currently U.S. Navy Reserves

"After leaving the Coast Guard, the decrease in stress and responsibility has been a welcome break. I'm a much better husband and father these last several months as I'm home a *ton*. My purpose has always been to honor Christ in all that I do, whether in uniform or not. I'm holding fast to that purpose as I continue my training and orientation with Delta Air Lines. The service to my country was done, in good faith, during the entirety of my active duty service obligation. I love my country, the role I played within an awesome organization, and I am proud to say that I served. I learned that, despite the naysayers in higher positions of authority, a great life could be lived outside of the service. Family time, vacation, financial compensation, and 401k options all greatly increased upon starting my career at Delta Air Lines."

—Lt. Cdr. Jono Parkhurst, U.S. Coast Guard Reserves

"Soldiering came easy for me. I was a gifted athlete, loyal, and brave. During my transition and early civilian career, I kept that mindset and it did not translate into the same success I had achieved in the military. I never trained to be a civilian. I entered West Point at seventeen, having lived my entire life with my mother, then trained to be a soldier. Once I got out, I just assumed that training would help me succeed in the civilian world. I soon realized it did not. After many bad decisions, it took me years of retraining before I could establish myself as a Civilian Warrior."

—James M. Shinn, captain, U.S. Army (Ret.)

"One of my mentors and author of *Never Enough*, Commander Mike Hayes, U.S. Navy (Ret.), asked me if I could go back and reread the last chapter of my life, would I change anything? Of course, we all have hardships we wish we could change to lessen the pain we felt and change the outcome for the better. But it is those transitions that strengthen us and allow personal growth. I cannot re-create the camaraderie and bonds I felt in the military: I have tried. Though I can reflect on the amazing men and women I worked with, draw from those experiences and transitions, and teach others what I have learned to help them grow personally. This gives me fulfillment."

—Rob Sarver, former U.S. Navy lieutenant; currently cofounder of Servius Group and co-CEO and cofounder of the Heroes Journey

"After I got out, I finally got to be a full-time mom, and I kinda hated it at first. Taking care of kids is long-term investment, but it's nothing like the mission satisfaction you get from the military. And your teenagers don't care if you retired as a captain or a master sergeant. They are not going to respond well to that E-7 voice. You have to relearn how to influence those around you without that nice stack of stripes and authority on your arm. And, consider therapy. Maybe you managed to make it through your career just fine. I did. Maybe you have a good support network. I did. But this

is a big transition. If I hadn't had a friend who was also transitioning to talk to, I would have needed a therapist."

—M.Sgt. Eileen Cobb, U.S. Air Force (Ret.); currently retired

"Honestly, I was extremely nervous when I left the Army, I was
newly married, I had a child on the way, and the only thing I could
think about was how I would support my family. I had no idea
what I was going to do; I just knew that I would out-work anyone.
This was my mission: to give my new wife and baby the best life I
could. I wanted to give them all the things I didn't have."

—Jesse Sargent, former staff sergeant, U.S. Army

"Anyone who tries to do this transition alone is a fool. Family
meant everything to me. It was my anchor when I was on deployment in Afghanistan. It is the reason I am fighting to be a success,
a well-rounded man, husband, and father today. I can't say that I
am perfect at these things, but if I don't give it everything I've got
for them, then I won't be able to look at myself in the mirror."

—Anonymous veteran, former sergeant, U.S. Marine Corps

"The military left me with a ton of positive things. It reinforced
core values and it taught me that I am the only one in charge
of my own life. That I need to get up every day, take a shower,
and care for myself. I can't just sit on my butt. At the same time,
I have learned that, at times, it's okay not to be okay, and that
that moment will pass. And then I get myself up again. What
helped me see these lessons was spending time with my former
teammates from the Navy. These conversations go deep fast; we
listen to each other; we have cried and mourned together; we
have gone through life after the Navy together. I am blessed to
have them in my life."

—John Sheehan, former petty officer third class (radioman),
U.S. Navy; currently CEO, Sheehan and Sons Security

"She stood in the storm,
and when the wind
did not blow her way,
she adjusted her sails."

—ELIZABETH EDWARDS

CHAPTER 16

THE TRANSITION FOR SPOUSES AND FAMILIES

"Transitioning from active-duty military life was a little like slipping and flying at the same time. When my husband transitioned out, it felt like we were finally embarking on the future we'd long anticipated. It also felt strange leaving behind the only adult life career I'd known him to have. The transition was a bigger thing than I'd expected. My advice? Prepare well in advance."

—RACHEL GRILLO, NAVY SPOUSE

The military spouse has equal standing to the veteran when it comes to the idea that they served—and the claim that they served side by side with their veteran. Some things that are worth repeating: Military spouses and families are the lifeblood of the armed services; they shoulder the weight more than anyone might understand as they stoically keep the family grounded, safe, and functioning while the service member performs their duty; their service defends our country and Constitution just as much as the warrior with a rifle in their hands; and depression, anxiety, suicide, and other great difficulties afflict military spouses far greater than their nonmilitary counterparts. These difficulties haven't been studied enough and they are currently not well understood.[1] When the veteran transitions to civilian life, the military spouse and family undergo a parallel transition process—parallel but not the same.

From our interviews with military spouses, we believe the following are critical points to bear in mind during the transition:

- *Anticipate.* Military spouses would do well to anticipate and engage in the transition process for themselves and their families just as much as the veteran. They deserve that, they will need it, and that anticipation and engagement will make the transition more effective for themselves, their families, and their veteran wife, husband, father, or significant other. Don't wait to figure this out.

- *Read this field manual—much of it applies to you.* Much of this book applies equally to military spouses—the need to prepare in advance about very practical issues, addressing and beginning to heal wounds they or their spouse have suffered that need tending to (whether physical or nonphysical), finding new purpose, and perhaps finding a new job or career. So, we urge military spouses to also read this book for themselves.

- *The veteran and the spouse both should read this field manual to understand the other.* Transitioning to civilian life is a dynamic exercise. Veterans would do well to know that their spouses and families will also be undergoing a major life transition—veterans need to read this chapter and participate as an equal member of the transition team. Military spouses need to understand as well as they can what their veteran is undergoing in the transition; reading this book is a step in the right direction.

- *Your process is also separate.* While military spouses undergo a transition parallel to that of veterans, the life and experience of the military spouse is also different from that of the veteran. The military spouses have issues unique to themselves that deserve care and attention.

- *Think in big categories of transition to manage.* As you prepare for and undergo the transition, many have found it helpful to assess the transition in terms of—and to stay focused on—the following major categories: work, family, health/general well-being, and community.[2]

The experiences of military spouses and families are critical and must be acknowledged and given attention—for themselves and to share the lessons they have learned along the way with others. In this chapter, we share the observations of lessons learned from spouses and families.

KEY TAKEAWAYS FOR SPOUSES

- The transition for yourself and your family will be bigger than you probably can imagine.
- Prepare in advance.
- Anticipate the many categories of things that need to be addressed in your life and the life of your family.
- Use this chapter as a checklist.
- Get advice and help where you need it. Many have traveled this road before. The military spouse community itself is the best resource available.

PREPARE IN ADVANCE

The military takes care of food, housing, health care, and a paycheck, and beyond the necessities, provides a sense of identity, community, and mission for military spouses, just as it does for veterans. After separation from the military, you will both need to take care of these needs on your own. In this regard, every military spouse with whom we spoke emphasized the importance of preparing for the transition in advance. The same process we identified in chapter 1 for preparing in advance applies to the military spouse and family. And while there can be much challenge and stress in the transition, this time also represents a profound and rare opportunity to re-form your life and that of your family. At these times, it may be valuable to ask yourself what a successful, happy, meaningful life looks like for you and your family after the military. Engaging in vision-making, as we described it in chapter 10, and planning can be profound, powerful tools.

One valuable planning resource is the MySTeP Military Spouse Transition Program (Stepping Beyond), which is available for a year after military separation. MySTeP raises several important topics to consider:

- Beginning the separation process
- Beginning the retirement process
- Out-processing at transition—how is it different?
- Understanding the survivor benefit plan
- Relocation considerations for families transitioning from the military
- Mentoring—sharing your military spouse experience to help your community
- Preparation for financial success after the transition from the military
- Debt management to prepare for the transition
- Building a transition fund
- Personal financial counseling to prepare for transition from the military[3]

There are many other resources available to military spouses and military families for the transition to civilian life. We list the best of what we have found in Annex 1 on our website, www.heroes-journey.net.

Back to brass tacks: What follows is a checklist of things to anticipate and possibly prepare for. It parallels some of the information in chapter 1 about preparing for the veteran's transition but is written for the spouse and family.

Where will you live? Where would you like to live? Will this involve relocating off-base or moving for work or family reasons? There are several factors to consider here, including proximity to family and friends, best job or education or career options, best schools for your children, cost of living, the presence of a veteran community, and a place that shares your values. There are many resources available to you, including numerous online resources for the best cities to live (go visit Veterans United Home Loans 2024 article "Best Cities for Veterans to Live" and the *Time Out* article "This Is the Best City in the U.S. for Veterans to Live"), prepared in partnership with Hiring Our Heroes (a foundation dedicated to helping veterans find jobs).

Moving logistics. If you need to move, consider the following:

- The military will pay for your move, but the only costs are those for travel to your home of record—and also, only one car to be shipped. Anything beyond that will be on you to pay for. However, and good news for pet lovers, as of January 1, 2024, the military has allowed a pet transportation allowance.
- If you are returning from overseas, your car will be shipped to the port closet to your home of record and will need to be retrieved from there.[4]
- When packing your things to ship to your new home:
    1. Make sure you supervise the movers—you don't want to have important items misplaced or taken or sent to the wrong place.
    2. Plan for how long it will take for your things to arrive at your new home. Shipping from overseas takes longer. Consider taking some essentials with you, like a few pots and pans, dishes, sheets, et cetera.
    3. Budget some extra money to deal with delays, lost items, or emergencies.
    4. Make your own records, with photographs and videos of valuable items, such as jewelry and electronics. This will help with the claims process if anything is damaged or lost.
- For all of your moving and PCS benefits, visit the "Plan My Move" section and "PCS & Military Moves" on Military OneSource.mil.
- In any move, be prepared for the possibility of your most precious family heirloom being broken or damaged. You can just

about count on it. After you express your frustration and sadness, it's also an opportunity to consider that sometimes, to make a new omelet, you need to break a few old eggs.

Will you buy a new home? This may involve researching schools, job opportunities, and a veteran's community, among other concerns. For some, taking time to research and find a community to live in is a good first step, and one that will allow you to do some looking around before you make a serious financial investment and commitment in purchasing a new home. Also, you may wish to look into VA home loans as well as private sources of mortgages that may be veteran friendly.

Will you want to get a new job or start a new career? Starting a new job or career while you and your veteran are transitioning can have advantages (a source of income; an avenue for a new sense of purpose for you; a sense of a new path in life that is yours and not just that of your veteran spouse at this moment) and disadvantages (you may not want too much change going on at the same time; you may need to be the quarterback of the transition). Most of the practical points we make in chapter 13 about finding a new job or career apply equally well to the military spouse.

There are many organizations dedicated to helping military spouses and families, such as:

- Association of Military Spouse Entrepreneurs
- Military Spouse Chamber of Commerce
- Bunker Labs (helping military spouses find jobs)
- U.S. Department of Labor: Military Spouse Interstate License Recognition Options (www.dol.gov/agencies/vets /veterans/military-spouses/license-recognition)
- Department of Defense: MySECo: Military Spouse Education and Career Opportunities
- Transition Employment Assistance for Military Spouses and Caregivers (TEAMS) is a series of Department of Labor (DOL) employment workshops that extend the department's Transition Assistance Program to assist military spouses and caregivers as they plan and prepare for their job search in

pursuit of their employment goals. All TEAMS workshops are instructor-led virtual training, provided at a variety of times, to meet the needs of individuals stationed throughout the world. TEAMS workshops are stand-alone training modules. You can take all of the workshops or just a few, and they can be taken in any order that fits your availability and schedule.

Will you want to continue your education? This may be a rare and opportune time to continue your education, and there are educational opportunities that support the military spouse.

- There are scholarships available to military spouses and children of service members, such as the Tillman Scholar Program.
- The Yellow Ribbon Program helps make college tuition affordable. If your veteran qualified for the Post-9/11 GI Bill at the 100 percent level, then a spouse using the transferred benefits of an active-duty service member who has served at least thirty-six months on active duty, or a dependent child using benefits transferred by a veteran, is eligible. We provide more detail below under the summary of VA benefits.
- Some master's degree programs allow spouses to attend class if the veteran is fully enrolled in a program.

Anticipate family financial health needs. Many military spouses shared that they wish they'd had a better financial plan. Amber McDonald, Army spouse, told us: "A financial plan is something I wished we had more assistance with. We planned for three years for him to transition, and even with ample conversations and intentionality it was still a shock for us. Without being the one transitioning out, it was hard for me to realize how huge of a change this was for his daily life."

- *Save money and budget your expenses.* While the military will pay for some transition costs, the reality is that it is usually more expensive than you think. If possible, start saving now before the transition begins.

- *Ask yourself if your finances are in line with your needs.* When your veteran separates from the military, are your finances, family financing plan, and budget under control, and do these things line up and support the kind of life you want to live and to pay for things that your family needs?[5]
- *Engage in family financial planning.* For several reasons, discussing finances with your veteran is perhaps the most important part of financial planning. Financial issues can often be a source of conflict in a marriage. Nothing beats preparing a financial plan—for which we offer some guidelines in Annex 3 on our website, www.heroes-journey.net. Consider the following questions to discuss together:
  - o   What are your financial needs and goals?
  - o   How does your current plan line up with these needs and goals?
  - o   If it doesn't, what is your plan B—what will that involve? Should you, as the military spouse, take on a job (if you don't already have one) to protect against the risk that your veteran may need more time to find a job?
- *Consider the reserves.* The veteran transferring from active duty to the reserves can ease the transition and help financially.
- *Plan for a delayed salary.* Financial stress can arise if it takes the veteran or spouse longer than expected to find the job they are looking for. Be prepared for this.

Research VA and other benefit programs for veterans, spouses, and dependents. There are many benefit programs available to military spouses and other dependents of veterans. Our point is that there are great resources out there, but you need to spend time looking into them. You might also benefit from getting help from others who have done it before. Begin the process of finding out about the requirements and the paperwork you need to complete for benefits at the VA. This can be time-consuming and may feel overwhelming, so it is wise to check on this before you need to access the benefits, particularly as you will be focusing on your new life.

Here is an initial checklist of benefits and programs that might be helpful to you:

- *Vet centers.* Families are eligible for help from the VA's Vet Centers, which is different from the standard counseling and other services provided by the local VA hospital. They offer discreet services, and the records are not filed into the standard VA system. Check out local Vet Centers near where you live.
- *eBenefits Portal.* This is a joint VA/DoD web portal (www .va.gov/eauth/ebenefits.asp) that provides resources and self-service capabilities to veterans, service members, and their families to research, access, and manage their VA and military benefits and personal information.
- *Health Care.* You can enroll online at the Department of Veterans Affairs website or at your local VA medical center. Be aware that VA health care does not extend to dependents and is available only for the veteran. So plan accordingly if you have dependents.
  - o If you have a spouse and they have a job, will their employer offer health coverage for you and your children?
  - o A practical recommendation: Get an electronic copy of your medical records.
- *College/graduate school tuition assistance.* There are many benefit programs, including ones that help pay for college, such as the Montgomery GI Bill and the Post-9/11 GI Bill.
  - o Know the difference between Chapter 33 (the Post-9/11 GI Bill, meant to support school or job training and covers monthly housing allowance and book stipend) and Chapter 31 (Veteran Readiness and Employment Program [VR&E], which covers tuition costs).
  - o The Post-9/11 GI Bill allows service members to transfer unused education benefits to immediate family members. This applies to officers and enlisted, active-duty, and selected reserve. Qualifying immediate family members are spouses and children. However, this transfer of benefits incurs a four-year commitment

to stay in the military, so think about transferring one month of eligibility to each dependent (the months can be adjusted later) as early as possible to make sure you fulfill the service obligation. This may affect how you choose your separation timing, especially if transferring those benefits to your dependents is a priority.

- *Disability.* You can file claims for a variety of disabilities.
- *Life insurance.* Your Servicemembers' Group Life Insurance (SGLI) coverage expires 120 days after leaving the military. Veterans can convert their coverage to Veterans' Group Life Insurance (VGLI), which is less expensive than other civilian options.
  - o Under certain conditions, the option to convert to a commercial insurance policy is extended to persons covered under the SGLI and VGLI programs, as well as spouses covered under Family Servicemembers' Group Life Insurance (FSGLI).
  - o Please visit this VA benefit site to review these options: Convert SGLI, VGLI, or FSGLI to a Commercial Policy—Life Insurance (va.gov).
- *Home loans.* As noted above in this chapter, there are VA home loans available as well as private sources of mortgages that may be veteran-friendly.
- *Small Business Administration (SBA) loans.* This may be helpful to you if you are starting a new business or looking to acquire a business. If you are acquiring a company with a commercial real estate component, you need to review the SBA 7a option.
- *Job search assistance.* Every branch of the armed forces offers seminars and courses, including some on résumé and cover letter preparation, interview coaching, career counseling, educational counseling, and job searches. Read chapter 13 of this book for a comprehensive guide to job searching.
- *Burial benefits.* The VA offers burial benefits to veterans. Beyond and in line with these benefits, you may wish to consider creating or reviewing your wills, powers of attorney, living will

and medical directives, burial instructions, transfer of assets, and tax planning around that and other inheritance matters. If you need to get a trustee or an executor of your wills, you should arrange that.

On our website, www.heroes-journey.net, Annex 1 contains a list of VA programs and benefits.

What will your children need? Kids may struggle and need support just as much as adults during transition. In many cases, their worlds get turned upside down if they have to leave their friends and communities. Besides that, kids tend to absorb their parents' stress—so if you are feeling it, your kids probably are, too. Consider the observation of Amber McDonald, Army spouse: "Our kids struggled with the transition because having their dad home more and not on such a structured schedule was something they weren't used to. We talked a lot to them about what this meant and why things were changing." While children need different things at different ages, here are a few considerations:

- What is the best choice of schools?
- If your children have special needs, have you researched public or private schools with resources that can support them?
- If you are looking at private schools, be sure to request financial aid packages and note any deadlines.
- What kind of community will you find yourself in and how do you find the best one for your children? Recall the adage: It takes a village to raise a child.
- Kids need routine. In many ways, the military community may be all they know. Most have endured the stress of moving, starting a new school, and making new friends many times over. Constantly starting over can induce its own stressors on a kid, even if, strangely, this also becomes routine. However, military transition can take this obscure safety net and common community away, giving the child no security. In this context, think about establishing in advance of the veteran's separation some routines and rituals that can be carried over during the transition. These may anchor your children and give them things to which they can look forward.

- Can you maintain your children's relationship with friends they are to move away from?
- Consider setting aside a modest portion of the family budget to invest in some small treats or new experiences for your children when they arrive at their new home or community or just after the veteran's separation. Maybe a new family dog would give them great joy and a new job with the opportunity for taking on responsibility.
- Engage your children in the transition—the change in your veteran's life, the great opportunities for this phase of their lives, positive things that they can look forward to—as well as recognizing and not sugarcoating the big change coming.
- Plan activities with your children. Inviting your kids to your new job, on planned family days or otherwise, can give them a sense of where you go during the day, among other benefits. Walking your new neighborhood is always valuable.
- Make time to be around. Parents are the constant in the life of a child, particularly if there is a lot of change going on.[6]
- Make time for play with younger children. Younger children experience, process, and even metabolize important and difficult life moments through play. Allowing them to play and playing with them during this important and sometimes destabilizing transition is key to their emotional health and their own success in the transition.

Dr. Charles Hoge said, "Children and adolescents need a sense of security, a consistent routine without too many disruptions, and a loving parent or guardian who is consistently present in their lives... [And] the most important things you can provide your children are your love, time, attention, reassurance, and encouragement, as well as a consistent, secure, stable, and safe environment for them to grow and develop."[7]

Some resources for military kids:

- *Sesame Street for Military Families* on Military OneSource has tools to help children understand the transition to civilian life.

- Thrive is a free online program that offers positive parenting, stress management, and healthy lifestyle practices for children from birth to age eighteen. Build on strengths you have and develop new resilience skills as your child grows and changes.
- Military Spouse (www.militaryspouse.com) is a website dedicated to military spouses, with articles on employment, education, entrepreneurship, life, and relationships.
- Babies on the Homefront is a free app from ZERO TO THREE, designed just for military and veteran parents. The app provides helpful tips for everyday interactions with babies and toddlers, including behavioral tips, playtime ideas, self-care for parents, and child development information.
- FOCUS, or Families OverComing Under Stress, is a program developed to help families and couples manage common challenges related to military life. It builds on strengths families already possess and teaches skills to help enhance communication, problem-solving, goal-setting, and more. The FOCUS On the Go! app will hold children's attention with fun games and activities that help them learn how to better communicate their feelings.

Find a mentor and resources for yourself. Military spouses often get great support, advice, life lessons, and encouragement from those who have traveled the path before them. In your networking and talks with friends, consider that finding a mentor may be a great resource for you, in ways practical and profound. Nothing beats having a mentor. This is true as a general matter and for military spouses or their veterans who come from diverse groups, such as African American, Asian American, female, LGBTQ+, and other communities or groups. But finding and developing a relationship with a mentor won't happen by accident—it should be developed with intention.

Considerations for the spouse of the injured veteran. Spouses of injured veterans walk a parallel pattern of challenge with their veterans. Depending on the circumstances, you may suffer an inner shock on hearing the news from your veteran. On your own, this may require you to come to grips with your veteran's injury—to process in your head and heart what it means and what to do next. We don't mean to be foreboding, but for some military spouses, there may be dark moments; you will experience your own fear, grief, anxiety, and uncertainty. You may feel like you have many questions with not a lot of answers. In these moments, the spouse of anyone afflicted with a physical injury, including one with life-threatening or life-altering consequences, will be tested. You will need to find your own way. This will be your own path to walk, but the support of family, friends, community, and, if applicable to you, a pastor of your own faith provides powerful resources, including for the soul. In chapter 6, we made many observations for injured veterans that may also be useful to you.

On a practical level—which may help you process where you are emotionally and move forward—there is a range of things to anticipate and to which to adapt:

- You may have to make adjustments to your home or even consider moving to accommodate the needs of your spouse. This may bring its own challenges if it means having to move off base.
- There may be economic consequences to grapple with if your veteran will not be getting the planned job after leaving the military, particularly if they leave the military earlier than expected. You may need to reevaluate your family financial plan and budget.
- You might need benefits from the VA that are unique to injured veterans. This may require a special search and assistance to find and access them.
- Your relationship and marriage may be impacted. Your role in the home may change. However, the hardship, though painful and perhaps difficult at first, has made it possible for some couples to find a new harmony and union.
- If you have children, spend some time thinking with your veteran about how to speak with them about their returning father or mother. How you spend time with and talk with them about their veteran parent's injury and this transition

period can help them understand and adjust to the transition, in emotional and other terms. We urge you to be aware of your own concerns and anxieties and put them aside before doing so since children have the best antennas and read us parents well. Whatever approach you take will need to take account of the nature of the situation, the ages of your children, and your transition plans, among other factors.

- At these moments, if you can, lean more heavily on family, friends, and community. You will also need to be the judge of how to involve others to balance what you need and the needs of your veteran and family.

There is no one-size-fits-all manual for adjusting to and addressing life with an injured spouse. With the suggestions above, we don't mean to take the situation for granted. Rather, with humility, we are attempting to provide assistance based on the feedback from spouses of injured veterans that have come before you.

Develop new rituals. Whether you were a military spouse for a short period or a long time, all military spouses have shared in, adapted to, or rejected some of the most common rituals of military life. Going to the exchange or commissary, the use of your military ID, and the annual military ball are simple examples. Everyone and every family has their own rituals. As we have written in an earlier chapter, rituals serve several important functions—they form a part of one's identity and sense of community, they mark important milestones in life, and they help us process or digest important moments in life. When you and your veteran leave the military, some of these rituals will go away and you will keep others. What we have learned from our conversations with military spouses is that being clear and intentional about what rituals to keep and the need to develop new ones is important and helpful.

Anticipate the change in community and the need to expand or build a new one. Many service members and spouses frequently say they feel lost after leaving military life, particularly if they were heavily involved in the military community. One of the challenges to the transitioning military spouse and family is the loss of their historic community and the perception that their new community does not understand them. In other words, their experience parallels that of the transitioning veteran. Navy spouse Katie Hancock shared how it felt when her husband transitioned: "The people he served beside were incredibly hard to leave. They are still family."[8]

Research shows that the nature of the civilian community to which the veteran returns, as well as the support that community provides, impacts how well the veteran manages the transition. Military spouses are commonly connected to their spouses' military units and locations.[9] These units include a built-in community support system. When the veteran leaves military service, spouses and families often relocate—thus, disconnecting from the local military community and the social support within that world. Leaving the military, therefore, involves a shift in community and the associated support networks.[10] Many have observed that successful transition requires military spouses to find new communities and develop new connections to derive social support. Where, after immersion into a new community, new connections are not made, military spouses may be at risk of becoming isolated if they find it difficult to develop and manage new relationships. In addition, the assumed challenges of connecting to new communities may be exacerbated for veteran families due to the perceived gap in understanding of military life and the life of the military spouse by civilians, particularly as experienced by military spouses.[11] This is understandable given that the vast majority of civilians have limited experience with the military, do not know anyone who served in the military,[12] and do not understand the impact of service on military families. The military-civilian gap can lead to misunderstandings and often leaves veterans feeling like outsiders.[13] It is likely that this gap also impacts veteran spouses and their ability to integrate into their new communities.[14]

Some practical suggestions:

- Before moving to a new community, research your choices and where you will end up living. Do you have friends or family there—or friends of friends and family?
- Develop a community around you, whether in the military or the civilian world. Tonya Waltors, Navy spouse, told us, "The

support we had was because we were prepared and created an amazing community outside the military." Nothing beats starting small—a group of friends or fellow current or former military spouses meeting to talk once a week for coffee or your drink of choice. There are many organizations that provide forums for veterans and their spouses to meet and listen to one another, as we mention in chapter 3.

- Consider volunteering as a way to meet new people in your community. As we have noted earlier, service and serving others is so woven into the DNA of many veterans that continuing it in and after the transition phase provides continuity and meaning for many.
- Project Sanctuary believes that everyone has the right and ability to heal. They assist military service members by reconnecting the family unit through a holistic approach. Their program heals the traumatic effects of military service, treating all family members at their level of need and enabling the service members to reintegrate into their families and communities in a healthy and sustainable manner. Project Sanctuary's work seeks to preserve the family unit, strengthening the community, the military, and the country.
- The VA TAP Social and Emotional Health Resources (www .benefits.va.gov/TRANSITION/docs/mlc-mental-health .pdf) provides a trove of resources for transitioning families and military spouses. A few items discussed are crisis help lines, insurance for children, moving checklist, TRICARE, mental health charities, and substance abuse charities

Some helpful resources, among many others available online:
- The Armed Services YMCA has created programs that are designed to help military families cope with their unique challenges while building family bonds, resiliency, and social connections with other military families.
- The programs for youth development support these ideals and assist in negating the effects of PTSD in children.

Try reading "4 Ways Armed Services YMCA Helps Operation Hero Kids and Their Parents" at www.asymca.org/blog/4-ways-armed-services-ymca-helps-kids.

Be prepared for some emotional stress and a feeling of loss. Major life transitions bring expected and unexpected forms of stress. Moving away from your community can give rise to a great sense of loss and even grief. Revisit chapter 4 on these topics—they may well apply to the military spouse just as much as the veteran. If you know these things may well come, anticipate them, speak with others, plan for them, and get help from your community, friends, family, and professional therapists. It is likely that neither of you has ever experienced this kind of a transition. If that's the case, train and prepare for it.

Here are some words of wisdom from military spouses of things to anticipate:

- *Expect new forms of emotional stress.* Such as when your in-laws or adult children move in with you, your cat or dog dies, or when you learn about the losses of others within your network of other military spouses. It will come and life will bring new challenges. How will you prepare for that?
- *It might be more challenging than expected.* As one military spouse told us, "We planned for my husband's transition for three years. We had our finances set, our business plan set, his plan set—and we still had to make adjustments along the way and even struggled sometimes."
- *Be prepared for lingering postwar effects on your veteran.* When a warrior returns home and is suffering from the effects of their experience, they are likely to bring it all back to the house. Fifty-five percent of military spouses surveyed found that family life was challenging after the veteran's reintegration from war and nearly half experienced an increase in conflicts and arguments at home after reintegration.[15] Family members are inevitably exposed to what the veteran is suffering from—it would seem impossible for that not to be the case. At times, family members may seem like they have "to walk

on eggshells" around the veteran.[16] Some common themes we have heard from spouses:

o   The veteran may expose their family to a variety of reactions, including anger or rage, a short temper, alcohol and drug abuse, disruption in sleeping patterns in the house, emotional detachment and withdrawal, a sense of helplessness, and even domestic abuse.[17]

o   By contrast, the veteran may present different challenges if they behave in an emotionless way around their families—reflecting the suppression of emotion as the persistence of a valid adaptation to combat.[18]

o   Be aware of the observation of a well-known therapist who treated Vietnam veterans: "The overwhelming majority of combat veterans whom I have known are painfully aware of the absence of intimacy, tenderness, light playfulness, or easy mutuality in their sex lives. For many, sex is a trigger of intrusive recollection and emotion from Vietnam as the sound of explosions or the smell of a corpse. Sex and anger are intertwined that they often cannot conceive of tender, uncoerced sex that is free of rage. When successful treatment reduces their rage, they sometimes report that they have to completely relearn (or learn for the first time) the pleasures of sex with intimacy and playfulness."[19]

o   The veteran may also resist your attempts to get them help, which can lead to conflict. Be prepared for these things, to the extent possible, and seek support, therapy, or counseling for yourself as you see fit. Of course, the veteran may engage in a loving, supportive way, but those are not things we need to prepare you for.

o   Look out for secondary PTSD. Spouses and children may experience secondary PTSD from their veterans. Many military spouses and children suffer symptoms that parallel and are consistent with PTSD even if they were never in combat. This can occur for several reasons, including due to repeated, deep concern for the active-duty spouse or returning veteran and also being sensitive to the veteran who has returned who is suffering from PTSD themselves.[20] Secondary PTSD can be deeply troubling particularly to children who do not have the background or training to understand what is happening inside their emotions and have few methods with which to cope with it. While well documented, secondary PTSD is not as well known in the veteran community as it should be from our research. That is unfortunate and a potential hurdle to recognizing it and getting help for it. Recent media reports have shined a light on secondary PTSD, its consequences and risks.[21] Jen Satterly has written about this in her book, *Arsenal of Hope*. There are resources available for getting help with secondary PTSD. We also recommend spouses read chapter 7.

Domestic abuse. Domestic violence is more prevalent within the military than the civilian population, even more so among veteran families and especially among families in which the veteran is suffering from one or more of the ailments we discussed in chapters 4–9 such as PTSD.[22] If the veteran is rageful, violent, or engages in domestic abuse, we urge you to get help. Contact the National Domestic Violence Hotline at 800-799-SAFE (7233) or 800-787-3224 (TTY). Annex 1 on our website, www.heroes-journey.net, lists some additional resources.

You may also experience the sense of a loss of purpose. Just as with the veteran, the transition can cause the military spouse to undergo a sense of loss of purpose. "Many spouses feel like it is now their time to be their own person but often aren't sure who that is anymore," says Victoria Terrinoni, author of *Where You Go, I Will Go: Lessons from a Military Spouse*.[23] See chapters 11 and 12 on refinding purpose.

You may need some healing. Just as with the veteran, the transition can cause isolation, emotional pain, and difficulties in your marriage—all things that are worthy of seeking therapy for. And, just as with the veteran, you are the only one who can be responsible for your own healing.

Prepare for and anticipate a new financial situation. Financial stress leads to relationship stress. Plan for that and anticipate your financial needs.

Develop new support systems. As Amber McDonald told us, "I think if I would have had a better support system to talk to others about what he would be feeling as he got out, it could have gone a lot smoother."

Make time for yourself. Many military spouses with children have had to continue to "get it all done" while their spouses were on assignment or deployment for long stretches of time. And, to boot, they rarely had time for themselves when their spouses came back and needed time to decompress. "When do *I* get time to decompress?" is a common refrain. The same goes, perhaps even more so, when the military spouse transitions to civilian life. Military spouses deserve and need time for themselves during this process. Time to relax, to figure out where the family ship is headed, and to just sit in silence.

Communicate with each other. As Sara Kono, a Marine Corps spouse, observed: "Wholeheartedly communicate! Don't go to bed angry, remember that we are in this together." As with many other parts of the transition, nothing replaces the value of speaking and listening to each other. It's also not just about speaking; it's about talking through your emotions together.

Amber McDonald, Army spouse, told us, "This is a huge move for your family as a whole, but also an even bigger move for your spouse. They have known nothing else but this for years—and the biggest lesson I learned was to not just assume because we had a plan, that he was going to be okay. Talk through your feelings and emotions together."

Support each other. When couples experience new challenges, one of two things tends to happen: They face it together and become stronger and more together than before, or they don't. Nothing beats committing to being patient, loving, and kind—and having your spouse by your side at those moments.

Be prepared to challenge each other. As in any good partnership, there are times when one must challenge the other for the greater good, for the purpose of clearing the air or moving the team to a higher standard or goal. One particular aspect of this arises in the context of understanding what your veteran is going through physically or medically. Shawn Prickett, colonel, U.S. Army (Ret.), relayed the following in our interview with him:

> Most spouses or those closest to the veteran do not know and they aren't privy to the diagnosis. They are oblivious to the signs and symptoms of pain and distress. In my case, my wife was afraid to cause further stress or damage to our relationship by saying anything...to anyone...including me. Spouses would do well at times to question their veterans, including in front of their doctors, and also question their doctors about the veterans' description of their pains or difficulties. Sometimes we veterans don't know how to recognize deeper diagnoses or have a hard time admitting to it, most of all to ourselves and our spouses. My mother, a nurse, did this for my father. Us veterans, we need that sometimes.

MARRIAGE TIPS FROM ROB AND ALEX

These recommendations actually come from some of the most renowned therapists and marriage counselors in the country today— not just Rob and Alex!

The transition to civilian life presents challenges for military couples that are often not expected. We have heard about so many marriages surviving decades of military life, multiple deployments, and separations, only to have things fall apart after they enter civilian life.[24]

Those who have regrets about a lost marriage will say that they didn't appreciate it or invest enough in it when they still had the chance. The difficulty of the transition poses some unique challenges for military couples, as expressed in the article "Will Your Marriage Become a Casualty of Transition?" from militaryspouse.com: "We thought the strain from old hardships would get better once he was out," the author recalled. "We thought all the stress that goes with the demands of military life would just dissolve away. Instead, our marriage dissolved."

As ironic as that may seem, there are many reasons why this occurs. The loss of the military community can be a significant challenge for the military spouse and family, as we've discussed. The need to reinvent oneself is likewise a major issue for both veteran and military spouse. While we've discussed these things separately above, it is important to realize that these may also represent challenges to the marriage.

Here are some important takeaways:

- The strains that accompany military life do not suddenly vanish once the veteran comes home. The enduring quality and bonds of a marriage will be tested in this new circumstance, as with any difficult moment in life.
- Ask yourself some important questions:
  o How is the state of our marriage and how will that change or be affected when my spouse leaves the military?
  o What resources for our marriage and family will be important to identify in advance?
- Before the veteran transitions, speak with one another about the path ahead, how to collaborate on it as a team, and what to expect from the change and from each other.
- For many couples, the benefits of health care, housing, and a predictable income sometimes serve as a barrier to divorce. It is difficult to do, but a time of major life transition is an opportunity to give an honest assessment to your marriage and the reasons for staying in it.
- Have a conversation with your spouse about each of your expectations for life after the military. This is an opportune time to revisit some aspects of your relationship. These may include finances, responsibilities with children, household chores, and more profound aspects of your relationship.
- This can be an opportunity to assess, repair (if needed), and invest in your relationship. The couples who do this work usually emerge on the other side of life transitions stronger and more unified. Those who don't usually see their relationships suffer and sometimes fall apart.

- While military life is itself difficult for many, it also offers many supports and sources of strength, fun, engagement, and identity. When those pieces go away, some partners will take the stress out on each other.
- Expect that you may need to be, at times, a cheerleader for your veteran. The transition is often exhausting, with setbacks and blows to the ego, and can bring out frustration, anger, and transition fatigue.[25] Any person going through a life transition needs friends and supporters. Your veteran certainly does.
- Make it clear to your veteran that you are interested and invested in supporting them.
- Manage the process together as a team.
- Get help. This is not a sign of weakness; it is a desire to improve. A skilled marriage therapist or couples' therapist can make a positive difference. Be mindful that finding a skilled therapist is like finding a good doctor, lawyer, or any other specialist; not all of them are effective. You need to interview them and find someone who is well suited to meet your needs.

We know from our research, interviews we have performed, and our own lives that the strength of a marriage is often tested in times of transition and stress. That is nowhere more true than in the transition to civilian life. From his years of working as a psychologist to veterans and their spouses, Dr. Ryan Rana, psychotherapist and couple's counselor whom we met in chapter 10, distilled some of his most important observations about what makes a successful marriage and relationship. He observed some fundamental principles, followed by some concrete, practical suggestions. First, he notes that emotional intimacy is a major predictor of the health of a marriage.[26] This means connecting with your spouse by expressing your feelings and thoughts, sharing vulnerabilities, and talking about what you are experiencing in small, mundane ways and in more profound emotional and even spiritual ways. In a word, it's sharing your hearts. At the center of this kind of intimacy is the sense of trust it builds in each other—knowing this intimacy will be embraced and reciprocated. The healthy pattern a couple creates by engaging in emotional intimacy builds a bond that is a cornerstone of the relationship, something that allows one to be oneself in the relationship and will serve as a ballast to weather the storms of life. Emotional intimacy serves to make marriage a safe place, a comfort zone, and a source of energy and rejuvenation to face the challenges of the transition.

Dr. Rana also offered some practical suggestions for supporting a healthy marriage. Doing this work takes commitment, practice, and some intentional behavior. What we're suggesting here is the wisdom to invest significant time and energy into what matters and what works.

- *Show up.* You don't always have to have solutions or even many words to say; showing up to be present, to be responsive, engaged, and to comfort when one is in distress makes all the difference—and even changes the brain. Sue Johnson, a noted clinical psychologist and couples therapist, refers to this kind of healthy bond as an "ARE" relationship—accessible, responsive, and engaged.
- *Overcome the past for your present.* Sadly, many veterans remain more attuned to even the inner world of their former comrades and fellow veterans who may be having a difficult time than they are to their spouses. From the perspective of the veteran mourning the loss of teammates or leaving the military, this attachment to the past may be understandable. But it comes at a great cost—that of living in the present and loving your spouse.
- *Leave no one behind.* Many veterans and their spouses overlook a fundamental rule of the former warrior that applies just as strongly in marriage as in the military—that is, never leave a comrade behind. The lesson is to never leave your spouse or your veteran behind when they are in pain, suffering, or having a difficult time. You can't always solve the issue, but you can always show, even if quietly, a presence from the heart.
- *Make time for connecting.* It's that simple.
- *Find a balance in your communications.* Effective communication in a marriage sometimes needs to balance between over- and

undercommunicating. Overcommunication can arise when there is discussion of the thousand details of daily life, without a true communication of what really matters. Undercommunication can arise, for example, when the veteran wants to protect their spouse from stress and, as a result, doesn't invite them into their world, head, and heart. By not sharing much of anything, you create isolation, loneliness, and a weakness in the relationship. You can usually measure the strength of a relationship by how much access the couple give to each other and how they respond during a time of distress. While warriors are trained to communicate, that often stops when it comes to opening their hearts. Every couple has to strike the right balance.

POINTERS FOR GOOD COMMUNICATION

Making marriage work sometimes—as we've discovered the hard way in our own lives and through the practical wisdom of Dr. Rana—has less to do with solving grand conflicts and more to do with how we communicate. What follows are general conversation pointers about a variety of possible topics.

Not likely to work in response to a variety of questions:

"Oh, I'm fine; I don't want to talk about it."

Explanation: This shuts down the bond and creates isolation. Taking this approach on occasion may not cause harm, but on a regular basis this approach is deadly—starving your bond.

Better but imperfect:

"Can you believe my boss said that? He said and did XYZ, ABC…Don't you agree? Don't you think I should (say or do)…"

Explanation: This invites dialogue, but it may be overly focused on details and an impersonal work situation rather than a discussion that will effectively bring people closer together.

Likely to work:

> "Hey, do you have a minute to talk about real stuff? So today was pretty tough, and I'm honestly feeling pretty beat up. My boss said XYZ to me, he even said ABC. I don't want to get into more of the details; I just don't want you to misread my frustration. To be honest I'm kind of in shock, really disappointed and hurt by this, and I wanted you to know."

Explanation: This approach tends to be very effective in that it gives just enough context to understand but is heavy on the sharing of impact and the heart, which tells your spouse how much they are valued and that they are invited to share in securing the emotional bond.

- *It's not the conflict; it's how you manage it.* Sixty-nine percent of conflict in successful marriages never gets solved, according to John Gottman's research.[27] What matters, rather, is how the couple anticipates conflict, manages it, and moves on. Speaking honestly, sincerely, and with open hearts, even about age-old conflicts in a relationship, allows the couple to remain united. We're not saying happy couples haven't found ways to minimize conflict—they have. Rather, the emotional intimacy bond at the center allows most conflicts to get out of the ditch faster. If you're not familiar with John Gottman's work, we encourage you to visit his website.
- Leave competitiveness behind. Though many components of a military attitude are actually positive for marriage, there are certainly a couple that are not. One of these is a competitive nature. Taking pride in one's service and an attempt to be the best is a great aspect of having been a soldier. This does not work so well in marriage. Selfish pride and always needing

to be right are deadly to the strength of a bond. Humility, a willingness to self-reflect on your own areas of weakness, forgiveness, and approaching your relationship with a curious, beginner's mind are key to making marriage work. Leave the pride with your uniform.

- *"Don't complain and work the problem" doesn't work in a good marriage.* The training soldiers receive to "adapt, improvise, and overcome" is helpful, to a point, for the veteran and spouse. However, the part of this that requires suppression or avoiding emotion is not. Conflict resolution and solutions to problems do not bond people—although of course a reasonable ability to do so is needed. In the military, "Work the problem" is a helpful concept; at home, "Be fully present" is better advice.

- *Assess your tool kit; it's more well-stocked than you think.* For many spouses, the hardships they've endured alongside their veteran have given them strength, a degree of independence, resiliency, and grit they never thought they would possess before getting married. For some spouses, their individuality and ability to live a fulfilling and meaningful life independently from their warriors is an important asset.[28] Friends, extended family, and community provide invaluable resources for nearly every spouse and military family. You may feel that your experiences while your spouse was in the military have prepared you for transitioning to civilian life; however, they have not. Just as subsequent deployments never got easier, you simply gained more tools in your tool kit to cope with separation. What we have laid out from our research, we hope, are tools to help manage this next phase in your life.

We're not marriage counselors, but we know the strain of transition can stress the bond between two people. Our hope is that this advice will help ease the challenges of your family's transition to civilian life.

MILITARY SPOUSES' VOICES

"Start thinking about what life will look like years before the transition looms. What does your spouse want to do when he exits military life? Does that require more college? Should you do that before he gets out? What doesn't he want to do? How does your role in the family change when you're no longer a military spouse? Come to agreements on where you want to live, and make sure you're on the same page about expectations. My husband took a pay cut when he left the military, and we knew to expect the unexpected.

"I also would have benefited from having someone give me a tutorial on how private insurance works. The military medical system was all I knew as an adult. My husband is still in the reserves so we still have some form of TRICARE, but it's not the same."

—Rachel Grillo, Navy spouse

"[Our children] spend their entire lives on and around military bases, but they get completely cut off. Can't go on base without a sponsor, so no longer able to shop at the grocery they knew, eat at the food courts they spent their teen years enjoying, or even run an errand for you. The things that were familiar to them no matter where you lived are cut off. Our children serve as much as their parents."

—Heather Forrey, military spouse[29]

"The biggest obstacle for me was not having anything for myself outside of the military community—that was where I had found my friends and my passion. Now here we are, far removed from a military community, and I've had to reinvent myself."

—Liz, military spouse

"One thing I would tell military spouses is to be patient with your spouse—they'll be bored most of the time. Also, my purpose, both before and after the transition, was to be a good mom to our daughter. That did not change."

—Tricia Bozung, U.S. Navy spouse

"I literally anguished over which grocery store to go to. I was used to shopping at the commissary, and then I moved to an area with grocery stores all over the place. It just takes time to settle in after a PCS, so I had to get used to a new location."

—Victoria Terrinoni, U.S. Marine Corps spouse and author of *Where You Go, I Will Go: Lessons from a Military Spouse*

"I would tell you that the start was horrible but the transition after a year was great, we opened up more than we ever did before and we were able to be more present with our kids. We had our ups and downs and still do, but we walk hand in hand with each other, our kids, and our faith in God. We know our worth and value now more than ever before and we are so truly grateful for that!"

—Sara Kono, U.S. Marine Corps spouse

"I think my husband lost himself quite a bit. He lost his identity when he got out and I don't think either of us predicted that would happen. It has been a continuous conversation and journey (we are one year into this new life), but now it is such an insane thing to see how much he has grown—how much he has worked to find the true him. I am so proud of him."

—Amber McDonald, U.S. Army spouse

"I would say that the transition probably goes best if an individual spends a lot of time planning and investigating options. It seems that many former military members fall into government-related work rather than pursuing other choices. If a person has civilian experience, skills, or education, they may reenter the job market relying on prior knowledge. Should they not have previous civilian participation, I would recommend they seek job fairs or counseling in order to study options. Depending on their financial circumstances, a military member needs to thoroughly review the economic impact of transition. Consider income, locale, spouse job opportunities, health care, and children's requirements."

—Helen Sarver, U.S. Air Force spouse

"As an Army helicopter pilot, my husband is a true patriot, and he devoted himself to our country for the first half of his life. The demons he faced as he transitioned out of the service were both real and imagined. Both were equally detrimental since, in his mind, they were the evils lurking in the unknown terrain of 'civilization' that lay before him in 'refinding' himself, and his purpose. I became aware of the fact that his struggles did not stem from character flaws, but rather a true 'identity crisis' that stemmed from a mindset that was so deeply indoctrinated into his psyche while he was still in his mind's formative years. Between his difficulty in opening up, speaking, and seeking help with his struggles, he certainly suffered and so did we as a family. In these moments, we found ourselves discouraged and vulnerable. However, in that vulnerability, he created the opportunity to find strength and meaning inside himself and from me as his wife and our families. We were fortunate to have been able to find it for us as a couple. For my fellow military spouses out there, I can tell you that there is light at the end of the tunnel. Perseverance is key."

—Penelope, registered nurse, healer, and U.S. Army spouse

"When it comes time for your spouse to separate or retire from the military, make sure they go through the steps to obtain a VA disability rating. They may not think they qualify because they don't feel 'disabled,' but it is very important to go through the steps with the VA. Just because they may not show outward signs at this time, years from now a service-related disability or medical condition may arise and that VA support will be vital. Additionally, there are states that will grant education benefits separate from the GI Bill to dependents of former service members who have disability ratings (sometimes to include a 0 percent rating). Talk through and understand the process with each other and encourage them to start the paperwork as soon as they are eligible (appointments can take weeks and months to schedule)."

—Becky Hilliker, U.S. Air Force spouse

"You will need emotional support in the transition. That mission-focused woman is now trying to figure out how she feels and what's next without some important pieces of her self-worth. Offer lots of hugs and reassurance. Notice if she is feeling overwhelmed. Be the person who tells her she might need more help than you can offer, and help her get scheduled to see someone. Talk about how things will change as you transition. What will the job situation be? How will you reallocate chores and childcare? Who will be in charge of the finances? In charge of shopping? In charge of cooking? Talk to the children as well. They can sense the anxiety even if they don't know what's happening."

—Command Sgt. Eileen Cobb, U.S. Air Force (Ret.)

"When my wife left the military, my part of the transition was not really difficult because I continued my full-time job at work and we continued to raise our four children together, as co-equal parents, with my very capable and attentive wife, the former Navy officer. I saw the good intentions of the military in providing for many things—but they end up coddling military spouses. Getting many needs taken care of while a part of the military community actually leaves many spouses ill-prepared to face civilian life, let alone get a job or find a career. When you combine that with the shock of having to rebuild your community and network, it's no wonder the transition proves difficult for many. Making life more 'real' while in the military cocoon will help you on the way back to civilian life. If I had a few words to pass on to other veteran spouses, I would say know and anticipate this and have your own things in life, with your veteran."

—Henry Crawford, U.S. Navy spouse

"Our transition was GOLDEN on paper—we planned for everything, it seemed. Guess what we did not plan to do? We did not once even consider me, the spouse, and my transition. I found myself struggling to make friends. Even my family did not understand us. I was lonely, I too had lost my identity and purpose. I too was failing as a civilian, wife, and as a mother. Our lives and relationships were embedded in the military community we had known over two decades. We were all logistics and planning in the never-ending deployment cycle. We were set up to fail as a military to civilian marriage. Our entire relationship was ruled by the military. Now we were 'free' and did not know how to survive, let alone thrive!

"We are five years post transition. It took work, it took time, it took a deep look at our marriage and who we were and who we wanted to be, together. Do the work, don't quit! Ask for help."

—Teresa Shick, U.S. Navy spouse

WHAT KIND OF A COUNTRY AND A PEOPLE ARE WE?

"The future of our Armed Services and the future of our country will be integrally linked with how we care for our veterans."
—GEN. GEORGE WASHINGTON

This field manual focuses on what veterans and their spouses can do in the transition to civilian life. Our premise is that it is the responsibility of veterans to plan for and carry out their transition—or, as Tom Satterly said, "We all need to own this part of ourselves, take responsibility for it, and act on it." But what if only a part of this equation is what the veterans can do, and the other part lies with our country and us as a people? What we mean to say is that the effectiveness of a veteran's transition and their well-being in doing so is necessarily impacted by the society that they sought to defend and to which they return. To have the right context, the problems veterans face, as Sebastian Junger has said, should be understood to be as much from their experience in combat as from the society to which they return, which doesn't understand or seem to care to try to do so. Dr. Tick takes it a step further: "What if the proper question is to focus less on veterans and more on our collective responsibilities regarding war? What if significant reasons our veterans suffer in epidemic numbers lies, to paraphrase Shakespeare, 'not in the veterans but in ourselves'?"[1] Dr. Tick backs up his view with evidence from history, including our own. From listening to poems, speeches, and plays about the return of ancient Greek warriors and the difficulties they faced in the transition, we learn that healing can fully happen only in community. From Native American warrior societies, Dr. Tick remarks on the understanding that was implicit in the fabric of their societies, in their social contract: "The entire tribe knew and accepted what [their warriors] were training for. Non-Warriors knew their responsibility and received their own training to welcome warriors back."[2]

We are not politicians or pundits, but the larger question that our work raises is, What is our duty as a country and as a people to help our warriors as they become civilians? Does our social contract with one another and our government require us to support our veterans in this transition—regardless of whether we, on an individual basis, supported particular military conflicts? Apart from the concept of a social contract, do we as a people have an individual and shared duty to those who stood on the wall for us? Dr. Tick wrote, "When we understand that invisible wounding is inevitable and it is everyone's responsibility to tend it, then our attitudes, relationships, and responsibilities change and we can find both new and time-honored directions for hope."[3] When we were less divided, we acted on these ideals—for example, in the Minutemen of Lexington and Concord and in the Greatest Generation of World War II. In doing so, we all were raised up.

Our earnest hope is that this book helps not only veterans and their families, but also changes the consciousness of our country, to ask for the better part of ourselves to show up by being part of the solution to veteran transition as a community, whether in our small towns or in our big cities. In this way, we all have a chance to be civilian warriors.

"He hits from both sides
of the plate.
He's amphibious."

—YOGI BERRA

ACKNOWLEDGMENTS

We have many people to thank, for whom we are profoundly grateful.

For all the veterans, doctors, pastors, healers, coaches, and others who made contributions to this book, whether your name is listed or not, we owe you a debt of gratitude. To those who did not come home and made the ultimate sacrifice: Your final act of service will never be forgotten, and may we live each day in debt to your uncommon courage that has allowed us to live each day free.

Our thanks to our friends and family who made this possible. In particular, Curt Cronin was an inspiration, set a high standard for us as with everything he does in life, challenged us, and is a true friend.

There are many others to whom we are indebted for their guidance and support for this project who are too numerous to name. But we nevertheless want to express special thanks to the following for their work on this book:

- Luca Gendzier-Imperiali (Alex's son), Daniel Billings (Alex's godson), Cam Burress (Rob's family friend), and Hayden Shin (Alex's family friend and the son of Cpt. Hyonwoo Shin) for their expert research and work.
- Becky Hilliker, our first editor.
- Byrd Leavell, cohead of publishing at United Talent Agency, our literary agent, who immediately understood our mission and went to bat for us; and for Woody Frehse, who vouched for us and got us to Byrd.

- Nana K. Twumasi and the whole team at Balance and Hachette, our publisher, who also saw what we are seeking to achieve and who worked tirelessly with us.
- Mimi Peak, Alex's coach, for traveling the road of the hero's journey with me, as my teacher.

SPECIAL THANKS FROM ROB

To Mom, Dad, and my sister Megan: I would like to express my deepest gratitude throughout the journey of writing this book. Your encouragement, patience, and unwavering belief in me over the years has been invaluable, and I am profoundly grateful.

To my friends, SEAL teammates, and veterans, who provided irreplaceable insights and collaborative spirit throughout writing this book: Your contributions, whether big or small, have made the journey all the more meaningful. I am indebted to you all. LLTB.

To my son Duke: Your middle name, Kekoa, carries a legacy of strength and sacrifice, and one day, you will come to understand its profound significance.

May you live life with the grace and courage befitting your name, honoring the memory of those who have paved the way before you.

For everyone who supported me during my transition from the military, thank you. While there are too many to name individually, I must give a special thank-you to Mike and Chandra Buress for generously opening their home to me. Additionally, I deeply appreciate Kurt Polk and Rich Gray for their invaluable guidance and assistance throughout my job search journey. Your support has meant the world to me during this significant period of change.

SPECIAL THANKS FROM ALEX

Carla, without you—my best friend, my advisor, my love—none of this would make sense: the mission, the journey, and my life. The book has cost us some sacrifice, so now let's have together tennis mornings, fires under the stars, and joy. Ours is a story of great love, self-discovery, and finding each other—our own hero's journey. Thank you with all my heart.

To my son Gabriel, who reminds me of what it is to serve the country, to serve something bigger than oneself, to put oneself out there at great risk to achieve great things and to defend those who cannot defend themselves. You leave nothing on the field and inspire us.

To my son Luca, who, with his heart of a warrior, inspires me to lift up others and to think big, to have courage, and to keep an open heart. If Gabriel is clearing a path in life for us, you are the one who shines a light on that path from above, with your heart and profound soul. You remind me to have fun while doing it—because, what else do we have?

To Beatrice, for you planted seeds in each of us to be the best version of ourselves and to live a heart-centered life, watered by each of us for each other, in your name and memory. We are grateful for your presence in our lives.

NOTES

PREFACE

1. Thomas Fleming, "Why Washington Wept," *New York Sun*, December 4, 2007; "Fraunces Tavern Museum, Sneak Peek, 2008" (New York: Sons of the Revolution in the State of New York), archived from the original on September 8, 2010, retrieved December 29, 2009); *Liberty's Kids*, episode 137, "The Man Who Wouldn't Be King," YouTube, released March 24, 2003, https://www.youtube.com/watch?v=SUMJWnQWCXc.
2. Jim Rohn, "Today Is Yesterday's Tomorrow," Get Motivation: Strategies for Success, accessed January 14, 2024, https://www.getmotivation.com/goals/goals_jrohntodaystom.html.

INTRODUCTION

1. One can find many statistics about veteran suicide. We have chosen the statistic of twenty-two suicides per day, which is viewed as generally accurate. In the past two years, the VA has reported slightly lower rates but that represents only a recent trend, measured over a short amount of time. See, for example, the VA's *2023 National Veteran Suicide Prevention Annual Report* at https://www.mentalhealth.va.gov/docs/data-sheets/2023/2023-National-Veteran-Suicide-Prevention-Annual-Report-FINAL-508.pdf.
2. Command Sgt. Maj. Tom Satterly, U.S. Army (Ret.), is a highly decorated combat veteran, having served in the Army for twenty-five years, the last twenty of which were in the First Special Forces Operational Detachment–Delta, also known as Delta Force. Tom is one of the heroes of the Battle of Mogadishu, which is portrayed in the movie *Black Hawk Down*. He is also the founder of the All Secure Foundation, which assists special operations active-duty and combat veterans and their families in recovery from post-traumatic stress through education, awareness, resources for healing, workshop retreats, and PTS resilience training.
3. Eric Potterat and Alan Eagle, *Learned Excellence: Mental Disciplines for Leading and Winning from the World's Top Performers* (New York: HarperCollins, 2024).

4. See, for example, William Bridges, *Transitions: Making Sense of Life's Changes* (New York: Da Capo Press, 2004).

5. Jonathan Shay, *Odysseus in America: Combat Trauma and the Trials of Homecoming* (New York: Scribner, 2002), 6.

CHAPTER 1

1. Janet I. Farley, *Military-to-Civilian Career Transition Guide* (St. Paul, MN: JIST Publishing, 2009).

2. Bill Watterson, *The Calvin and Hobbes Portable Compendium* (Kansas City, MO: Andrews McMeel, 2023).

3. Farley, *Military-to-Civilian.*

4. National Public Radio, "A Former Navy SEAL Went to College at 52. His Insight Led to a New Class," September 18, 2023.

5. Farley, *Military-to-Civilian.*

CHAPTER 2

1. Jonathan Vespa, "Those Who Served: America's Veterans from World War II to the War on Terror," June 2, 2020, U.S. Census Bureau, https://www.census.gov/library /publications/2020/demo/acs-43.html. Vespa reports that roughly 18 million Americans, or about 7 percent of the adult population, were veterans of the U.S. Armed Forces in 2018, spanning from World War II to the War on Terror. This is a modest number when compared to the entire U.S. adult population (77.9 percent of the total U.S. population).

2. Dennis McGurk, Dave I. Cotting, Thomas W. Britt, and Amy B. Adler, "Joining the Ranks: The Role of Indoctrination in Transforming Civilians to Service Members," in *Military Life: The Psychology of Serving in Peace and Combat*, vol. 2, *Operational Stress*, ed. Amy B. Adler, Carl A. Castro, and Thomas W. Britt (Westport, CT: Praeger Security International, 2006), 13–31.

3. Rebecca D. Folkerth, "PTSD—Seeking the Ghost in the Machine," *New England Journal of Medicine* 386, no. 23 (2022): 2233–34.

4. Folkerth, "PTSD," xxi.

5. "Transition Resources," Military-Transition.org, accessed January 22, 2023, https://military-transition.org; Lewis Lin, "7 Secrets for Successful Military Career Transitions," May 10, 2011, accessed January 22, 2023, https://www.military.com /veteran-jobs/career-advice/military-transition/secrets-for-successful-military -career-transition.html; "Common Challenges During Re-adjustment to Civilian Life," U.S. Department of Veterans Affairs, last updated August 6, 2021, https: //www.va.gov/VETSINWORKPLACE/docs/em_challengesReadjust.asp.

6. Brienna N. Meffert et al., "US Veterans Who Do and Do Not Utilize Veterans Affairs Health Care Services: Demographic, Military, Medical, and Psychosocial Characteristics," *Primary Care Companion for CNS Disorder* 21, no. 1 (2019), https: //doi:10.4088/PCC.18m02350.

7. Jen Satterly is an Army spouse, award-winning filmmaker and photographer, and cofounder and co-CEO with her husband, Command Sgt. Maj. Tom Satterly, of the All Secure Foundation. We recommend her book *Arsenal of Hope*, her podcasts, and the All Secure Foundation, which assists veterans with PTSD, individual and couples coaching, and other things. Jen Satterly and Holly Lorincz, *Arsenal of Hope: Tactics for Taking on PTSD, Together* (New York: Post Hill Press, 2021).

8. Mental Health First Aid for Veterans, from National Council for Mental Wellbeing (accessed July 4, 2024).

9. U.S. Department of Veterans Affairs, Office of Mental Health and Suicide Prevention. 2023 National Veteran Suicide Prevention Annual Report. 2023. from https://www.mentalhealth.va.gov/docs/data-sheets/2023/2023-National-Veteran -Suicide-Prevention-Annual-Report-FINAL-508.pdf (retrieved September 25, 2024); Myers, Brittany. "The State of Veteran Suicide (2024)." *Mission Roll Call*, March 26, 2024. http://missionrollcall.org/veteran-voices/articles/the-state-of-veteran suicide.

10. Meghann Myers, "Four Times as Many Troops and Vets Have Died by Suicide as in Combat, Study Finds," *Military Times*, June 21, 2021.

11. U.S. Department of Veterans Affairs, Office of Mental Health and Suicide Prevention. 2023 National Veteran Suicide Prevention Annual Report. 2023. from https://www.mentalhealth.va.gov/docs/data-sheets/2023/2023-National-Veteran -Suicide-Prevention-Annual-Report-FINAL-508.pdf (retrieved September 25, 2024).

12. Ron Zaleski, *The Long Walk Home: A Veteran's Barefoot Journey Across America* (Kamel Press, November 2021), 4.

13. U.S. Department of Veterans Affairs, "PTSD in Iraq and Afghanistan Veterans," https://www.publichealth.va.gov/epidemiology/studies/new-generation/ptsd.asp (last accessed September 25, 2024).

14. Miriam Reisman, "PTSD Treatment for Veterans: What's Working, What's New, and What's Next," *Pharmacy and Therapeutics* 41, no. 10 (2016): 623–624.

15. Miriam Reisman, Ibid.

16. Leah Miller, "Statistics on Veterans and Substance Abuse," August 19, 2021, VeteranAddiction.org, accessed December 12, 2023, https://veteranaddiction.org /resources/veteran-statistics/. Last accessed August 7, 2024.

17. Kristy N. Kamarck and Barbara Salazar Torreon, "Military Sexual Assault: A Framework for Congressional Oversight," February 26, 2021, Congressional Research Service, https://crsreports.congress.gov/product/details?prodcode=R44944.

18. T. James and J. Countryman, "Psychiatric Effects of Military Deployment on Children and Families: The Use of Play Therapy for Assessment and Treatment," *Innovations in Clinical Neuroscience*, 9(2), 16-20. https://www.ncbi.nlm.nih.gov/pmc /articles/PMC3312898/.

19. Jenni B. Teeters et al., "Substance Use Disorders in Military Veterans: Prevalence and Treatment Challenges," *Substance Abuse and Rehabilitation* (2017): 69–77; National Institute on Drug Abuse, "Substance Use and Military Life Drug Facts," October 2019 (National Institutes of Health; U.S. Department of Health and Human Services), https://nida.nih.gov/publications/drugfacts/substance-use-military-life; U.S. Department of Veterans Affairs, *2019 National Veteran Suicide Prevention Annual*

Report (USA: Office of Mental Health and Suicide Prevention), accessed January 22, 2023, https://www.mentalhealth.va.gov/docs/data-sheets/2019/2019_National _Veteran_Suicide_Prevention_Annual_Report_508.pdf.

20. U.S. Department of Housing and Urban Development, *The 2020 Annual Homeless Assessment Report (AHAR) to Congress, Part 1: Point-in-Time Estimates of Homelessness* (January 2021), https://www.huduser.gov/portal/sites/default/files /pdf/2020-ahar-part-1.pdf.

21. Terri L. Tanielian and Lisa H. Jaycox, eds., *Invisible Wounds of War: Psychological and Cognitive Injuries, Their Consequences, and Services to Assist Recovery* (Santa Monica, CA: RAND Corporation and RAND Center for Military Health Policy Research, 2008); Miriam Reisman, "PTSD Treatment for Veterans: What's Working, What's New, and What's Next," *Pharmacy and Therapeutics* 41, no. 10 (2016): 623–27, 632–34, https://www.ncbi.nlm.nih.gov/pmc/articles/PMC5047000/.

22. Jennifer Silva and Jose Ramos, "We Need to Consider the Unique Challenges Facing Women Vets," *Fortune*, May 2, 2022, https://fortune.com/2022/05/02 /congress-women-vets-military-veteran-affairs-health-employment-silva-ramos/. This article cites their 2021 Annual Warrior Survey and others'.

23. Silva and Ramos, "We Need to Consider."

24. VAWnet, "Challenges Specific to Female Veterans," accessed February 13, 2023, https://vawnet.org/sc/challenges-specific-female-veterans.

25. Silva and Ramos, "We Need to Consider."

26. VAWnet, "Challenges Specific to Female Veterans."

27. Teeters et al., "Substance Use Disorders"; U.S. Department of Veterans Affairs, *Veteran Benefits Administration Annual Benefits Report Fiscal Year 2020*, accessed January 22, 2023, https://www.benefits.va.gov/REPORTS/abr/docs/2020_ABR.pdf.

28. Valerie L. Dripchak, "Issues Facing Today's Female Veterans—'Feeling Invisible and Disconnected,'" *Social Work Today* 18, no. 6, 2018: 24, accessed February 13, 2023, https://www.socialworktoday.com/archive/ND18p24.shtml.

29. Teeters et al., "Substance Use Disorders."

30. Silva and Ramos, "We Need to Consider."

31. Dripchak, "Issues Facing Today's Female Veterans."

32. United States Government Accountability Office, *VA Health Care: Better Data Needed to Assess the Health Outcomes of Lesbian, Gay, Bisexual, and Transgender Veterans* (Report to Congressional Committees, October 2020), https://www.gao.gov/assets/gao-21-69.pdf.

33. United States Government Accountability Office, *VA Health Care.*

34. Dripchak, "Issues Facing Today's Female Veterans."

35. Lindsay Mahowald, "LGBTQ+ Military Members and Veterans Face Economic, Housing, and Health Insecurities," April 28, 2022, Center for American Progress, https://www.americanprogress.org/article/lgbtq-military-members-and -veterans-face-economic-housing-and-health-insecurities/.

36. Mahowald, "LGBTQ+ Military Members and Veterans."

37. Mollie A. Ruben et al., "Lesbian, Gay, Bisexual, and Transgender Veterans' Experiences of Discrimination in Health Care and Their Relation to Health

Outcomes: A Pilot Study Examining the Moderating Role of Provider Communication," *Health Equity* 3, no. 1 (2019): 480–88.

38. United States Government Accountability Office, *VA Health Care*; Ruben et al., "Lesbian, Gay, Bisexual, and Transgender Veterans' Experiences."

CHAPTER 3

1. Dr. Edward Tick is best known for his work in treating veterans, particularly for trauma and the stress and challenges of reentering civilian life. Some of his works include *War and the Soul: Healing our Nation's Veterans from Post-traumatic Stress Disorder* (Wheaton, IL: Quest Books, 2005); *Warrior's Return: Restoring the Soul After War* (Boulder, CO: Sounds True, 2014); and *Coming Home in Viet Nam* (Evanston, IL: Northwestern University Press, 2021).

2. Charles W. Hoge, *Once a Warrior, Always a Warrior: Navigating the Transition from Combat to Home, Including Combat Stress, PTSD and mTBI* (Guilford, CT: Lyons Press, 2010), 176. Dr. Hoge directed the U.S. military's premier research program on the mental health and neurological effects of the wars in Afghanistan and Iraq from 2002 to 2009 at Walter Reed Army Institute of Research. He deployed to Iraq in 2004 to improve combat stress care, and continues to work as a staff psychiatrist treating service members, veterans, and family members. His book *Once a Warrior, Always a Warrior* is essential reading for veterans and their spouses on these topics.

3. Jonathan Shay, *Odysseus in America: Combat Trauma and the Trials of Homecoming* (New York: Scribner, 2002), 21.

4. Shay, *Odysseus in America*, 168 (referring to the work of Judith Herman). Judith L. Herman, *Trauma and Recovery: The Aftermath of Violence—from Domestic Abuse to Political Terror* (New York: Basic Books, 2015).

5. Eric Burleson, *Separating from Service: The Mental Health Handbook for Transitioning Veterans* (Austin, TX: Varime, 2019).

6. Vets Town Hall is a nonprofit organization created and run by Sebastian Junger, which promotes town hall–style meetings of veterans to allow them to speak about what it was like to serve their country. The principle behind these meetings is that humans are resilient when part of a community and fragile when they are not. The Vets Town Hall website points out that while veterans are more likely to be connected to one another rather than their families and communities, that is not healthy.

7. Bessel A. van der Kolk, *The Body Keeps the Score: Brain, Mind, and Body in the Healing of Trauma* (New York: Penguin, 2014).

8. Shay, *Odysseus in America*, 242–43 (citing Herman, *Trauma and Recovery*).

9. Shay, *Odysseus in America*, 168, 175 (referring, in part, to the works of Judith Herman).

10. Erwin Raphael McManus, *The Way of the Warrior: An Ancient Path to Inner Peace* (New York: Waterbrook, 2019), 197.

11. Tick, *Warrior's Return*, xvi. Also see Dr. Tick's book *War and the Soul*.

12. We have been influenced by the works of Dr. Tick and the writings of Native American warriors, such as Sitting Bull, Tecumseh Chief Red Cloud, and others too numerous to name here.

CHAPTER 4

1. Mayo Clinic, "What Is Grief?," October 19, 2016, https://www.mayoclinic.org /patient-visitor-guide/support-groups/what-is-grief.

2. Elisabeth Kübler-Ross and David Kessler, *On Grief and Grieving: Finding the Meaning of Grief Through the Five Stages of Loss* (New York: Scribner, 2007). The works of Kübler-Ross are often cited as the key to understanding the pattern of grief, and from that understanding, one can begin to navigate a way through the grief to a better state. From her works, we have come to understand that there are five stages of grieving: denial, anger, bargaining, depression, and acceptance. A point of clarification: The five stages of grief described by Kübler-Ross and Kessler are different from the stages that many veterans go through that Dr. Glick has conceived of.

3. Simon S. Rubin, "A Two-Track Model of Bereavement: Theory and Application in Research," *American Journal of Orthopsychiatry* 51, no. 1 (1981): 101–9; Ruth Malkinson, *Cognitive Grief Theory: Constructing a Rational Meaning to Life Following Loss* (New York: W. W. Norton, 2007).

4. Ryan Rana, PhD, Licensed Marriage and Family Therapist (LMFT), Licensed Professional Counselor (LPC), is an ICEEFT certified Emotionally Focused Therapy (EFT) trainer, supervisor, and therapist. He is the current president and founder of the Arkansas EFT Center. He and his wife, Anne, founded the Joshua Center, where he currently practices and is executive director. His specializations include work with couples, sexuality, depression, and traumatic stress. In addition to psychotherapy, Dr. Rana works with people on organization and leadership approaches as well as studying military training/process and performance psychology. He has worked extensively with veterans and veteran/spouse couples. He is an extraordinary therapist.

5. U.S. Department of Veterans Affairs, "Veterans Employment Toolkit," accessed January 22, 2023, https://www.va.gov/vetsinworkplace/.

6. Reverend Thomas Evans, senior pastor of Brick Presbyterian Church of New York, pointed out to us that monasteries, or their equivalent in other religions, often allow visitors to stay with them and become a part of their structured days and rhythms. This can be healing and centering. He explained that many find a renewed closeness to God, or find God, during hardship that in turn creates hope.

7. The rage that can come from grief for warriors has been described throughout history. In his comparison to Achilles, a warrior from Homer's *Iliad*, Dr. Jonathan Shay draws a powerful lesson for modern-day veterans by summarizing one scene of *Iliad* in which Achilles unleashes in an uncontrolled manner berserk rage after the death of his closest friend and comrade, Patroclus. Dr. Shay's point is that Achilles holds on to that anger as a way of unconsciously trying to hold on to his friend in his heart because the fear is that, somehow, when we let go of anger, we have to

come to terms with letting go of the friend who died. As Dr. Shay points out, "The friend is constantly alive; letting go of the rage lets him die." Jonathan Shay, *Achilles in Vietnam: Combat Trauma and the Undoing of Character* (New York: Scribner, 1995).

CHAPTER 5

1. National Institute on Drug Abuse, October 2019; Jenni B. Teeters et al., "Substance Use Disorders in Military Veterans: Prevalence and Treatment Challenges," *Substance Abuse and Rehabilitation* (2017): 69–77.
2. U.S. Department of Veterans Affairs, "PTSD and Substance Abuse in Veterans," October 17, 2019, https://www.ptsd.va.gov/understand/related/substance_abuse _vet.asp.
3. U.S. Department of Veterans Affairs, "PTSD Basics," June 15, 2021, https://www .ptsd.va.gov/understand/what/ptsd_basics.asp.
4. Teeters et al., "Substance Use Disorders"; National Academies of Sciences, Engineering, and Medicine, "Need, Usage, and Access and Barriers to Care," in *Evaluation of the Department of Veterans Affairs Mental Health Services* (Washington, DC: National Academies Press, 2018); RAND Corporation, *Improving the Quality of Mental Health Care for Veterans: Lessons from RAND Research* (Santa Monica, CA: RAND Corporation, 2019), https://doi.org/10.7249/RB10087.
5. National Institute on Drug Abuse, "Substance Use and Military Life DrugFacts," October 2019 (National Institutes of Health, U.S. Department of Health and Human Services), https://nida.nih.gov/publications/drugfacts/substance-use-military-life; Teeters et al., "Substance Use Disorders"; U.S. Department of Veterans Affairs, *2019 National Veteran Suicide Prevention Annual Report (Office of Mental Health and Suicide Prevention),* accessed January 22, 2023, https://www.mentalhealth.va.gov/docs /data-sheets/2019/2019_National_Veteran_Suicide_Prevention_Annual_Report _508.pdf.
6. National Institute on Drug Abuse, "Substance Use and Military Life DrugFacts."
7. Teeters et al., "Substance Use Disorders."
8. Teeters et al., "Substance Use Disorders."
9. Substance Abuse and Mental Health Services Administration, *2018 National Survey on Drug Use and Health: Veterans* (U.S. Department of Health and Human Services), https://www.samhsa.gov/data/sites/default/files/reports/rpt23251/6_Veteran _2020_01_14_508.pdf.
10. National Institute on Drug Abuse, ibid; Teeters et al., "Substance Use Disorders"; Substance Abuse and Mental Health Services Administration, ibid.
11. National Institute on Drug Abuse, "Substance Use and Military Life DrugFacts."
12. Teeters et al., "Substance Use Disorders."
13. National Institute on Drug Abuse, "Substance Use and Military Life DrugFacts"; Teeters et al., "Substance Use Disorders."
14. Teeters et al., "Substance Use Disorders."
15. National Institute on Drug Abuse, "Substance Use and Military Life DrugFacts"; U.S. Department of Veterans Affairs, "How Common Is PTSD in Veterans?,"

October 23,, 2019, https://www.ptsd.va.gov/understand/common/common _veterans.asp.

16. National Institute on Drug Abuse, "Substance Use and Military Life DrugFacts."

17. Teeters et al., "Substance Use Disorders."

18. Teeters et al., "Substance Use Disorders."

19. U.S. Department of Veterans Affairs, "VA Research on Mental Health," (accessed June 26, 2024), https://www.research.va.gov/topics/mental_health.cfm#top.

20. Mayo Clinic, "Alcohol Use Disorder," accessed January 22, 2023, https://www.mayoclinic.org/diseases-conditions/alcohol-use-disorder/symptoms -causes/syc-20369243.

21. Sarah O. Meadows et al., *2015 Department of Defense Health Related Behaviors Survey (HRBS)* (Santa Monica, CA: RAND Corporation, 2018); Substance Abuse and Mental Health Services Administration, *2018 National Survey on Drug Use and Health: Veterans,* accessed January 22, 2023, https://www.samhsa.gov/data/sites/default /files/reports/rpt23251/6_Veteran_2020_01_14_508.pdf; Shehan Karunaratne, "Alcohol Abuse in the Military," Texas Addiction Treatment Centers, July 31, 2021, https://novarecoverycenter.com/alcohol-abuse/alcohol-abuse-in-the-military/.

22. Substance Abuse and Mental Health Services Administration, "Behavioral Health Treatment Services Locator," https://www.samhsa.gov/resource/dbhis /behavioral-health-treatment-services-locator.

23. National Institute on Drug Abuse, "General Risk of Substance Use Disorders," accessed February 18, 2024.

24. Make the Connection, "Substance Use Disorder," accessed February 19, 2024, https://www.maketheconnection.net/conditions/substance-use-disorder/.

25. Make the Connection, "Substance Use Disorder."

CHAPTER 6

1. Mandy Oaklander, "Unbroken Wounded Warriors Overcome Injury to Find New Strength," *Time,* June 23, 2015, https://time.com/3932182/wounded-warriors-military -veterans/.

2. Shira Maguen and Sonya B. Norman, "Moral Injury," *PTSD Research Quarterly* 33, no. 1 (2022): 1050–1835.

3. Danae King, "US Withdrawal from Afghanistan Prompted Talk of 'Moral Injury' in Veterans. What Is It?," *Columbus Dispatch*, November 15, 2022.

4. "Moral Injury," *Psychology Today*, March 10, 2018.

5. Tick, *Warrior's Return*, 93. See also the articles and books by Dr. Rita Nakashima Brock, including, with Gabriella Lettini, *Soul Repair: Recovering from Moral Injury After War* (New York, Beacon Press, 2013).

6. Tick, *Warrior's Return*, 93.

7. Tick, *Warrior's Return*, 72.

8. Rick Waters, "Invisible Wounds…Brite Divinity School's Soul Repair Clinic," *Texas Christian University Magazine* (quoting Rita Nakashima Brock) (accessed June 26, 2024).

9. Maguen and Norman, "Moral Injury."

10. Maguen and Norman, "Moral Injury."

11. Elizabeth Svoboda, "Moral Injury Is an Invisible Epidemic That Affects Millions," *Scientific American*, September 19, 2022. Also see Brett T. Litz et al., "Moral Injury and Moral Repair in War Veterans: A Preliminary Model and Intervention Strategy," *Clinical Psychology Review* 29, no. 8 (2009): 695–706.

12. Litz et al., "Moral Injury and Moral Repair."

13. Nakashima, "Returning to Life."

14. David Brooks, "The Moral Injury," *New York Times*, February 17, 2015.

15. Harold G. Koenig, Nagy A. Youssef, and Michelle Pearce, "Assessment of Moral Injury in Veterans and Active Duty Military Personnel with PTSD: A Review," *Frontiers in Psychiatry*, June 27, 2019, https://pubmed.ncbi.nlm.nih.gov/31316405/; Jennifer H. Wortmann et al., "Spiritual Features of War-Related Moral Injury: A Primer for Clinicians," *Spirituality in Clinical Practice* 4, no. 4 (2017): 249–61.

16. Disabled American Veterans, "What Is Moral Injury?," DAV.org, accessed January 28, 2024, https://www.dav.org/get-help-now/veteran-topics-resources/moral-injury/.

17. Erwin Raphael McManus, *Chasing Daylight: Seize the Power of Every Moment* (Nashville, TN: Thomas Nelson, 2006), 78.

18. Volunteers of America, "Moral Injury FAQ," voa.org, accessed January 28, 2024, https://www.voa.org/services/moral-injuryfaq/.

20. Pauline Jelinek, "Veterans Suffer 'Moral Injury' from Warfare," NBC News, February 22, 2013, https://www.nbcnews.com/health/health-news/veterans-suffer-moral-injury-warfare-flna1c8496782.

CHAPTER 7

1. Less than half of returning veterans needing mental health services receive any treatment, and of those receiving treatment for PTSD and major depression, less than one-third are receiving evidence-based care. Dr. Glick makes the poignant point that many combat veterans can have "adrenaline junkies" qualities: "They are wired for mission-ready combat while in training and deployed. The effects of repeated dopamine, cortisol, adrenaline transforms the brain. It takes 1/300th of a second to respond to this reflex in our 'reptilian brain' with only three options: flight, fight, or freeze. Upon returning home those reflex reactions are triggered in most combat veterans, especially those with PTSD."

2. This section was written with the particular assistance, instruction, and insights of Dr. Bob Koffman and Dr. Kamran Fallahpour; Robert Koffman, MD, MPH, is a Navy medical corps captain (Ret.), continuing to serve active-duty and veteran populations as the military and veteran liaison for Sunstone Therapies. Dr. Koffman capped an acclaimed thirty-two-year career in uniform as the inaugural chief of clinical operations at the National Intrepid Center of Excellence (NICoE), located on the Walter Reed campus in Bethesda, Maryland. A recognized

expert in the management of war-related psychological trauma and brain injury, he is also a passionate advocate for the promotion of nonstigmatizing and nontraditional psychological services and integrative modalities. Dr. Koffman left active service in 2015 to begin his education in Psychedelic Assisted Therapies (PAT), a career choice that culminated in 2020 when he completed his training at the Center for Psychedelic Treatment and Research at the California Institute of Integral Studies (CIIS). Dr. Koffman currently conducts vital psychedelic research and provides FDA-approved expanded access care using these breakthrough treatments at the Bill Richards Center for Healing in Rockville, Maryland. He is known as a leading figure in the treatment and healing of veterans after decades of experience, including in downrange. Kamran Fallahpour, MD, PhD, is a licensed clinical psychologist and director of the Brain Resource Center in New York City (www.brainresourcecenter.com). He has worked with patients with PTSD for the past twenty years and has developed neurotechnology solutions to help stress-related conditions such as anxiety, PTSD, and sleep disorders. Based on his research and clinical work in the areas of health psychology, applied neuroscience, and neuropsychology, Dr. Fallahpour has developed neuroscience-based treatment methodologies for stress disorders, including PTSD, that utilize brain mapping and neuromodulation techniques to treat the neurodynamics and the root cause of such conditions.

3. Based on interviews with Dr. Koffman in November 2023.

4. Bessel A. van der Kolk, *The Body Keeps the Score: Brain, Mind, and Body in the Healing of Trauma* (New York: Penguin, 2014).

5. Mayo Clinic, "PTSD—The Silent Assassin," accessed March 15, 2023.

6. Mayo Clinic, "Post-Traumatic Stress Disorder: Symptoms and Causes," December 13, 2022, https://www.mayoclinic.org/diseases-conditions/post-traumatic-stress-disorder/symptoms-causes/syc-20355967.

7. These remarks are based on our interviews in 2023 with Dr. Fallahpour and others.

8. Jake Wood, *Among You: The Extraordinary True Story of a Soldier Broken by War* (Edinburgh: Mainstream Publishing, 2013).

9. From our interview with Dr. Tick on February 13, 2024.

10. Mattia I. Gerin et al., "Real-Time fMRI Neurofeedback with War Veterans with Chronic PTSD: A Feasibility Study," *Frontiers in Psychiatry* 7 (2016): 111, https://doi.org/10.3389/fpsyt.2016.00111.

11. Akbari Yeganeh Zahra, Dolatshahi Behrouz, and Rezaee Dogaheh Ebrahim, "The Effectiveness of Neurofeedback Training on Reducing Symptoms of War Veterans with Posttraumatic Stress Disorder," *Practice in Clinical Psychology* 4, no. 1 (2016): 17–23.

12. See, for example, van der Kolk, *The Body Keeps the Score*; and Jonathan Shay, *Odysseus in America: Combat Trauma and the Trials of Homecoming* (New York: Scribner, 2002).

13. American Psychiatric Association, "What Is Posttraumatic Stress Disorder (PTSD)?," December 2022, https://www.psychiatry.org/patients-families/ptsd/what-is-ptsd.

14. Dr. Charles Hoge directed the U.S. military's premier research program on the mental health and neurological effects of the wars in Afghanistan and Iraq from 2002 to 2009 at the Walter Reed Army Institute of Research. He deployed to Iraq in 2004 to improve combat stress care, and continues to work as a staff psychiatrist treating service members, veterans, and family members. His book *Once a Warrior, Always a Warrior: Navigating the Transition from Combat to Home, Including Combat Stress, PTSD and mTBI* (Guilford, CT: Lyons Press, 2010) is essential reading for veterans and their spouses on these topics.

15. Hoge, *Once a Warrior*, xx, 3.

16. Hoge, *Once a Warrior*.

17. Tick, *Warrior's Return*, ix, xvi.

18. Tick, *Warrior's Return*.

19. Tick, *Warrior's Return*, 75.

20. Tick, *Warrior's Return*.

21. Tick, *Warrior's Return*, x.

22. Robert Kroger, *Death's Revenge* (CreateSpace Independent Publishing, 2013).

23. Michael Anthony, *Civilianized: A Young Veteran's Memoir* (San Francisco, CA: Pulp, 2016).

CHAPTER 8

1. Charles Hoge, *Once a Warrior, Always a Warrior: Navigating the Transition from Combat to Home, including Combat Stress, PTSD and mTBI* (Guilford, CT: Lyons Press, 2010), 41.

2. Patricia Kime and Rebecca Kheel, "They Said the Rise in Military Suicide Is a Mystery. Traumatic Brain Injury May Be an Answer," Military.com, November 8, 2022, https://www.military.com/daily-news/2022/11/08/they-said-rise-military -suicide-mystery-traumatic-brain-injury-may-be-answer.html.

3. Kime and Kheel, "They Said the Rise in Military Suicide Is a Mystery."

4. Johns Hopkins Medicine, "Traumatic Brain Injury," accessed March 15, 2023, https://www.hopkinsmedicine.org/health/conditions-and-diseases/traumatic -brain-injury.

5. Kime and Kheel, "They Said the Rise in Military Suicide Is a Mystery."

6. Kime and Kheel, "They Said the Rise in Military Suicide Is a Mystery."

7. U.S. Department of Veterans Affairs, "Effects of TBI: In Veterans' Own Words," accessed February 1, 2023, https://www.mentalhealth.va.gov/tbi/index .asp.

8. U.S. Department of Veterans Affairs, "Effects of TBI."

9. Make the Connection, "Trauma, Transitioning and Treatment," accessed February 1, 2024, https://www.maketheconnection.net/read-stories/trauma-transitioning -and-treatment/.

10. Make the Connection, "About Getting Support, Marine Veteran Says: 'It Felt Good to Talk to Somebody That Listened,'" accessed February 2, 2024, https://www .youtube.com/watch?v=8llvIDp2Qco.

CHAPTER 9

1. Deborah Hufford, "Hallucinogens & Native Spirituality," *Notes from the Frontier* (blog), May 4, 2023, https://www.notesfromthefrontier.com/post/hallucinogens-native -american-spirituality.

2. Shelly Womack, "'You Deserve to Be Healed': Exploring Veteran Psychedelic Healing with Founder of No Fallen Heroes Foundation," Big Country Homepage, last updated October 16, 2023, https://www.bigcountryhomepage.com/big-country -politics/you-deserve-to-be-healed-exploring-veteran-psychedelic-healing -with-founder-of-no-fallen-heroes-foundation/.

3. Adam Janos, "G.I.s' Drug Use in Vietnam Soared—with Their Commanders' Help," History.com, August 29, 2018, https://www.history.com/news/drug-use-in -vietnam.

4. See, for example, Alan K. Davis et al., "Psychedelic Treatment for Trauma-Related Psychological and Cognitive Impairment Among US Special Operations Forces Veterans," *Chronic Stress* 4 (2020): 1–11.

5. Michael Pollan, *This Is Your Mind on Plants* (New York: Penguin, 2021).

6. Michael Pollan, *How to Change Your Mind: What the New Science of Psychedelics Teaches Us About Consciousness, Dying, Addiction, and Transcendence* (New York: Penguin, 2018).

7. Richard Louis Miller, *Psychedelic Medicine: The Healing Powers of LSD, MDMA, Psilocybin, and Ayahuasca* (Rochester, VT: Park Street Press, 2017)

8. George W. Bush Institute, "We Need to Explore Psychedelic-Assisted Therapy for Veterans," *Catalyst* 26 (Winter 2023).

9. Johns Hopkins Center for Consciousness and Psychedelic Research, https: //hopkinspsychedelic.org/.

10. Matt Saintsing, "The Potential Healing Power of Psychedelics," DAV.org, November 27, 2023, https://www.dav.org/learn-more/news/2023/veterans-and-the -new-psychedelic-renaissance/.

11. "From Resistence to Resilience—A Veteran's Renewal with Ketamine" https:// marketplace.va.gov/innovations/from-resistance-to-resilience-a-veteran-s -renewal-with-ketamine (last viewed Sept. 19, 2024).

12. Harrington, "VA Studying Psychedelics as Mental Health Treatment."

13. Robert L. Koffman and Janis Phelps, "SITREP: New Directions in Treatment for Veterans with Psychedelic-Assisted Therapy," Wellbeing for LA Learning Center, accessed April 22, 2024, https://learn.wellbeing4la.org/detail?id=401006&k =47756311.

14. Harrington, "VA Studying Psychedelics as Mental Health Treatment."

15. Harrington, "VA Studying Psychedelics as Mental Health Treatment."

16. Tiffany Kary, "US Veterans Are Accelerating the Push for Psychedelics," Bloomberg .com, June 5, 2023, https://www.bloomberg.com/news/newsletters/2023-06-05 /us-veterans-are-accelerating-the-push-for-psychedelics.

17. Berkely Lovelace Jr., "FDA Panel Rejects First MDMA Treatment amid Deep Concerns about Flawed Trials," NBC News, June 4, 2024.

18. Charles W. Hoge et al., "Combat Duty in Iraq and Afghanistan, Mental Health Problems, and Barriers to Care," *New England Journal of Medicine* 351, no. 1 (2004): 13–22, https://doi.org/10.1056/NEJMoa040603.

19. Maria M. Steenkamp et al., "Psychotherapy for Military-Related PTSD: A Review of Randomized Clinical Trials," *JAMA* 314, no. 5 (2015): 489–500, https://doi.org/10.100/jama.2015.8370.

20. Jennifer M. Mitchell et al., "MDMA-Assisted Therapy for Moderate to Severe PTSD: A Randomized, Placebo-Controlled Phase 3 Trial," *Nature Medicine* 29, no. 10 (September 14, 2023): 2473–80, https://doi.org/10.1038/s41591-023-02565-4.

21. Mitchell et al., "MDMA-Assisted Therapy for Moderate to Severe PTSD."

22. Davis et al., "Psychedelic Treatment for Trauma-Related Psychological and Cognitive Impairment."

23. Davis et al., "Psychedelic Treatment for Trauma-Related Psychological and Cognitive Impairment."

24. Robin L. Carhart-Harris and K. J. Friston, "REBUS and the Anarchic Brain: Toward a Unified Model of the Brain Action of Psychedelics," *Pharmacological Reviews* 71, no. 3 (June 20, 2019): 316–44, https://doi.org/10.1124/pr.118.017160.

25. Paul Best, "US Veterans with PTSD Turn to Psychedelic Drugs Overseas as VA Frustration Grows," Fox News, November 3, 2022, https://www.foxnews.com/us/us-veterans-ptsd-turn-psychedelic-drugs-overseas-va-frustration-grows.

26. Roberta Murphy et al., "Therapeutic Alliance and Rapport Modulate Responses to Psilocybin Assisted Therapy for Depression," *Frontiers in Pharmacology* 12 (2022): 788155, https://doi.org/10.3389/fphar.2021.788155.

27. David E. Nichols, Matthew W. Johnson, and Charles D. Nichols, "Psychedelics as Medicines: An Emerging New Paradigm," *Clinical Pharmacology & Therapeutics* 101, no. 2 (2017): 209–19, https://doi.org/10.1002/cpt 557. Epub 2016 Dec 26. PMID: 28019026.

28. Samuel Turton, David J. Nutt, and Robin L. Carhart-Harris, "A Qualitative Report on the Subjective Experience of Intravenous Psilocybin Administered in an fMRI Environment," *Current Drug Abuse Reviews* 7, no. 2 (January 27, 2014): 117–27, https://doi.org/10.2174/1874473708666150107120930.

29. Nichols, Johnson, and Nichols, "Psychedelics as Medicines."

30. Torsten Passie, *The Science of Microdosing Psychedelics* (London: Psychedelic Press, 2019).

31. Eduardo Ekman Schenberg, "Psychedelic-Assisted Psychotherapy: A Paradigm Shift in Psychiatric Research and Development," *Frontiers in Pharmacology* 9 (2018): 323606, https://doi.org/103389/fphar.2018.0733.

32. Don Lattin, "Timothy Leary's Legacy and the Rebirth of Psychedelic Research," *Harvard Library Bulletin* 28, no. 1 (Spring 2017): 65–74.

CHAPTER 10

1. Eric Potterat and Alan Eagle, *Learned Excellence: Mental Disciplines for Leading and Winning from the World's Top Performers* (New York: HarperCollins, 2024).

2. Loren W. Christensen, *Meditation for Warriors: Practical Meditation for Cops, Soldiers and Martial Artists* (North Charleston, SC: CreateSpace Independent Publishing, 2013); "Commander Divine on Meditation and Positivity," *Mark Divine Show*, https://www.youtube.com/watch?v=0GnyFiMDRDE; and "Box Breathing and Meditation Technique with Mark Divine of SealFit-TechniqueWOD," *Barbell Shrugged*, accessed March 15, 2023, https://www.youtube.com/watch?v=GZzhk9jEkkI.

3. Madhav Goyal et al., "Meditation Programs for Psychological Stress and Well-Being: A Systematic Review and Meta-Analysis," *JAMA Internal Medicine* 174, no. 3 (2014): 357–68.

4. Jon Kabat-Zinn, *Full Catastrophe Living: Using the Wisdom of Your Body and Mind to Face Stress, Pain, and Illness* (New York: Random House, 1990); and the online clinics of Kabat-Zinn and others. In fact, his work has been used by the military to improve operational effectiveness of combatants.

5. The hooded box drill, or black-hood drill, which was designed by Duane Dieter as part of his close quarters defense, is no longer done in SEAL training. It used to be part of the close quarters defense system trainees would go through after the initial six months of BUD/S. The training was used to condition trainees to control the amygdala signals. The drill involved a trainee standing in a three-foot by three-foot square on the ground (think of the box as safety, or "home base"; if the trainee makes the decision to leave the box, the scenario can become more chaotic and complex). The trainee, in protective headgear, stood in the middle of the square and a black hood was lowered over his head—making the trainee deaf and blind—from a pulley affixed to the ceiling. Various scenarios then played out with the hood being pulled off and the trainee being instantly bombarded with different types of stimuli that would require different but immediate responses. One time he would be struck in the face and his response should be rapid and lethal. Next, a scenario might be an innocent person asking directions to the nearest gas station. In this case the response should be nonlethal. More intense scenarios would involve someone striking the trainee and retreating back to try to coax them to follow him outside the box, where other threats were present (for example, other attackers waiting). Once the trainee left the box they were no longer in a safe region and it was game on.

6. Eric Potterat and Alan Eagle, *Learned Excellence: Mental Disciplines for Leading and Winning from the World's Top Performers* (New York: HarperCollins, 2024).

7. Diane K. Osborne, *Reflections on the Art of Living* (attributed to Campbell) (New York, NY, HarperCollins, 1991), 8 and 24. Campbell was influenced by the works of many, including Carl Jung and Friedrich Nietzsche.

8. Edward Tick, *Warrior's Return: Restoring the Soul After War* (Boulder, CO: Sounds True, 2014), xvi.

9. Charles W. Hoge et al., "Combat Duty in Iraq and Afghanistan, Mental Health Problems, and Barriers to Care," *New England Journal of Medicine* 351, no. 1 (2004): 9.

10. From our interview with Dr. Ryan Rana, February 17, 2024.

11. Megan Anna Neff, "Up and Down Regulation: How to Regulate Your Nervous System," *Neurodivergent Insights by Dr. Neff* (blog), January 23, 2023, https://neurodivergentinsights.com/blog/up-and-down-regulation.

12. Hoge et al., "Combat Duty in Iraq and Afghanistan," x.

13. William H. McRaven, "University of Texas at Austin 2014 Commencement Address," YouTube, accessed March 15, 2023, https://www.youtube.com/watch?v=pxBQLFLei70.

14. Maggie BenZvi, "This Is Not Where You Die," November 10, 2018, Coffee or Die, https://coffeeordie.com/not-where-you-die-crispy-avila.

15. BenZvi, "This Is Not Where You Die."

16. BenZvi, "This Is Not Where You Die."

17. Tick, *Warrior's Return*, 235–36.

18. David Lynch Foundation, Center for Resilience, "Leshonda Gill, Iraq War Veteran," accessed January 22, 2023, https://www.davidlynchfoundation.org/veterans-day.

CHAPTER 11

1. Rich Morin, "The Difficult Transition from Military to Civilian Life," Pew Research, December 8, 2011, https://www.pewresearch.org/social-trends/2011/12/08/the-difficult-transition-from-military-to-civilian-life/.

2. Joseph Campbell, *The Hero's Journey: Joseph Campbell on His Life and Work* (Novato, CA: New World Library, 2003); *The Hero with a Thousand Faces* (Novato, CA: New World Library, 1998).

3. Edward Tick, *Warrior's Return: Restoring the Soul After War* (Boulder, CO: Sounds True, 2014), 169–70.

4. We are aware that there are different views about the hero's journey. One of them is presented eloquently by Dr. Jonathan Shay: "As beasts are beneath human restraints, gods are above them…It would be foolish and untruthful to deny the appeal of exalted, godlike intoxication…We have seen the paradox that these godlike exalted moments often correspond to times when the men who have survived them say that they have acted like beasts…Above all, a sense of merely human virtue, a sense of being valued and of valuing anything seems to have fled their lives…However, all of our virtues come from not being gods. Generosity is meaningless to a god, who never suffers shortage or want. Courage is meaningless to a god, who is immortal and can never suffer permanent injury. The godlike berserk state can destroy the capacity for virtue. Whether the berserker is beneath humanity as an animal, above it as a god, or both, he is cut off from all human community when he is in this state.

"As products of a biblical culture, most veterans believed it is nobler to strive to be like God than to want to be human. However, all of our virtues come from not being gods: Generosity is meaningless to a god, who never suffers shortage or want; courage is meaningless to a god, who is immortal and can never suffer permanent injury; and so on. Our virtues and our dignity arise from our mortality, our humanity—and not from any success in being God. The godlike berserk state can destroy the capacity for virtue." Jonathan Shay, *Odysseus in America: Combat Trauma and the Trials of Homecoming* (New York: Scribner, 2002).

5. "You Can Do Something About This," *Daily Stoic*, https://dailystoic.com/you-can-do-something-about-this/.

6. "Hierocles, a Conservative Stoic," *How to Be a Stoic*, wordpress.com, January 12, 2016, https://howtobeastoic.wordpress.com/2016/01/12/hierocles-a-conservative-stoic/.

7. A corollary point: We can control only the space immediately around us; we cannot worry anymore about what we cannot affect. Clausewitz: "Everything in war is easy, but the easy things are difficult."

8. Admiral William H. McRaven, "A Sailor's Perspective on the United States Army," War on the Rocks, February 4, 2014, https://warontherocks.com/2014/02/a-sailors-perspective-on-the-united-states-army/.

9. "Hierocles, a Conservative Stoic."

CHAPTER 12

1. Audie Murphy is the most decorated American combat soldier in U.S. history. He received every military combat award for valor available from the United States Army, including the Medal of Honor, as well as French and Belgian awards for heroism. He was also an actor and a songwriter.

2. Jake Wood, *Once a Warrior: How One Veteran Found a New Mission Closer to Home* (New York: Sentinel, 2020).

3. Wood, *Once a Warrior*.

4. Wood, *Once a Warrior*.

5. Colonel Benjamin Tallmadge's memoirs, written in 1830, are stored in the collection of Fraunces Tavern Museum, New York City, https://www.frauncestavernmuseum.org/tallmadge-memoir.

6. Many have written of combat and the lives of veterans but few with such deep understanding, with such compassion and power derived from the eye of a journalist, anthropologist, and deep soul. Sebastian Junger's words could fill a book—and in fact have filled three of them: *War* (New York: Twelve, 2010); *Tribe: On Homecoming and Belonging* (New York: Grand Central, 2016); and *Freedom* (New York: Simon & Schuster, 2021). He was also the codirector along with Tim Hetherington of the documentary *Restrepo: One Platoon, One Valley, One Year* (National Geographic Entertainment, 2010), and has given numerous talks.

7. Junger finds corroboration in the societies of Israel and the Apache, Lakota, and Navajo, all warrior societies, in which there is an implicit recognition of what warriors have done and how to welcome them back. From this, he puts in context the PTSD rates of Israel (about 1 percent) with those of the U.S. (where 10 percent were in combat but PTSD rates are estimated to be at about 25 percent with almost 50 percent putting in for related benefits). https://mwi.westpoint.edu/sebastian-junger-talk/

8. "The Story of Capt. Derek Herrera, USMC (Ret.)," Marine Raider Foundation, May 31, 2017, https://marineraiderfoundation.org/the-story-of-capt-derek-herrera-usmc-ret. Much of our summary of Derek's story is derived from this article and our interview with him.

9. Dan Bozung, *This Civilian Sh*t Is Hard: From the Cockpit, Cubicle, and Beyond* (self-pub., 2020).
10. Bozung, *This Civilian Sh*t Is Hard.*
11. Bozung, *This Civilian Sh*t Is Hard.*
12. Bozung, *This Civilian Sh*t Is Hard.*

CHAPTER 13

1. Dr. Cotton, CEO and executive coach at Elevate Tempus, is a renowned researcher and has been instrumental in helping companies recruit and hire talent for both military and civilian companies for sixteen years. In 2009, he had the unique opportunity to work as a personnel research psychologist for multiple branches of the military, using people analytics to advise senior leaders in the military and in private companies. Collaborating with selection and assessment counterparts within and outside the Navy, including the U.S. Naval Academy, the Navy Health Research Center (NHRC), the Marine Special Operations Command (MARSOC), the FBI, the NFL, and other organizations, he has created innovative, cutting-edge solutions for the modern personnel issues of his clients. Since 2006, he has overseen the assessment of more than 150,000 applicants. Using proven techniques in Industrial-Organizational (I-O) Psychology, he has improved organizational effectiveness for the U.S. Navy, DuPont, Service Master, CSX, Flowserve Corporation, and multiple other Fortune 500 and smaller organizations. Our summary of his points comes from his participation on the #TEAMVETERAN Show (Episode 9) and our interview with him.
2. Mathew J. Louis, *Mission Transition: Navigating the Opportunities and Obstacles to Your Post-Military Career* (New York: HarperCollins, 2019).
3. Malcolm Gladwell, *Blink: The Power of Thinking Without Thinking* (New York: Back Bay Books, 2007).
4. Jonathan Shay, *Odysseus in America: Combat Trauma and the Trials of Homecoming* (New York: Scribner, 2002), 51.
5. Jordan Peterson, interview, Facebook (November 9, 2021).

CHAPTER 14

1. Jonathan Shay, *Odysseus in America: Combat Trauma and the Trials of Homecoming* (New York: Scribner, 2002), 56.

CHAPTER 15

1. Edward Tick, *Warrior's Return: Restoring the Soul After War* (Boulder, CO: Sounds True, 2014), 12.
2. Tick, *Warrior's Return*, x.
3. Tick, *Warrior's Return*, 9.

4. Robbins, Tony, "Wake Up Every Day with a Warrior Mindset," June 24, 2022 email to subscribers.

5. Dan Millman, *Way of the Peaceful Warrior* (California: H. J. Kramer/New World Library, 2000).

6. Paulo Coelho, *Warrior of the Light* (New York: Harper Perennial, 2004).

7. Erwin Raphael McManus, *The Way of the Warrior: An Ancient Path to Inner Peace* (New York: Crown Publishing Group, 2019).

8. Tick, *Warrior's Return*, xix.

9. Command Sgt. Maj. Tom Satterly, U.S. Army (Ret.) is a highly decorated combat veteran, having served in the Army for twenty-five years, the last twenty of which were in the Delta Force. He is also the founder of the All Secure Foundation, which assists special operations active-duty and combat veterans and their families in recovery of post-traumatic stress through education, awareness, resources for healing, workshop retreats, and PTSD resiliency training.

10. Jen is a force on her own, as an award-winning filmmaker and photographer, author of *Arsenal of Hope*, as well as her co-founding and co-CEO-ing the All Secure Foundation. Jen Satterly and Holly Lorincz, *Arsenal of Hope: Tactics for Taking on PTSD, Together* (New York: Post Hill Press, 2021).

11. Maureen Mackey, "Combat Veteran and His Wife Help Others Fight PTSD—and Find Healing and Hope," Fox News, May 27, 2022, https://www.foxnews.com /lifestyle/combat-veteran-wife-ptsd-strength.

CHAPTER 16

1. Mary Keeling et al., "Military Spouses Transition Too! A Call to Action to Address Spouses' Military to Civilian Transition," *Journal of Family Social Work* 23, no. 1, (2020): 3–19, https://www.tandfonline.com/doi/abs/10.1080/10522158.2019.1652219.

2. Carl A. Castro and Sara Kintzle, *Military Transition Theory* (New York: Springer, 2018).

3. "Stepping Beyond," Military One Source: Spouse Education and Career Opportunities, accessed January 22, 2023, https://myseco.militaryonesource.mil /portal/mystep/stepping-beyond.

4. "Transitioning to Civilian Life: Benefits," Military OneSource, accessed March 15, 2023, https://www.militaryonesource.mil/transition-retirement/transition-to -civilian-life/benefits/.

5. "These spouses experience a transition to civilian life alongside their veteran, with the associated disruptions to career trajectories, yet we have virtually no empirical research on their experiences and outcomes." Keeling et al., "Military Spouses Transition Too!"

6. G.I. Jobs, "5 Ways to Help Transition Military Kids into Civilian Life," Military Spouse, accessed January 22, 2023, https://www.militaryspouse.com/military-to -civilian-transition/how-to-help-transitioning-military-kids-integrate-into-civilian -life/.

7. Charles W. Hoge, *Once a Warrior, Always a Warrior: Navigating the Transition from Combat to Home, Including Combat Stress, PTSD and mTBI* (Guilford, CT: Lyons Press, 2010), 268.

8. Victoria L. Terrinoni, *Where You Go, I Will Go: Lessons from a Military Spouse* (self-pub., 2021).

9. Keeling et al., "Military Spouses Transition Too!"

10. Keeling et al., "Military Spouses Transition Too!"

11. Keeling et al., "Military Spouses Transition Too!"

12. Keeling et al., "Military Spouses Transition Too!"

13. Keeling et al., "Military Spouses Transition Too!"

14. The Armed Services YMCA reports that 43 percent of military families feel isolated from their communities. Jeanine Rickman, "Building a Military Support Community Wherever You Are," Armed Services YMCA, https://asymca.org /blog/building-a-military-support-community-wherever-you-are/.

15. Helga Luest and Trina Parker, *Veterans and Domestic Violence: The Traumatic Impact on Women*, n.d., accessed January 4, 2023, https://vawnet.org/sites/default/files/assets /images/NRCWebinar_TraumaticImpact.pdf.

16. Hoge, *Once a Warrior, Always a Warrior*, 257.

17. Hoge, *Once a Warrior, Always a Warrior*, 257.

18. Shay, *Odysseus in America: Combat Trauma and the Trials of Homecoming* (New York: Scribner, 2002), 136 (citing Patience Mason, the wife of Vietnam veteran).

19. Shay, *Odysseus in America*, 136. See also the works of Aphrodite T. Matsakis: *Vietnam Wives: Facing the Challenges of Life with Veterans Suffering Post-Traumatic Stress* (Lutherville, MD: Sidran Press, 1996); *Loving Someone with PTSD: A Practical Guide to Understanding and Connecting with Your Partner After Trauma* (Oakland, CA: New Harbinger Publications, 2013); and *In Harm's Way: Help for the Wives of Military Men, Police, EMTs & Firefighters* (Oakland, CA: New Harbinger Publications, 2005), among others.

20. Amanda Mineer, "Married to PTSD: What is Secondary PTSD?" Veteranslaw .com (May 20, 2021); K. Gilbert, "Understanding the Secondary Traumatic Stress of Spouses (1988) appearing in C. R. Figley (ed.), *Burnout in Families: The Systematic Costs of Caring*, pages 47–74 (CRC Press/Routledge/Taylor & Francis Group); Keith D. Renshaw et al., "Distress in Spouses of Service Members with Symptoms of Combat-Related PTSD: Secondary Traumatic Stress or General Psychological Distress?," *Journal of Family Psychology*, 25, no. 4 (2011): 461–469, https://doi.org /10.1037/a0023994 (2011); and "Partners of Veterans with PTSD," U.S. Department of Veterans Affairs (last viewed May 4, 2024).

21. Scott Pelley, Aliza Chasan, Aaron Weisz, and Ian Flickinger, "Home from War: Veterans Trauma Still Ripples Through Families," *60 Minutes Overtime* (aired April 28, 2024).

22. Michael Kraut, "Domestic Violence Among Military Families," *Los Angeles DUI Attorney Blog*, March 16, 2022, https://www.losangelesduiattorneyblog.com/domestic -violence-among-military-families/.

23. Terrinoni, *Where You Go, I Will Go*.

24. "Will Your Marriage Become a Casualty of Transition?," Military Spouse, accessed January 22, 2023, https://www.militaryspouse.com/military-to-civilian-transition /will-your-marriage-become-a-casualty-of-transition/.

25. "The Transition from Military to Civilian Life," *Angel Blog*, June 6, 2022, https://soldiersangels.org/the-transition-from-military-to-civilian-life/.

26. Sue Johnson, *Love Sense: The Revolutionary New Science of Romantic Relationships* (New York: Little, Brown Spark, 2013).

27. John Gottman, "Managing vs. Resolving Conflict in Relationships: The Blueprints for Success," Gottman.com (accessed July 5, 2024).

28. Hoge, *Once a Warrior, Always a Warrior*, 258.

29. Nikki Madison, "Making the Transition from Service Easier for Military Families," Military Times, May 1, 2022, https://www.militarytimes.com/education-transition/2022/05/01/making-the-transition-from-service-easier-for-military-families/.

POSTSCRIPT

1. Edward Tick, *Warrior's Return: Restoring the Soul After War* (Boulder, CO: Sounds True, 2014), xii.

2. Tick, *Warrior's Return*, 120–21.

3. Tick, *Warrior's Return*, xvi.

INDEX

ABOUT THE AUTHORS

Rob Sarver is a 2004 graduate of the U.S. Naval Academy, where he transferred after attending the Virginia Military Institute. He initially served as a surface warfare officer and ultimately as a Navy SEAL assigned to SEAL Team 3, where he completed seven deployments, including three tours in support of Operation Iraqi Freedom and two tours in support of Operation Enduring Freedom. Rob's military awards and decorations include: the Bronze Star Medal with combat "V" device and oak leaf cluster, the Joint Commendation Medal, the Navy and Marine Corps Commendation Medal, the Combat Action Ribbon with gold star device, and various other personal and unit awards. Rob has served in multiple leadership and executive positions since leaving the military in 2013 with organizations including Goldman Sachs, Cognizant Technology Solutions, Employer Direct Solutions, Sycamore Tree Capital Partners, MicroTraks, and Wild-Life Partners, and is the cofounder of Servius Group and co-CEO and cofounder of The Heroes Journey, LLC. Rob also completed his Executive MBA with a major in Entrepreneurial Management at the University of Pennsylvania's Wharton School of Business in May 2016. He regularly speaks about transition to companies, veteran support groups, government agencies, foundations, and universities, with Alex. He is recognized as one of the experts about veteran transition in the United States from the years' worth of interviews and research for this field manual and the interviews and talks that have arisen out of it.

Alex Gendzier is a partner at a top law firm. In college, he studied Ancient Greek philosophy, literature, and plays, which he continues to this day. At his firm, he leads teams, wins and maintains key client relationships, and has developed training and mentoring programs for associates and partners. At his prior firm, he was a senior advisor to the VALOR Group, which provides pro bono legal services to veterans and their families, and where he led his law firm's efforts to assist Afghan allies and friends. Although Alex has no military experience, his own journey through losses and life transitions, a sense of his own successes and failures, and a desire to make a contribution to our service members and their families led to his collaboration with Rob Sarver. He regularly speaks with Rob about transition to companies, veterans' groups, government agencies, foundations, and universities. He is recognized as one of the experts on veteran transition in the United States from the years' worth of interviews and research for this book and the interviews and talks that have arisen from it.